# Terrorism
# in the Twenty-First
# Century

SECOND EDITION

# Terrorism in the Twenty-First Century

*Cindy C. Combs*

University of North Carolina–Charlotte

PRENTICE HALL, UPPER SADDLE RIVER, NEW JERSEY 07458

Library of Congress Cataloging-in-Publication Data

Combs, Cindy C.
    Terrorism in the twenty-first century / Cindy C. Combs.
        p.      cm.
    ISBN 0-13-020887-6
    1. Terrorism.    2. Terrorism—Forecasting.    I. Title.    II. Title:
    Terrorism in the 21st century.
    HV6431.C6472    1999
    303.6'25—dc21                                          99-21272
                                                           CIP

Editorial Director: Charlyce Jones Owen
Editor in Chief: Nancy Roberts
Senior Acquisitions Editor: Beth Gillett Mejia
Editorial Assistant: Brian Prybella
Project Manager: Merrill Peterson
Prepress and Manufacturing Buyer: Ben Smith
Cover Director: Jayne Conte
Cover Designer: Joe Sengotta
Cover Photo Credit: Gamma Liaison Network
Marketing Manager: Christopher DeJohn

This book was set in 10/12 Times by Stratford Publishing Services
and was printed and bound by Courier Companies, Inc. The cover
was printed by Phoenix Color Corp.

© 2000, 1997 by Prentice-Hall, Inc.
Upper Saddle River, New Jersey 07458

Printed in the United States of America

10   9   8   7   6   5   4   3   2   1

ISBN   0-13-020887-6

PRENTICE-HALL INTERNATIONAL (UK) LIMITED, *London*
PRENTICE-HALL OF AUSTRALIA PTY. LIMITED, *Sydney*
PRENTICE-HALL CANADA INC., *Toronto*
PRENTICE-HALL HISPANOAMERICANA, S.A., *Mexico*
PRENTICE-HALL OF INDIA PRIVATE LIMITED, *New Delhi*
PRENTICE-HALL OF JAPAN, INC., *Tokyo*
PEARSON EDUCATION ASIA PTE. LTD., *Singapore*
EDITORA PRENTICE-HALL DO BRASIL, LTDA., *Rio de Janeiro*

# Contents

# 12   Security Measures: A Frail Defense   198

# 13   Future Trends   *214*

# Preface

This project had its roots in my inability to find a book which made clear, to students as well as instructors, not only what terrorism *is* and has been, but also what it may be like in this new world as we begin a new century. The new edition, materials for which I have collected, organized, and written while teaching my undergraduate course in Political Violence, includes analyses of new threats of "terrorism" which impact the peace and stability of our world. Again, I have tried to focus on the responses of individual nations and of the international community, legally and politically, to terrorist attacks, which are becoming increasingly lethal, indiscriminate, and widely dispersed.

It is important, from my perspective, that the book be easy for both students and professors to use, with material organized clearly and concisely and presented without prejudice. In order to prevent, as far as possible, a pejorative use of the material, the concept of "terrorism" is examined with emphasis on a legal, operational definition applicable to terrorist *acts,* rather than to the individuals, groups, or states that carry out such acts. This makes the term much less likely to be applied with prejudice; if the term is applied in the legally correct fashion, it can be done objectively rather than subjectively. It also facilitates the use of the book by a wider audience, since each individual, group, and state can be evaluated in the context of the nature of the actions taken.

In order to keep this new edition "user friendly" for students, I have retained the original structure, adding a chapter on the role of the media in terrorist events, new material on state responses to terrorism, and vital changes noted on the trends in terrorism today. The book still begins with a chronology of a few terrorist incidents, designed to make the reader aware of the dimensions of the problem. This is followed by a brief look at terrorism in historical perspective, with emphasis given to understanding the cyclical nature of these acts of violence. Evaluation sections at the end of each chapter, designed to challenge readers to apply their understanding to current events, have been useful in provoking excellent student discussion of the concepts. This historical analysis is particularly useful, since many of the "new" terrorist events have historical roots which contribute significantly to an understanding of the phenomenon.

In addition to building an interest in the study of terrorism, I have tried to high-light criteria useful in studying the types of modern terrorism. Applying such criteria to individuals, groups, and states makes it possible to differentiate to some degree between "crusaders" and "criminals," between state-sponsored and state-tolerated terrorism, and between "separatist" and "nationalist" groups. Familiarity with opera-tionalized terms makes it easier to apply such terms without prejudice and, more sig-nificantly, to evaluate the response options for each type.

The text is organized in a manner intended to be quite comfortable for course use in a lecture or seminar. Inclusion of lists of key concepts, case studies, evaluation sections, and strategically significant endnotes are designed to allow people with a variety of learning styles and reading approaches to master the content fairly easily. Faculty can readily accentuate, elaborate, or correlate examples that are similar, par-allel, or contrary, with a sound framework for student understanding. With this for-mat, I have sought to engage the interest of, and to motivate, a wide range of readers of varied preparatory background and academic experience in the vitally interesting subject of terrorism.

*Cindy C. Combs*

# Acknowledgments

The University of North Carolina–Charlotte has a strong commitment to the integration of research and teaching, encouraging faculty to generate materials that are useful in the classroom. I have been particularly fortunate in that the Political Science Department offered me a reduction in course load, a chance to teach a course on this topic each year, and continuous friendly support as I struggled to complete the research, writing, and editing of this text. Particular thanks must go to Cheryl Almond, the administrative assistant, without whom little of this work would have been possible; and to Ted Arrington, who helped me stay focused on this task. My thanks also to Richter Moore of Appalachian State University for encouraging me to begin this task several years ago.

My husband, Lee, stood before me and behind me, pushing and pulling me forward, editing, and encouraging me not to give up in spite of the many frustrations. His help on the computer, particularly, made it possible for me to meet my deadlines within a very crowded schedule. Our daughters, Sara, Elizabeth, and Katherine, with their assessments of the inherent "dullness" of social science from a student's perspective, helped me to remember to try to keep this second edition interesting and exciting to students, who will be its primary consumers.

# Introduction

*To get anywhere, you have to walk over the corpses.*

This ruthless declaration by Ilyich Ramirez Sanchez in 1975, made while holding 11 OPEC ministers hostage, evokes the image of terrorists as they have menaced so many lives during the latter part of the twentieth century. When Sanchez, known to the public as "Carlos the Jackal," was taken from his home in the Sudan by French police in the summer of 1994, many believed that this capture might mark the beginning of the end of terrorism. Just as the end of the cold war has made many governments less willing or able to engage in state-sponsored or state-protected terrorism, many hoped that the capture of Carlos was symbolic of a willingness among states to cooperate to end the decades of bloody terrorist acts.

Less than one month later, nations reeled from the alarm of weapons-grade plutonium "on sale" from former Soviet arsenals. During the spring and summer of 1994, German police uncovered four attempts to sell smuggled nuclear material that could actually be used to make an atomic bomb. On August 10 of that year, Lufthansa Flight 3369 from Moscow to Munich was found to contain 350 grams of atomic fuel aboard in a lead-lined suitcase carrying MOX. A Colombian and two Spaniards were arrested. A 35-year-old German man was arrested two days later trying to sell an extremely pure sample of plutonium to a police informant.

None of the recovered materials were sufficient to produce even a small, crude atom bomb. But the fact that weapons-grade plutonium was on the market has acted as a red alert for many terrorist experts in Western governments. Frightening questions have been raised about the possibilities of nuclear terrorism, a potential threat largely written off during the past few decades as too expensive, too heavily safeguarded, and too politically costly to be an attractive option for most groups engaged in terrorist activities. Now many of those who study terrorism wonder whether, with bomb-grade plutonium finally on sale, a rogue state or group will try to buy enough to build a bomb. Although it is reassuring to know that these small amounts captured in Germany are not enough to build a bomb, it is disturbing to worry about whether larger deals, perhaps, are taking place undetected in other parts of the world. The detonations by India and Pakistan in the summer of 1998 dramatized the problems of

1

nuclear proliferation and increased the credibility of the potential for nuclear terrorism. As more states become nuclear powers, the ability to control access to dangerous nuclear materials decreases.

Terrorism in the twenty-first century may well be quite different from that
experienced in the twentieth. The wave of terror that Carlos the Jackal embodied is,
apparently, fading. Just as the extreme left-wing ideology that Sanchez and others
of the 1960s and 1970s embraced is fading in much of the world, so is the terrorism
of the extreme left that plagued much of Europe also becoming less common. The
1980s witnessed the beginning of the shift in contemporary terrorism from ideologies of the extreme left toward fundamentalism from the extreme right. Both types of
terror continue to play an important role in international politics, but the pattern for
the twenty-first century is less clear.

To understand what terrorism may well be like in the twenty-first century, it is
important to first examine what is known about terrorism in the twentieth century.
Political science is founded on a need to be able to both explain and predict actions in
the political realm. For that purpose, this text will examine the known facets of contemporary terrorism, attempting to explain the primary characteristics of what, who,
why, and how. Prediction about forthcoming patterns of terrorism can then be based
on an understanding of previous and present patterns of behavior.

Terrorism, in spite of Carlos's capture, has not gone away. It continues to exist,
but it may be changing. Evaluating present conditions, and attempting to predict
future trends, can offer useful insights for policy makers and for citizens in the new
century.

# An Idea Whose Time Has Come?

## Key Concepts

terrorism

mass terror

dynastic assassination

random terror

focused random terror

tactical terror

## Chronology of Terror

08/31/81    Twenty people are injured when a powerful bomb explodes at the U.S. Air Force base in Ramstein, West Germany. The Red Army Faction claimed responsibility.

01/18/82    Lieutenant Colonel Charles Robert Ray is shot and killed while walking to his car in Paris. The Lebanese Armed Revolutionary Faction claimed responsibility.

08/09/82    Gunmen throw a grenade into a Jewish restaurant in Paris then fire with automatic weapons, killing 6 people and wounding 27 others. The leftist group, Action Direct, first claimed then denied responsibility for this attack.

09/23/83    One hundred eleven people are killed when a bomb explodes on board an Omani Gulf jet en route from Karachi to Abu Dhabi.

01/18/84    Malcolm Kerr, president of American University in Beirut, is shot and killed as he steps off the elevator to his office on the West Beirut campus. Islamic Jihad claimed responsibility.

06/14/85    Shiite gunmen hijack TWA Flight 847 from Athens. The hijackers shoot and kill one passenger then disperse the remaining hostages throughout Beirut.

3

10/07/85   Four Palestinian gunmen hijack the Italian cruise ship *Achille Lauro* off the coast of Egypt. One passenger, an American in a wheelchair, is shot before the hijack ends.

12/27/85   Palestinian gunmen attack airports in Rome and Vienna with grenades and automatic weapons, killing men, women, and children. Abu Nidal's Revolutionary Army Fatah group claims responsibility.

04/02/86   Four people are killed, including one infant, and nine are injured in a bomb explosion aboard TWA Flight 840 en route from Rome to Athens. The Hawari Group, a radical Palestinian organization, claims responsibility.

04/05/86   A Turkish woman and two U.S. Army sergeants are killed, and nearly 200 people are injured, in a bomb explosion in a West Berlin discotheque. Intelligence data link Libya to the bombing.

04/17/86   Peter Kilburn, a librarian at the American University of Beirut, Lebanon, and two British schoolteachers are killed by their captors in apparent retaliation to the U.S. air raids on Libya on April 15. The pro-Libyan Arab Fedayeen cells claim responsibility for Kilburn's death.

09/05/86   Pan Am Flight 73 is hijacked in Pakistan. At 5:55 P.M. (Eastern Standard Time), four members of Abu Nidal's organization seized a 747 at Karachi International Airport. The hijackers held 374 passengers and 15 crew members hostage for 16 hours. When the ground power units ran out of gas and the lights dimmed on the plane the following night, the gunmen panicked and began firing indiscriminately at the huddled passengers. Twenty-one hostages were killed, and more than 60 were seriously injured.

12/27/87   Ronald Strong, an American sailor, died from wounds received December 26 in a grenade attack on a temporary USO club in Barcelona, Spain. The Catalan Red Liberation Army claimed responsibility.

04/05/88   Hizballah fighters hijack Kuwait Airways Flight 422 en route from Bangkok, Thailand, to Kuwait. Two Kuwaiti passengers were killed, in an effort to dramatize the hijackers' demands.

04/14/88   A car bomb explodes outside the USO club in Naples, Italy, killing five people. The Organization of Jihad Brigades (a Japanese Red Army—associated group) claims responsibility.

05/15/88   ANO members fire machine guns and throw grenades in the British Sudan Club and the Acropole Hotel in Khartoum. Eight people are killed.

12/21/88   A Pan Am 747 passenger aircraft was destroyed in flight over Lockerbie, Scotland, by a bomb, killing 259 people on board and another 11 on the ground. Two Libyans have been indicted for this operation.

Were the 1980s truly a decade of violence? Perhaps. But it was clearly less violent than those decades during which the world experienced the trauma of global war. There was certainly less loss of life than during the years in which the Indo-China conflict raged. Fewer lives were claimed by political violence during the 1980s than by traffic accidents on U.S. highways annually.

So why is so much attention directed toward developing policies to cope with the terrorist violence of recent years? As experts such as Walter Laqueur point out, it has attracted what could be considered an inordinate amount of attention, compared with other major problems of our times, such as global debt and world hunger. Terrorism has been the subject of countless speeches by political leaders throughout the world and the impetus for numerous initiatives and conferences by foreign policy experts. The drama of terrorist-directed events such as those outlined earlier attracts enormous attention in the press and on television worldwide. Terror-violence, some have argued, became an accepted method of warfare during the latter part of the twentieth century.

Certainly terrorism has been waged by a wide variety of individuals and groups. It has become a favored tactic to national and religious groups, by groups on both the left and the right of the political spectrum, by nationalist and internationalist movements. It has been used as an instrument of state policy. It has been directed against autocratic as well as democratic regimes, although political democracies have been the most frequent target. At times it has been an instrument of last resort for movements of national liberation whose political attempts to change the system have failed; at other times it has been deliberately chosen by such movements *before* other such political options have been attempted.

States have sponsored terrorism outside their own frontiers and have used terrorism as a weapon against their own citizens. Terrorism has become, paradoxically, both an instrument designed to force radical social and political changes and an instrument of oppression to try to prevent such changes.

Even with the increased use of terrorist violence, or perhaps because of its proliferation, a great deal of confusion remains as to what the term *terrorism* really encompasses. Many definitions of terrorism are, in fact, encoded political statements. Too often the term is used in a pejorative sense, attached as a label to those groups whose political objectives one finds objectionable. To study this phenomenon, we must first establish a workable and useful definition—workable in that it has sufficient precision to allow us to identify the phenomenon when it occurs, and useful in that it is acceptable to a fairly broad range of political persuasions. For *terrorism* is a politicized term, just as terrorism is a political crime. Its definition must therefore be politically acceptable.

## MODERN DEFINITIONS OF AN OLD CONCEPT

Terrorism is a phenomenon that is becoming a pervasive, often dominant influence in our lives. It affects the manner in which governments conduct their foreign policy and corporations transact their business. It causes alterations in the role and even the structure of our security forces. It forces us to spend huge amounts of time and money to protect our public figures, vital installations, citizens, and even our system of government. It influences the way we travel and the places we travel to see. It even affects the manner in which we live our daily lives. Our newspapers, radios, and televisions inundate our lives with vivid details of terrorist spectaculars from all corners of the globe.

But what is terrorism, this "it" to which we attribute so much influence today? Before we can assess just how great a threat it poses and exactly whom it threatens, we need to determine what terrorism is. And it is precisely this problem of definition that has caused political, legal, and military leaders to throw up their hands in discouragement and dismay.

Because terrorism is a political as well as a legal and military issue, its definition in modern terms has been slow to evolve. Not that numerous definitions are not available—there are hundreds. But few of them are of sufficient legal scholarship to be useful in international law, and most of those that are legally useful lack the necessary ambiguity for political acceptance.

Thus, the problem of defining terrorism is not insuperable, but it must be handled with caution for subsequent use of the term to have meaning. To say that the number of terrorist incidents is rising annually will have little meaning unless it is clear precisely what such an incident is and is not.

Moreover, it helps to put the term into a historical perspective. Terrorism is not a modern phenomenon. The admixture of religion and politics fomenting terrorism in many areas today has a counterpart in the hashashin of the Middle Ages. Incidents such as the *Achille Lauro* hijacking have precedents dating back many centuries. The statement that "one man's terrorist is another man's patriot" illustrates the historical continuum of conflict under which terrorism is operationally defined.

Ideology has always had an ambiguous relationship with terrorism, at one point justifying and at another condemning the same act. Theorists (and practitioners) of both the left and right have advocated the use of what has been termed "terrorist" violence. Understanding the context of the ideological debate helps to deal with the "justifications" offered in contemporary times for terrorist acts.

It also helps to assess the ideological commitment of the perpetrators of terrorism. Profiling modern terrorists is one way of assessing what terrorism is committed for today. An understanding of the impact of group dynamics is also useful in critiquing the rationale behind such acts. Patterns in the type of recruiting done among groups committing terrorist acts lends substance to these profiles of modern terrorists.

But terrorism is not strictly a phenomenon committed by individuals or groups. In fact, *terrorism* as a political term derived from *state* terror. So analysis of ways in which states use terrorism as an instrument of foreign and domestic policy offers interesting insights.

Some states are even involved in the network emerging among individuals and groups involved in the commission of terrorist acts. Opinions differ as to the extent, cohesiveness, and ideological commitment of this network, but evidence of its existence is beyond reasonable dispute. Nations such as Libya, Syria, and Iran have repeatedly been accused of involvement in state-sponsored terrorism. The linkage between these states and terrorism will be explored in depth later, focusing on questions such as, How is the terrorism financed? What are its targets? These and other fascinating questions offer opportunities to plumb the murky depths of the "terror network."

Understanding of *why* and *who* leads to questions of *how.* Profiles of terrorist events offer thumbnail sketches and interesting insights into the how of terrorism. The depth of media involvement in the making of a "terrorist spectacular," for instance, can provide useful clues to understanding why this is so sensitive an area of democratic policy making. Analysis of potential targets and weapons raises crucial and frightening questions for democratic systems.

The responses of the systems—legal, military, and political—to the threat and reality of terrorism are, of course, crucial to any understanding of the problem of terrorism today. The willingness as well as the capacity of the international community, and of an individual nation, to respond to this form of "warfare" are critical to any assessment of the role of terrorism in shaping our world. The difference between the responses to domestic, as opposed to international, terrorism may also be critical as democratic nations seek ways to respond to terrorism without sacrificing fundamental principles of democracy.

Ultimately, the question may not be how nations can eliminate terrorism—if it is indeed a centuries-old practice and well entrenched as a useful tool in warfare—but rather how much terrorism a state can tolerate. New laws and new technology are changing the face of terrorism, but because it is not vanishing, new thresholds for "acceptable" violence may well be emerging.

This discussion in no sense covers all that could be said about terrorism. This is a contemporary review of current acts of terrorism. Definitions of terrorism, like the acts themselves, continue to undergo changes. The definition suggested in the following section highlights certain important facets of the issue, answering some questions while raising a multitude of others. Such a study can only provide a frame of reference from which it should be possible to analyze this phenomenon—the instrument and the nemesis of rulers, governments, and citizens.

## CRUCIAL COMPONENTS OF TERRORISM

Although it has not been possible yet to create a universally acceptable definition of terrorism, it is both possible and necessary to specify certain features common to the phenomenon. This in turn makes it feasible to create an operational definition of this term. Acts with *all* of these attributes could then be identified as terrorist acts with some consistency. Without falling into the political quagmire of attempting to label individuals or groups as "terrorist," certain types of *actions* could be identified as terrorism, regardless of who commits them, for however noble a cause.

Let us consider a loose definition of contemporary terrorism. It must necessarily be loose, because its elements tend to form a wide variety of compounds that today fall within the rubric of terrorism. For the purposes of this investigation, **terrorism** will be defined as a synthesis of war and theater, a dramatization of the most proscribed kind of violence—that which is perpetrated on innocent victims—played before an audience in the hope of creating a mood of fear, for political purposes.

This description of terrorism has a number of crucial components. Terrorism, by this definition, involves an act of violence, an audience, the creation of a mood of fear, innocent victims, and political motives or goals. Each of these elements deserves some clarification for us to formulate a clear set of parameters for this frequently misunderstood and misused term.

## Violence, Audience, and a Mood of Fear

First, it is important to note that terrorism is fundamentally a violent act. Sit-ins, picket lines, walkouts, and other similar forms of protest, no matter how disruptive, are *not* terrorist acts. Violence—the threat of violence in which the capacity and the willingness to commit violence are displayed—is endemic to terrorism. The violence need not be fully perpetrated—that is, the bomb need not be detonated or all of the passengers aboard an airliner killed—for it to be considered a terrorist act. But the capacity and the willingness to commit a violent act must be present.

This means, then, that it is the *perception* of the audience of that violent potential that is crucial to classifying an act as terrorism. Terrorism is, essentially, theater, an act played before an audience, designed to call the attention of millions, even hundreds of millions, to an often unrelated situation through shock—producing situations of outrage and horror, doing the unthinkable without apology or remorse. Unlike similar acts of murder or warfare, acts of terrorism are neither ends in themselves nor often more than tangentially related to the ends sought. They are simply crafted to create a mood of fear or terror in that audience.

This mood is not the result of the numbers of casualties caused by the act of violence. Automobile accidents cause greater numbers of injuries and deaths each year in the United States, without necessarily invoking a mood of terror among other drivers or pedestrians. Nor is it the deliberate nature of the death inflicted that causes the audience response. Individuals are murdered in nonpolitical, nonterrorist acts throughout the world each year, without provoking widespread fear.

## Victims: The Right Place,
## But It Must Have Been the Wrong Time

The creation of this mood of intense anxiety seems to be specifically linked to the nature of the victim of terrorist acts. As one scholar notes:

> To qualify as an appropriate victim of a terrorist today, we need not be tyrants or their sympathizers; we need not be connected in any way with the evils the terrorist perceives; we need not belong to a particular group. We need only be in the wrong place at the wrong time.[1]

Terrorism is thus distinguished from guerilla warfare by deliberate attacks on innocent persons and the separation of its victims from the ultimate goal: the "playing to an audience" aspect of a terrorist act. Terrorism can also be distinguished from legal acts of warfare and ordinary crimes of murder. As David Fromkin points out:

> Unlike the soldier, the guerilla fighter, or the revolutionist, the terrorist . . . is always in the paradoxical position of undertaking actions the immediate physical consequences of which are not particularly desired by him. An ordinary murderer will kill someone because he wants the person to be dead, but a terrorist will shoot somebody even though it is a matter of complete indifference to him whether that person lives or dies.[2]

Put more simply, the difference between a terrorist act and a similar crime or war activity is that terrorist acts are perpetrated *deliberately* on innocent third parties in an effort to coerce the opposing party or persons into some desired political course of action. Victims are thus chosen not primarily because of their personal guilt (in terms of membership in an opposing military or governmental group) but because their deaths or injuries will so shock the opposition that concession can be forced to prevent a recurrence of the incident or will focus attention on a particular political cause. Terrorist acts, in other words, are constructed to "make war" deliberately on innocent persons.

This distinction needs some explanation. The laws of war permit waging war between national armies, within certain humanitarian limits. Even for the enemy in a violent protracted conflict, some types of behavior (e.g., genocide and torture) are expressly forbidden, and certain basic amenities are required to be preserved (regarding such issues as the treatment of prisoners of war).[3] "War" as waged by terrorist acts violates these rules in that those deliberately destroyed are not principally armed military opponents but hapless civilians. Rules of international behavior, particularly those pertaining to political responsibility and military obligations, offer maximum protection to the innocent person. Terrorism makes a practice of persistent, deliberate harm to precisely that type of person.

The distinction between a terrorist act and a legitimate act of guerrilla warfare is not always clear. General George Grivas, founder and head of the Cypriot EOKA, asserted in his memoirs, "We did not strike, like a bomber, at random. We shot only British servicemen who would have killed us if they could have fired first, and civilians who were traitors or intelligence agents."[4] The French Resistance, the Polish Underground, and the Greek Guerillas were called terrorists by the Nazi Occupation; yet they, like the EOKA, attacked primarily military personnel, government officials, and local collaborators.

During World War II, the Polish Underground planted explosives at the Cafe Cyganeria in Kraków, a meeting place for Nazi officers, which no doubt resulted in injury to Polish waiters as well as to the desired military targets.[5] The point here is that the terrorist deliberately chooses to invoke injury on the innocent in an effort to shock the "guilty" political or military audience. Injury to the innocent thus is not an undesirable accident or by-product but the carefully sought consequence of a terrorist act.

A terrorist act is committed not against a military target, necessarily, as the individual or group perpetrating the act does not seek to overthrow by military force, or against the person in direct opposition to the perpetrators, as the ultimate goal is not usually the death of one leader. Unlike the terrorism practiced by nineteenth-century anarchists, twentieth-century terrorist acts are deliberately aimed against non-combatants, unarmed third parties whose loss of well-being can be expected to evoke a desired response from the opposition or from the "audience" watching the event throughout the world.

Until recently it appeared that, although most of the victims of terrorism were innocent of any crime, they were also relatively few in number. In those terrorist incidents recorded in the 1950s and 1960s, the actual number of casualties was relatively small. It has been speculated that perhaps the terrorists felt a need to avoid alienating certain groups of people or portions of society. Perhaps it was also true that terrorists "want a lot of people watching, not a lot of people dead."[6]

But the recent bombings of crowded passenger airplanes and the slaughter of family groups at airports would appear to herald a loosening of the threads that have constrained terrorists in their search for victims. As the craving for a worldwide audience increases among groups using terrorism, the increasing tolerance of that audience for violence may actually be pushing terrorists to widen their target range, to create a more spectacular event for their audience.

Thus, as the violence becomes more randomized, it is being directed against a wider range of innocent persons. Children are becoming targets, as the massacres at the Rome and Vienna airports demonstrated. Ironically, this increase in innocent targets may well be a direct result of a viewing audience that is no longer as interested in attacks on military attaches or political figures.

## Political Quicksand

Terrorism, then, is an act of violence, perpetrated on an innocent person to evoke fear in an audience. One further component, however, is necessary to this definition; otherwise, such a definition could be reasonably applied to actions taken by professional sportsmen on the playing field!

The addition of a "political purpose" to the concept of terrorism continues to create enormous legal problems. Although it is obviously crucial to establish parameters for this concept of political purpose, particularly in light of the fact that political crimes and criminals have enjoyed special status under international law for centuries, the concept remains largely undefined.

Much of the confusion today results from a misperception that the presence of political *motivation* is sufficient to establish the political character of an action. An extradition case clearly states, "An offense is not of a political character simply because it was politically motivated."[7] The prevailing Anglo-American rule of law has been derived from *in re Castroni,* in which two basic criteria are given for determining the political quality of an action: (1) the act at issue must have occurred during a political revolt or disturbance, and (2) the act at issue must have been incidental to and have formed part of that same revolution or disturbance.[8]

A political motive thus may be termed *necessary* but is not sufficient to earn for an action a "political offense" status under international law. Nicholas Kittrie has suggested that a "pure political offense" would consist of acts "which challenge the State but affect no private rights of innocent parties."[9] By this definition, a political revolution or disturbance is an essential ingredient, in which the political offense plays only a part. Moreover, the offense must bring harm *only* to the state, while protecting innocent parties from harm through reasonable precautions. This view has the effect of narrowing the classes of acceptable victims and eliminating random acts of lone assassins.

Political assassination by committed revolutionaries careful to cause as little harm as possible to innocent persons thus remains protected to some extent within the political offense provisions of international law. Hence, the assassination of the Grand Duke Sergius might qualify for political offense status, whereas the mob violence of the Paris Commune would certainly not.

Obviously, the political element of an act of terrorism adds considerable confusion, in both the legal and the political realm. Although it is a necessary component to a definition of terrorism, it is so ambiguous a concept that it is often a two-edged sword, offering insights into the causes of an act while providing gaping loopholes in the law through which perpetrators of heinous acts continue to slither.

One legal expert has described the problem in this manner:

> In order to maintain a proper balance between human rights and world order, it is imperative that the world community in rejecting the proposition that all forms of violence are justified if supported by political goals, avoid the trap of supporting the other extreme, that violent opposition to an established regime is never permissible by international standards. Consequently, the principles of self-defense and the requirement of proportionality need to be re-examined, refined and injected more vigorously into this area.[10]

What distinguishes terrorism, then, from purely political actions may be the illegality of the violence employed, primarily in terms of the victims of the offenses. As noted earlier, many activities, including some sports and many movies, have as a goal the instilling of fear in an audience or opponent. What distinguishes the terrorist of today from the football player, the political assassin, and the revolutionary engaged in regular or irregular warfare may be the *lack* of legitimacy that his or her actions enjoy under international norms. By its very nature, terrorism involves the deliberate disruption of norms, the violation of generally accepted standards of decency, including the laws of war as they apply to the innocent and helpless.[11]

Because this area of the definition of terrorism is very confusing and contradictory, it is useful to review the issue once more. What is it, then, that distinguishes the terrorist act from other acts of war, as well as from other political or common crimes? Few would argue that wars, whether between or within states, could or should occur without violence, without the inflicting of injury and death. As individuals we may deplore the violence, but as nations we have recognized its inevitability and accorded war a limited legitimacy.

But international rules have been created and accepted that govern the acceptable types of violence, even in war. The international community does not forbid the use of *all* violence; it does, however, suggest basic rules for the use of violence. Many of these rules are directed toward the protection of innocent persons. Even in the life-and-death struggles between nations, these laws focus on the minimizing of danger of injury or death to noncombatants, civilians with neither military nor political rank or involvement in the conflict.[12]

Political motivation, then, is not a lever by which acts of terrorism can be justified under international law. On the contrary, international law makes it clear that, regardless of the motive, some acts of political violence are never acceptable.

## TYPOLOGIES OF TERRORISM: USEFUL TOOLS

It is appropriate at this point to look at some typologies of terror that may help us distinguish between types of terrorism as they pertain to revolutionary and guerilla movements. Feliks Gross, a leading authority on revolutionary terror, has suggested that at least five types of terror-violence exist:

1. **Mass terror** is terror by a state, in which the regime coerces the opposition in the population, whether organized or unorganized, sometimes in an institutionalized manner.

2. **Dynastic assassination** is an attack on a head of state or a ruling elite, precisely the kind of terrorism that the international community tried to criminalize in the mid–nineteenth century.

3. **Random terror** involves the placing of explosives where people gather (e.g., post offices, railroads, and cafés) to destroy whoever happens to be there. "Algerian revolutionaries left bombs in public places in Paris," one scholar notes, "apparently convinced that one Frenchman blown to bits was pretty much like any other."[13]

4. **Focused random terror** restricts the placing of explosives, for example, to where significant agents of oppression are likely to gather (as in the aforementioned case of the Polish Underground).

5. Finally, **tactical terror** is directed solely against the ruling government as a part of a "broad revolutionary strategic plan."[14]

It is obvious that such a typology leaves some guerrilla activity enmeshed in the terrorist label. Although similar difficulties afflict other such typologies, several important points can be derived concerning the phenomenon of terrorism by examining some of them. J. Boyer Bell's excellent study of terrorist types yields many insights into the kinds of terrorism prevalent today, thus contributing to an understanding of what is encompassed by the modern meaning of the term.[15]

In addition to psychotic and criminal terror, which Bell links to air piracy and kidnapping, four other categories are suggested: endemic, authorized, vigilante, and revolutionary. *Endemic terror* in terms of societal anarchy offers an interesting insight into the internal chaos that characterized Uganda under Idi Amin, for example. *Authorized terror* is used by the state to intimidate internal enemies or hostile governments, whereas *vigilante terror* is carried out by nonstate actors with the tacit permission of the state, and *revolutionary terror* is, like Gross's tactical terror, "purely political."

Unlike Gross, however, Bell suggests that this final category could be subdivided into at least six types of terror: organizational, allegiance, functional, provocative, manipulative, and symbolic. These subdivisions, however, somewhat overlap with the types of terrorism in general discussed by Gross, particularly the focused random type. Bell's typology adds, in effect, diversification as to the specific targets and audiences of focused random terror and broadens the spectrum of types of state terror.

Although numerous other typologies of terrorism have been offered by various scholars, review of them in detail would not significantly contribute to the development of a workable definition of contemporary terrorism. However, a few important points can be made about these typologies. First, virtually every major typology developed today includes some form of state terrorism as well as individual and group terrorism. What Gross terms "mass" terror and Bell calls "authorized" or even "endemic" terror is described by U.S. State Department analyst Thomas Thornton as "enforcement" terror[16] and by political scientist Paul Wilkinson as "repressive terror."[17] Whatever the label applied to this particular type of terror, it is obvious that some consensus exists on the propriety of including some repressive state tactics in the classification of terrorist acts.

Second, the typologies suggest that a wide variety of acts have been encompassed under the rubric of terrorism, including many engaged in by revolutionary groups, and composed of both internal activities and activities that cross state lines, but all of which are politically motivated and directed toward some end other than the immediate act of violence. These observations serve both to fortify the conclusions already drawn concerning the distinctive nature of terrorist acts and to highlight certain points of dissension that may contribute to cloud our understanding of this term.

Table 1.1 summarizes some of the typologies of terrorism in use today. Although not all of the possible categories of terrorism are included, it is useful to compare the tactics, targets, and perpetrators of such types of terrorism.

**TABLE 1.1**

| Type | Committed by | Target | Tactics |
| --- | --- | --- | --- |
| Mass terror<br>　Endemic<br>　Authorized<br>　Enforcement<br>　Repressive | Political leaders<br>(e.g., Idi Amin's rule in Uganda) | General<br>population | Coercion,<br>organized or<br>unorganized |
| Dynastic assassination | Individuals or groups<br>(e.g., Russian anarchists) | Head of state<br>or ruling elite | Very selective<br>violence |
| Random terror | Individuals or groups<br>(e.g., bombing of<br>Pan Am Flight 103) | Anyone in "the<br>wrong place at<br>the wrong time" | Bombs in<br>cafés,<br>markets, and<br>similar places |
| Focused random<br>　terror | Individuals or groups<br>(e.g., PIRA and UDF<br>bombings in<br>Northern Ireland) | Members of the<br>"opposition" | Bombs in<br>*specific* cafés<br>and markets |
| Tactical terror<br>　Revolutionary | Revolutionary movements<br>(e.g., M19's attacks<br>on Colombian justices) | The government | Attacks on<br>politically<br>attractive<br>targets |

## TACTICS AND LABELS

Before we summarize the conclusions concerning a working definition of terrorism, one further point needs to be emphasized. Both the typologies of terrorism and the working definition of terrorism being offered treat terrorism as a *tactic,* not as a *goal.* This is important to remember, if the term *terrorism* is not to be used or misused by governments unsympathetic to a group's cause. To describe a particular action as a terrorist action does not, and should not, in any sense define either the group or the cause for which it uses that tactic as terrorist.

It is true that if an individual, group, or government chooses to use this particular tactic repeatedly, those observing the actions will probably associate the tactic with those individuals. Continued or prolonged use of such a tactic by any group or government contributes to the perception of that group or government as terrorist by the audience for whom the crime is committed. This view is not necessarily accurate, nor is it inaccurate; it is simply a natural phenomenon. A congressperson who repeatedly supports war efforts and defense buildups may well expect to be labeled a "hawk" both by those who agree with his or her position and by those who disagree with it. It is simply a recognition of this politician's patterns of action.

The same point is to some extent true of groups that repeatedly engage in terrorist acts. The frequency with which they engage in such actions, and to some degree the openness with which they do so, will certainly have an effect on whether their audience views them as being terrorists. This does not mean that the ends toward which they strive are "bad," somehow tainted with the opprobrium of terrorism. It simply means that the audience for whom the terrorist acts are generally staged have associated in their minds the actors with the actions taken in pursuit of that cause.

This perspective is, of course, a very narrow line of reasoning, one not clearly understood by the general public, which is often the audience for terrorist events. That same public frequently attaches a terrorist label to individuals and even to groups who engage fairly regularly in terrorist acts. But in terms acceptable in the legal and political community, it is only the *act* that can accurately be labeled as terrorist, not the individual or the group, and certainly not the cause for which the tactic is employed.

It is true that members of a group cannot engage in questionable or even blatantly illegal actions on a regular basis and not be tainted with the negative labels associated with such actions. Members of Mafia families, although they themselves may be several steps removed from the actual commission of organized crimes, are nevertheless viewed by both the general public and law enforcement agencies as being linked to, and a part of, those deplorable actions.

So it is with terrorism. Those who commit it, and those whose groups or governments have chosen to use it as a tactic, cannot escape the label of "terrorist" given them not by governments but by the very audience toward which such acts are directed. The justice of a cause rarely is sufficient, in that audience's view, to excuse the use of such a tactic. Although politicians and ideologues may accept the rationale, covertly or openly, that the ends for which they struggle justify the means that they choose to employ, most of the civilized world remains unwilling to accept this rationale. Certain acts can be described by definition as terrorist acts whether they are carried out by democratic governments in pursuit of reasonable policy goals or by armed revolutionaries fighting for freedom against tyranny.

## CONCLUSION

Terrorism is an *act* comprised of at least four crucial elements: (1) It is an act of violence, (2) it has a political motive or goal, (3) it is perpetrated against innocent persons, and (4) it is staged to be played before an audience whose reaction of fear and terror is the desired result. This definition eliminates football players, lunatics on a killing spree, and the assassin who tries to kill a "bad" ruler from the label of "terrorist." All acts of violence are not terrorist acts, however heinous they may be.

The line between acceptable types of violence and unacceptable types is, unfortunately, not always clear. Violence by revolutionaries and by the state is sometimes difficult to categorize clearly as terrorist, even given the working definition evolved here. Further study of the history, ideology, and individuals involved in terrorist acts may increase our understanding of this important but confusing term.

## *Evaluation*

Using the definition in a practical application is one method of increasing one's understanding of the usefulness and limitation of the definition. Listed here are two brief sketches of what were termed by some observers to be terrorist acts. Use the four criteria in the definition of terrorism suggested in this chapter to decide whether these incidents were, in fact, terrorist acts. Try also to decide which type of terrorism, if any, was involved, using any one of the typologies mentioned.

1. At 2:30 P.M. on March 30, 1981, Pres. Ronald Reagan was shot in the chest by a gunman. The would-be assassin, John W. Hinckley, Jr., shot the president as he walked to his limousine after addressing the AFL-CIO meeting at the Washington Hilton Hotel. Shooting from a distance of about ten feet, Hinckley shot Reagan, Press Secretary James Brady, Secret Service Agent Timothy J. McCarthy, and Washington police officer Thomas K. Delahanty. Evidence at the subsequent trial indicated that Hinckley was motivated by a desire to impress actress Jodie Foster.

2. Just before dawn on October 23, 1983, a suicide vehicle laden with about 2,500 tons of TNT blew up the U.S. Marine headquarters near the Beirut, Lebanon, airport. About 230 persons were reported killed, most of them as they slept. The Free Islamic Revolutionary Movement claimed responsibility for the action.

## *Suggested Readings*

Friedlander, Robert. *Terrorism: Documents of National and International Control.* Vol. 1. Dobbs Ferry, NY: Oceana, 1979.

Jenkins, Brian, and Janera Johnson. *International Terrorism: A Chronology, 1968–1974.* A report prepared for the Department of State and the Defense Advances Research Projects Agency, R-1587-DOSIARPA (March 1975). Santa Monica, CA: Rand, 1975.

Leeman, Richard W. "Terrorism." In *Morality and Conviction in American Politics: A Reader,* ed. Martin Slann and Susan Duffy. Upper Saddle River, NJ: Prentice Hall, 1990.

Schmid, Alex. *Political Terrorism.* New Brunswick, NJ: Transaction, 1983.

Wilcox, Ambassador Philip, Jr. "Terrorism Remains a Global Issue." *USIA Electronic Journal,* February 1997.

Wilkinson, Paul. *Terrorism and the Liberal State.* New York: New York University Press, 1979.

## *Endnotes*

1. Irving Howe, "The Ultimate Price of Random Terror," *Skeptic: The Forum for Contemporary History* 11 (January–February 1976): 14.

2. David Fromkin, "The Strategy of Terror," *Foreign Affairs* 53 (July 1975): 689.

3. See T.I.A.S., no. 3365.

4. Robert A. Friedlander, *Terrorism: Documents of National and International Control* (Dobbs Ferry, NY: Oceana, 1979), vol. 1, 40.

5. Howe, "The Ultimate Price of Random Terror," 14–15.

6. Brian M. Jenkins, *International Terrorism: A New Kind of Warfare* (Santa Monica, CA: Rand, 1974), P-5261, 4.

7. *Escabedo v. United States,* 633 F2d. 1098, 1104 (5th Cir. 1980).

8. *In re Castroni,* 1 Q.B. 149, 156, 166 (1891).

9. Nicholas N. Kittrie, "Patriots and Terrorists: Reconciling Human Rights with World Order," *Case Western Reserve Journal of International Law* 13, no. 2 (Spring 1981): 300.

10. Kittrie, "Patriots and Terrorists," 304.

11. Friedlander, *Terrorism,* 286.

12. *Principles of the Nuremberg Charter and Judgment,* formulated by the International Law Commission, 1950 (UN General Assembly Records, 5th Session, Supp. 12 A/1315).

13. Howe, "The Ultimate Price of Random Terror," 15.

14. Feliks Gross, *Political Violence and Terror in Nineteenth and Twentieth Century Russia and Eastern Europe* (New York: Cambridge University Press, 1990), 8.

15. J. Bowyer Bell, *Transnational Terror* (Washington, D.C.: American Institute for Public Policy Research; and Stanford, CA: Hoover Institution on War, Revolution and Peace, 1975), 10–25.

16. Thomas Thornton, "Terror as a Weapon of Political Agitation," in *Internal War,* ed. H. Eckstein (London: International Institute for Strategic Studies, 1964), 77–78.

17. Paul Wilkinson, *Political Terrorism* (Cambridge, MA: Harvard University Press, 1974), 38–44.

# Not a Modern Phenomenon

**Key Concepts**

assassination

hashashin

narcoterrorism

tyrannicide

political asylum

state terrorism

privateers

guerrilla warfare

cycle of violence

Even though the word *terrorism* originated during the French Revolution and the Jacobin Reign of Terror (1792–1794), individual acts of terror-violence can be traced back at least to the ancient Greek and Roman republics. By definition, the assassination of Julius Caesar in 44 B.C. was an act of terrorism in so far as a modern political assassination is defined as terrorism. Modern political science, at any rate, tends to treat **assassination,** the murder of a head of state, as a terrorist act.[1]

Group terrorism became more common as early as the Middle Ages. In fact, the word *assassin* comes from an Arabic term **hashashin,** which literally means "hashish eater," or "one addicted to hashish."[2] It was used to describe a sectarian group of Muslims who were employed by their spiritual and political leader (the local caliph) to spread terror in the form of murder and destruction among religious enemies, including women and children.

Accounts of Marco Polo's travels include lurid tales of murder committed by these assassins, acting, it was supposed, under the influence of hashish or other such drugs. It was reported that these early terrorists were motivated not only by religious promises of eternal reward but also by promises of unlimited access to hashish (and other drugs). Even the Crusaders made mention of this group of fanatics and the terror they inspired.[3]

The potent combination of religious and political fanaticism with intoxicating drugs made the legacy of the "Brotherhood of Assassins" formidable. It is still evident to some extent in the unrest that plagues the Middle East today. **Narcoterrorism,** as the linkage between drugs and terrorism is often termed today, will be described in more depth in a later chapter. It is interesting to note here that the region from which the assassins emerged is in the modern nation of Iran. The former Ayatollah Khomeini, leader of the Shiites in this nation during its revolution in the late 1970s, was from the same area that, hundreds of years before, was the home of the infamous caliph.

Another Brotherhood of Assassins emerged from a combination of religion and politics in the 1890s. The Hur Brotherhood, whose roots were in the Sind region of British India, resembled the earlier Islamic Brotherhood of Assassins. Although this latter brotherhood was suppressed, after considerable bloodshed, another Hur rebellion occurred in Pakistan in the mid–twentieth century. Indeed, much of modern Pakistan's terrorism from its Sikh minority derives from that group's religious and political dissatisfaction with Muslim Pakistan's leaders. Religion and politics continue to take innocent lives in this turbulent region.

Islam is not, in any sense, a violent religion. Nor are Christianity, Judaism, or any of the other religions in whose name violence has been carried out. However, the mixture of religion and politics has quite often resulted in violence, frequently against innocent victims, which makes it, according to the definition suggested in the preceding chapter, terrorism. The Middle East, as the home of three major world religions, has been plagued by a variety of violent sects. Today, nations such as Iran have witnessed, and perhaps fostered, the creation of several violent sects, whose blending of religion and politics looks a lot like that of the Brotherhood of Assassins. Table 2.1 offers a brief insight into two of the larger of these radical groups, their location, and their violent activities.

The fedayeen, the Islamic "self-sacrificers" in the "holy war" being waged by more militant sects today, are similar in many respects to the Brotherhood of Assassins of the Middle Ages. Like the Assassins, modern fedayeen find strength in the promise of a reward in "paradise." Unlike the earlier sect, however, these modern zealots believe that they will receive their reward in a spiritual paradise, not in the caliph's courtyard. Religion is the narcotic that serves to both motivate their terrorist actions and to deaden their consciences to the horror of the slaughter that they inflict on innocent persons.

Thus, the mixture of religion and politics in the commitment of terrorism today is not new but continues to be quite deadly. History enables us to place current mixtures such as these in context, which makes understanding easier. It has not, however, yet made it possible for governments or organizations to prevent the explosion of these potentially lethal elements.

## TYRANNICIDE: "TO GO TOO FAST"

Assassination has become both an ideological statement and a powerful political weapon, using the vehicle of the doctrine of **tyrannicide**, the assassination of a political leader (tyrant). Throughout Italy during the Renaissance, tyrannicide was fairly widely practiced, whereas in Spain and France during the Age of Absolutism it was at least widely advocated. The leading advocate of the doctrine of tyrannicide as an

**TABLE 2.1**

| Group | Description | Activities |
|---|---|---|
| Hizballah (Party of God) a.k.a. Islamic Jihad, Revolutionary Justice Organization | Radical Shiite group formed in Lebanon; close ties to Iran | • Bombing of U.S. Marine barracks in Beirut (1983) • Held most, if not all, Western hostages in Lebanon |
| Armed Islamic Group a.k.a. GIA | Islamic extremist group, operating in Algeria against sectarian state | • Civilian massacres, often of entire villages |
| Sikh groups Includes, among others, *Dashmesh* (active in India, Germany, and Canada); *Dal Khalsa* (active in India, Pakistan, and Germany); *Babbar Khalsa* (active in India, Germany, and Canada) | Several domestic and international groups | • Regular and bloody attacks against Hindus • Blamed for bombing of Air India airline (329 people killed, 1979) • Desecration of Hindu holy places, bombings, and assassinations |
| The All India Sikh Students Federation | Seek to establish an independent Sikh state called Khalistan | • Hijacked an Indian airline to Pakistan (1981) |

acceptable solution to political repression was a Spanish Jesuit scholar, Juan de Mariana, whose principal work, *De Regis Institutions,* was banned in France.[4]

In the words of Mariana we find much of the same political justification as that used by leaders of national liberation movements today. Mariana asserted that people necessarily possessed not only the right of rebellion but also the remedy of assassination, stating that "if in no other way it is possible to save the fatherland, the prince should be killed by the sword as a public enemy."[5]

Only ten years after Mariana's words were uttered, Henry III, king of France, was assassinated by the monk François Favaillac. Many leaders since that time have been struck down by persons who claimed to have acted as instruments of justice against a tyrant. Even President Lincoln's assassin, John Wilkes Booth, saw his act in such a light, as evidenced by his triumphant shout, "Sic semper tyrannis!" (Thus always to tyrants!).[6]

Political assassins, like those committing murder in the name of religion, have frequently claimed to be acting as "divine instruments" of justice. At the very least, such assassins have viewed themselves as the chosen instruments of a popular legitimacy, rightly and even righteously employed in the destruction of illegitimate regimes and tyrannical rulers. The robes of martyrdom have been donned as readily by political as by religious zealots. Like the religious fanatics, political assassins have had no hesitation in acting as judge, jury, and executioner, assuring themselves and others that their appointment to these offices was made not by themselves but by a higher will or authority.

During the latter part of the eighteenth century and early nineteenth century, the divine right of kings theory, which stated that kings rule by divine appointment, began to lose its political grip on Europe. As the theory of the existence of a social contract between a people and their government began to gain acceptance, those who carried out political offenses such as tyrannicide gradually found a more benign atmosphere in which to act.

As one acting to "right the wrongs" committed by government, the political assassin was no longer regarded with universal disfavor. Vidal, a leading French legal scholar, noted:

> Whereas formerly the political offender was treated as a public enemy, he is today considered as a friend of the public good, as a man of progress, desirous of bettering the political institutions of his country, having the laudable intentions, hastening the onward march of humanity, his only fault being that he wishes to go too fast, and that he employs in attempting to realize the progress which he desires, means irregular, illegal, and violent.[7]

Not until the middle of the twentieth century was the murder of a head of state, or any member of his or her family, formally designated as terrorism. Even today, those who commit the "political" crime of murder of a head of state can often enjoy a type of special protection, in the form of **political asylum,** a type of sanctuary or refuge for a person who has committed such a crime granted by one government against requests by another government for extradition of that person to be prosecuted for this political crime.

## STATE TERRORISM: FRANCE'S REIGN OF TERROR

The use of "irregular, illegal, and violent means" was not, of course, limited to lone political assassins. The execution of Marie Antoinette on October 16, 1793, was one of the first incidents actually called terrorism. In this instance, the terrorists were not trying to overthrow the government—they *were* the government! The Committee of Public Safety, led by Robespierre, chief spokesman of the Jacobin party, governed France during the tumultuous period known as the Reign of Terror (September 1793–July 1794). It is from this period, during which an estimated 20,000 persons were killed, that the word *terrorism* has evolved.

It is interesting, is it not, that modern "terrorism" derives its name from a gross example of **state terrorism,** acts of terrorism that a state commits against defenseless victims, rather than from terror-violence by a lone assassin or small, fanatic, nonstate group? States have been, and continue to be, involved from time to time in a wide variety of violent acts against their own citizens and those of other nations.

Consider the case of piracy. From the sixteenth century forward, lawmakers have considered pirates and piracy to be the "common enemies of humanity." Blackstone's *Commentaries* referred to piracy as "an offense against the universal law of society."[8] Yet both England (for whom Blackstone wrote) and America (whose law frequently cites his precepts) licensed **privateers,** private ships outfitted as warships and given letters of marque and reprisal, allowing them to make war on vessels flying foreign flags.

Under the reign of Queen Elizabeth I of England, the Elizabethan Sea Dogs, privateer ships sailing under the protection of the English flag, carried out violent acts of piracy against the Spanish fleet. American privateers, too, played a fairly significant role in both the American Revolution and the War of 1812. Both nations, then, have commissioned pirates to carry out acts of terror-violence for them on the high seas, acts that both nations publicly deplore as "offenses against humanity" in their courts today. Modern terrorism continues occasionally to take the form of piracy, but today the piracy is often of aircraft rather than sea vessels. This interesting change will be discussed later, with particular attention to its impact on legal remedies for terrorism.

## GUERRILLA WARFARE: SELECTIVE VIOLENCE

Since the French Revolution, terrorism and guerrilla warfare have become increasingly difficult to separate clearly. **Guerrilla warfare** is, essentially, an insurrectionary armed protest, implemented by means of selective violence. To the extent that the violence remains selective and the choice of targets military rather than civilian, it is possible to distinguish between guerrilla warfare and terrorism.

The term *guerrilla,* meaning "little war," evolved from Spanish resistance to the invasions of Napoleon in 1808. This war on the Iberian Peninsula, in which Spanish guerrillas were aided in making increasingly successful attacks on French encampments by the British military, has become in some measure a prototype for the twentieth-century wars of national liberation. In such contemporary struggles, indigenous vigilante groups are often supported openly (as were the Spanish) or covertly, by the military of other nations.

Ideology and nationalism combined with terror-violence in the Internal Macedonian Revolutionary Organization (IMRO), a group that made its first appearance in 1893. For several years the IMRO waged guerrilla warfare, sometimes employing terrorist tactics, against the Turkish rulers of their region. As in the Iberian conflict, other nations both assisted and interfered in the struggle. Bombings and kidnappings, as well as the murder of civilians and officials, were frequent in this "little war." Violence escalated into the Saint Elliah's Rebellion in August 1903, which was dealt with ruthlessly by Turkish authorities. This struggle left thousands dead on both sides, at least 70,000 homeless, and 200 Macedonian villages in ashes.

Turkey's suppression of similar nationalist struggles on the part of its Armenian population in the early part of the twentieth century helped to create

Armenian groups willing to engage in terrorist activities today. These activities, which include bombings and murder reminiscent of the IMRO, have been directed less by nationalism than by a desire to have revenge for the ruthless suppression of that earlier nationalism. In this case, savagely suppressed nationalism has spawned vengeful terrorism by individuals and groups whose demands are perhaps even harder to satisfy than were those of the nationalists of earlier decades.

Events in the 1990s in the former Yugoslavia give credence to the concept that repressed nationalism can, in a resurgent form, exact a bloody toll on innocent civilian populations. In the turbulent years before the outbreak of World War I, the Balkan states were engaged in a wide variety of revolutionary violence. Brigands, calling themselves *comitatus* ("committee men") and covertly sponsored by Greece, Serbia, and Bulgaria (which was also involved in the IMRO struggles), roamed the countryside. In the worst, not the best, tradition of revolutionaries, these brigands terrorized their own countrymen, burning, murdering, and robbing all who stood in their way. The incredible destruction and genocidal murders that took place in the Balkans in the 1990s parallel, and even exceed, this pattern.

World War I was, in fact, triggered by a transnational assassination that had its roots in revolutionary terrorism. A secret Serbian terrorist organization, popularly known as the Black Hand, was both an organization employed by the Serbian government as an unofficial instrument of national foreign policy and a lethal weapon of political protest against the Austro-Hungarian Empire. On June 28, 1914, a 19-year-old Serbian trained by the Black Hand murdered the heir to the imperial throne of that empire, Archduke Franz Ferdinand, in Sarajevo. This assassination was the catalyst for a series of events that, within a month's time, grew into a global conflagration. Revolutionary terror-violence triggered international devastation on a scale unprecedented at that time.

Conflict in and around Sarajevo in the 1990s is partially explained, too, by this early pattern of revolutionary terror-violence. At least twice within the twentieth century, revolutionary terror-violence has been unleashed by groups, governments, and militias against a civilian population. This type of violence makes reconciliation extremely difficult, if not impossible, to achieve. Memories of violence against women and children within families are hard to relinquish, and repetition of such violence within less than a century makes the creation of a sense of common identity (nationalism) and reconciliation between populations within that region perhaps an impossible goal.

Revolutions are not by definition terrorist events. Indeed, some have been successfully carried out without resort to terrorist tactics. It is increasingly difficult, however, for an untrained and sparsely equipped indigenous army to wage a successful guerrilla war against a national standing army. With mounting frustration in the face of apparently insurmountable odds, it is increasingly easy to resort to terror-violence to achieve by psychological force what it is not possible to achieve by force of arms.

Perhaps nowhere else in this century has the role of liberationist combined more thoroughly, until recently, with that of terrorist than in the actions of the militant group usually known as the Irish Republican Army (IRA). This group's guerrilla campaign of murder and terror, growing out of the Sinn Fein movement in 1916, provoked the British to respond in kind, with a counterterror campaign. While this revolutionary terrorism may be said to have stimulated the creation of an independent Irish republic, the violence did not end with this "success." In the mid-1950s the Provisional IRA began a second wave of anti-British terror, which continued until 1994.

This struggle offers insights in several historical respects. In addition to being, in part, a blend of nationalism and terrorism, it is also a contemporary example of the potent mixture of religion and politics. Catholic Ireland has long resented Protestant Britain's domination of its politics. Northern Ireland, which remains under British rule, is predominantly Protestant, with a Catholic minority.

Thus, the lines of battle are drawn along both nationalistic and religious lines. Catholics in Northern Ireland have tended to support a unification of those northern provinces with the Irish republic, whereas Protestants in Northern Ireland have demanded continued British rule. The legacy of hatred and mistrust bred by generations of violence is so bitter that an end to the violence seemed, until the end of the twentieth century, unlikely. The cyclical nature of violence can indeed create a deadly spiral.

## CYCLICAL NATURE OF TERROR

Violence, particularly terrorist violence, has too often created a **cycle of violence,** with those against whom the terror-violence is first carried out becoming so angered that they resort to terrorism in response, directed against the people or institutions regarded as being responsible for the initial terrorist acts. Each violent act frequently causes equally violent reactions. When the violence is unselective, when innocent people are victimized, the reactive violence is also likely to "break all the rules" in the selection of targets and thus be terrorist.

Most revolutionary groups assert that it is terrorism by the *state* that provokes, and by its presence justifies, acts of terror-violence by nonstate groups seeking to change the government or its policies. The relationship between terror-violence by the state and that of nonstate groups and individuals is evident in the history of many modern nation-states. But the nature of that relationship is still the subject of much debate.

From the time of the French Revolution, terrorism and guerrilla movements have become inextricably intertwined. Perhaps the most prominent proponents of individual and collective violence as a means of destroying governments and social institutions were the Russian anarchists, revolutionaries within Russia who sought an end to the czarist state of the latter nineteenth century. "Force only yields to force," and terror would provide the mechanism of change, according to Russian radical theorist Alexander Serno-Solovevich.[9] In the writings of two of the most prominent spokesmen for revolutionary anarchism, Mikhail Bakunin and Sergei Nechaev, one finds philosophies often echoed by modern terrorists. Bakunin, for example, advocated in his *National Catechism* (1866) the use of "selective, discriminate terror." Nechaev, in his work *Revolutionary Catechism* (1870), went further in advocating both the theory and practice of pervasive terror-violence. He asserted of the revolutionary:

> [D]ay and night he must have one single thought, one single purpose: merciless destruction. With this aim in view, tirelessly and in cold blood, he must always be prepared to kill with his own hands anyone who stands in the way of achieving his goals.[10]

This is surely a very large step in the evolution of a terrorist from the lone political assassin of earlier centuries. Even the religious fanatics of the assassins genre and the privateers of Elizabethan times were arguably less willing to kill anyone to achieve a political objective. But this difference may well have existed more on paper than it did in practice. In spite of this written willingness to kill anyone who stood in the way, even the Socialist Revolutionary Party resorted primarily to selective terror-violence and took special pains to avoid endangering innocent bystanders. For instance, the poet Ivan Kalialev, who assassinated the Grand Duke Sergius on the night of February 2, 1905, had passed up an opportunity earlier that evening to throw the bomb because the Grand Duchess and some of her nieces and nephews were also in the Grand Duke's carriage.[11]

Although an attempt was made to kill Alexander II as early as 1866, the first generation of Russian terrorists generally resorted to violence only to punish traitors and police spies or to retaliate against brutal treatment of political prisoners. (Odd, isn't it, that these same reasons are frequently quoted today as justifications for similar use of "extralegal violence"?)

With the creation of the *Zemiya I Volva* (Will of the People) in 1879, political assassination of a wide range of targets began to become a normal form of political protest, becoming part of an intense cycle of terror and counterterror. This revolutionary group believed that terrorism should be used to compromise the best of governmental power, to give constant proof that it is possible to fight the government, and to strengthen thereby the revolutionary spirit of the people and their faith in the success of the cause.[12]

It is quite easy to note the blending of revolutionary and state terror-violence during this time. The assassinations of Czar Alexander II in 1881 and First Minister Peter Stolypin in 1911 were incidents that produced periods of counterterrorism (in the form of state repression). This repression probably accelerated the revolutionary movement responsible for those assassinations. Thus, the terrorist acts of assassination, inspired by brutal repression in the czarist state, provoked further state terrorism, which in turn the inspired revolutionary movement to further acts of violence.

The formation of the Union of Russian Men to combat the growing revolutionary movement "by all means" not only was sanctioned by the czar, but granted special protection by him. This reactionary group engaged in a variety of terrorist activities, including but not limited to political murders, torture, and bombing. The Okrana (the czarist secret police) also wreaked fierce counterterror against the militant revolutionaries in an unabated attack, until World War I.

George Kennan, commenting on the rising tide of terrorism in Russia during the last half of the nineteenth century, explained the relationship of state and revolutionary terrorism in this way: "Wrong a man . . . deny him all redress, exile him if he complains, gag him if he cries out, strike him in the face if he struggles, and at the last he will stab and throw bombs."[13]

Still, while some of the seeds of more widespread and random terror-violence were sown in the revolutionary and anarchistic movements of the late nineteenth century, by the beginning of the twentieth century, terror-violence was still principally directed toward political assassination. Between 1881 and 1912, at least ten national leaders had lost their lives to assassins, as Table 2.2 indicates.

The cyclical nature of terror is also evident in the events surrounding the creation of the state of Israel. The terrorism spawned in Nazi Germany helped to create a cycle of violence that still grips the Middle East today. After the military collapse of the Central Powers and the armistice agreement of November 1918, within Germany a large number of largely right-wing paramilitary organizations grew. In ideology, terrorist method, and political role, these groups were in many respects the historical heirs of the Brotherhood of Assassins. They were also the nucleus for the German *Reichswehr.*

Under the leadership of such men, Germany perpetrated on innocent persons the greatest atrocities the world has ever recorded. Organized state terrorism reached its zenith in Nazi Germany, and its victims numbered in the millions. Of those victims, the majority were Jewish. Many who sought to flee the terror tried to emigrate to Palestine, which at that time was under British mandate. But the British Mandate Government, by 1940, was closing the gates to Jewish immigration into this land, which was, in fact, already occupied by Arabs. As the population balance began to

**TABLE 2.2**

| *Individual* | *Nation* | *Date of Death* |
| --- | --- | --- |
| President James Garfield | United States | 1881 |
| Czar Alexander II | Russia | 1881 |
| Lord Frederick Cavendish, chief secretary | Ireland | 1882 |
| President Sadi Carnot | France | 1894 |
| Premier Antonio Canavos del Castillo | Spain | 1897 |
| Empress Elizabeth | Austria-Hungary | 1898 |
| King Umberto I | Italy | 1900 |
| President William McKinley | United States | 1901 |
| Premier Peter Stolypin | Russia | 1911 |
| Premier Jose Canalejas y Mendez | Spain | 1912 |

swing away from the indigenous Arab population toward the immigrant Jews, the British government sought to stem the tide of refugees.

The Haganah, a Zionist underground army, and the Irgun Zvai Leumi, a Zionist militant force willing to use terrorist tactics, waged terrorist warfare on the British forces in Palestine. Bombing, murder, and assassination became the order of the day, as British counterviolence met with escalating Irgun and Haganah intransigence. With the Irgun bombing of the King David Hotel, in which many innocent persons died or were seriously injured, British determination to quell the rebellion diminished.

But during the struggle to gain a homeland free of Nazi terror, the Irgun had practiced terror against the indigenous population. When Israel declared itself to be an independent state in 1948, some of the dispossessed people within its borders and those who fled to surrounding states began a war of revolution and of terror against Israel.

Israel's revolutionary terror-violence against the Palestinian people has spurred a conflict that continues to rend the fragile fabric of peace in the Middle East. Born in bloodshed, violence, and desperation, Israel continues to struggle against the terrorist violence that its very creation evoked.

## Contemporary Events, Historical Roots

*Is* contemporary terrorism "different"? In what ways? One reason for briefly reviewing the historical pattern and roots of terrorism is to be able to discover whether that pattern remains accurate in the contemporary world. If terrorism today is just like terrorism of previous centuries, then we can use historical patterns to predict behavior and to construct responses based on successful attempts to combat this phenomenon in the past.

If terrorism today is different, however, then historical patterns will be less useful in designing responses, though still helpful in understanding the dynamics of the phenomenon. Terrorism has clearly existed before this century. What we need to know as we prepare for yet another century is whether twentieth-century terrorism was significantly different from its historical counterparts.

### Political Assassinations

Terrorist acts are no longer directed solely or even primarily at heads of state. Security precautions to guard such persons against attack have made it very difficult for a lone assassin to successfully murder such a person. The assassination of Yitzhak Rabin, prime minister of Israel, in 1995 demonstrated that it is not, of course, impossible for such an attack to occur with success. However, in the latter part of the twentieth century, attacks have been made with greater frequency on individuals of less significance but easier access. This broadens the range of acceptable victims well beyond the realm justified under the doctrine of tyrannicide.

## Drugs, Religion, and Political Murders

Although this lethal combination still exists in the contemporary world, the relationship among these elements has changed considerably. During the Middle Ages, the caliph rewarded his assassins with drugs for successfully completed murders of religious opponents. Today, drugs are used to finance the lethal expeditions of religious zealots whose targets are not only those of another religion within their community, but include whole nations or groups of nations whose citizens are regarded by the zealots as legitimate targets for murder. Again, this is a drastic broadening of the category of acceptable potential victims.

## Piracy

While piracy of the sea has waned somewhat in recent years (although the incident involving the *Achille Lauro* reminded us that such piracy still occurs), air piracy has more than taken its place. During the 1970s and 1980s, airline hijacking became fairly commonplace. Whereas pirates of old, however, sought primarily material gain (with political gain a pleasant by-product for certain governments), modern air pirates tend to seek political gain first. So although the treatment of victims of piracy has remained essentially the same (pirates throughout the ages have tended to treat their victims as completely expendable), the purpose or goal of the act has changed radically.

## State-Sponsored Terrorism

Modern governments have expanded the concept of "licensed" pirates. Terrorism has, in fact, become an institutionalized form of foreign policy for many nations. Governments privately and sometimes publicly sponsor groups involved in terrorist activities. Moreover, in the latter half of the twentieth century, governments increasingly became involved in revolutionary movements, providing assistance for either the revolutionaries or the regime against which the revolution was fighting. This has blurred the lines between those involved in the fighting of a war and those who are merely innocent bystanders. Chapter 5 takes a closer look at state-sponsored terrorism.

## Modern Travel and Communication

Related to these differences between historical and modern terrorism are important developments in the contemporary world. Modern methods of travel, for example, make it possible to carry out an assassination in the morning of Country Q and be halfway around the world from that nation within a matter of hours.

Modern communication, too, has made this a smaller world in that events in, for instance, Nigeria are of immediate notice and interest in New York. Such communications, too, have served to expand the theater to which the terrorist plays. Thus, to catch the attention of America, the terrorist need not travel to New York City with a bomb; he need only plant a bomb in Lagos.

# Weapons

The dramatic increase in the arsenal of weapons available to modern terrorists is also worth noting. No longer need the would-be assassin rely on a small handgun to eliminate his or her victim. A letter bomb will do the job without endangering the perpetrator, as the Unibomber in the United States has demonstrated. Revolutionaries are no longer confined to simple rifles; SAMs (surface-to-air missiles) are all too accessible.

The potential for destruction through chemical and biological weapons has not yet been fully tapped, although the events in Japan in 1995 gave ample evidence of the potential for such weapons when used in the very vulnerable mass transit systems of a modern nation. Perhaps, until recently, the consequences of using such weapons were too dramatic for most groups to contemplate. But modern technology has certainly put at the terrorist's disposal a vast array of lethal and largely indiscriminate weapons, of which the sarin toxin apparently used in Japan represents only a very simple example. With the arsenal, the selection of victims has become devastatingly indiscriminate. One can be a victim simply by riding a subway train to work—a necessary act for millions of innocent people.

As historical precedents for terrorism grow, it becomes very hard to distinguish between legitimate and illegitimate violence. As the nation born in illegitimate violence, such as occurred in Northern Ireland and Israel, becomes the state, it becomes increasingly difficult to condemn as terrorist (and thus illegitimate) the methods employed in the struggles for independence and survival of those within those states. The longer the history of terrorism grows, the harder it is to make a label of "terrorism" stick to the actions of any group or nation.

## *Evaluation*

### *Modern Piracy and Government Responses*

In October 1985, the news flared across the world: a group of American and European tourists had been taken hostage aboard a pleasure ship, the *Achille Lauro,* by a handful of Palestinian terrorists. The ship wandered north along the coast of Lebanon as the hijackers sought safe haven. Bit by bit, news of the horror aboard leaked out: 69-year-old Leon Klinghoffer of New York City was murdered in his wheelchair.

The Egyptian government called in a negotiator, Abu Abbas, leader of the Palestinian splinter group to which the hijackers claimed to belong. He ordered them to release the ship and come into port, where they were promised safe passage out of the country.

At the same time, U.S. intelligence sources, who were monitoring the exchanges between President Hosni Mubarak of Egypt and Yasir Arafat, leader of the Palestinian Liberation Organization (PLO), gained enough information to enable the United States to spring a trap. The Egypt Air plane aboard which the hijackers were being smuggled out of Egypt was ambushed by U.S. war planes and forced to land in Italy, where the hijackers were taken into custody by the Italian government.

This modern incident of terrorism and counterforce raises some important questions for discussion:

1. Were the hijackers pirates, "common enemies of humankind," or revolutionaries using the means at their disposal to wage war on oppressive governments?

2. Was Egypt wrong to allow the hijackers into port and assist them in leaving the country, since in doing so they secured the release of the rest of the hostages?

3. Was the United States justified in its actions against the hijackers, or was it guilty of terrorism as well?

4. Do, in fact, "rights" (to commit acts of terror-violence) derive from "wrongs"?

## *Suggested Readings*

Laqueur, Walter. "PostModern Terrorism." *Foreign Affairs* (September/October 1996).
Maranto, Robert. "The Rationality of Terrorism." In *Multidimensional Terrorism,* ed. Martin Slann and Bernard Schechterman. New York: Rienner, 1987.
Rose, Paul. "Terror in the Skies." *Contemporary Review* 248 (June 1986).
Schultz, George. "Low-Intensity Warfare: The Challenge of Ambiguity." Address to Low-Intensity Warfare Conference, Washington, D.C., January 15, 1986.
Slann, Martin. "The State as Terrorist." In *Multidimensional Terrorism,* ed. Martin Slann and Bernard Schechterman, New York: Rienner, 1987.

## *Endnotes*

1. Robert Friedlander, *Terrorism: Documents of International and Local Control* (Dobbs Ferry, NY: Oceana, 1979), 7.

2. Funk and Wagnall's *Standard Dictionary: Comprehensive International Edition,* vol. 1, 86, col. 3.

3. See M. Hodgson, *The Order of the Assassins* (San Rafael, CA: Presidio Press, 1960); B. Lewis, *The Assassins: A Radical Sect in Islam* (San Rafael, CA: Presidio Press, 1968).

4. See O. Zasra and J. Lewis, *Against the Tyrant: The Tradition and Theory of Tyrannicide* (Boston: Little Brown, 1957).

5. Quoted by B. Hurwood, *Society and the Assassin: A Background Book on Political Murder* (London: International Institute for Strategic Studies, 1970), 29.

6. Carl Sandburg, *Abraham Lincoln: The War Years* (Cambridge: MIT Press, 1939), vol. 4, 482.

7. Vidal, *Cours de Droit Criminal et de Science Pententiare,* 5th ed. (Paris: Institute de Paris Press, 1916), 110–112.

8. William Blackstone, *Commentaries on the Laws of England* (1749), vol. 4, 71.

9. Quoted by F. Venturi, *Roots of Revolution: A History of the Populist and Socialist Movements in Nineteenth Century Russia,* trans. F. Haskell (New York: Norton, 1966), 281.

10. Venturi, *Roots of Revolution,* 366.

11. Irving Howe, "The Ultimate Price of Random Terror," *Skeptic: The Forum for Contemporary History* 11 (January–February 1976): 10–19.

12. Sandra Stencel, "Terrorism: An Idea Whose Time Has Come," *Skeptic: The Forum for Contemporary History,* 11 (January–February 1976): 4–5.

13. Quoted by Friedlander, *Terrorism: Documents,* 26.

# 3

# Ideology and Terrorism: Rights from Wrongs?

## Key Concepts

anarchism
*jus ex injuria non oritur*
right of self-determination
image of the enemy
image of themselves
image of the victims
nature of the conflict
theme of millianarianism

religious fanaticism
neo-Nazism/neofascism
separatism
nationalism
issue orientation
ideological mercenaries
pathological terrorists
counterterror terrorists

Can rights ever derive from wrongs? Can one injustice truly justify the commission of another injustice? There are, of course, no easy answers to such loaded questions. In the same manner, there may be no clear or absolute answer to the question of whether there could be a "justifiable" terrorist act.

Most individuals or groups who claim that an act is justified mean that it has a purpose that is "just," one that can be given a "reasonable explanation." So to determine whether terrorism is justified, we must study the reasons or justifications given for the terrorist acts. Because we have already reviewed the transformation of terrorism over the centuries, from the lone assassin executing an unjust ruler to the revolutionaries of czarist Russia, we will confine our study to the "reasons" for terrorism to the terrorism that has existed in the twentieth century.

This approach will not limit the usefulness of our observations, because the basic reasons for terrorism have not, in fact, changed as rapidly as have the tactics of terror. The forces of oppression that have caused men to rebel have not changed over the centuries; what has changed is the willingness of the oppressed to use previously unthinkable means to achieve their objectives.

The reasons for this willingness to use extraordinary means are important; they are, in many ways, the "justification" for modern terrorism. It has always been possible to murder innocent persons. Why is it no longer an unthinkable option for so many revolutionary groups?

This is the crucial question. It is unarguable that states throughout history have used terrorism on their citizens, on the citizens of other nations, and as an instrument of war. Biblical and historical accounts abound of conquering armies who slaughtered innocent men, women, and children; who took slaves and captives and perpetrated all manner of atrocities on their innocent heads.

But those rebelling against such tyrannous brutality have heretofore eschewed a comparable brutality. Indeed, the lodestar of revolutionary theory has been its vehement condemnation of the brutality of the existing regime.

Why, then, have twentieth-century revolutionary groups become more and more willing to perpetrate equally brutal acts against similarly innocent persons? Oppression is not new, nor is the presence of a few desperate persons willing to risk all to oppose a system they abhor. What is new is the willingness of these "desperate people" to use tactics that, until very recently, were the sole province of the despised state?

This, it seems, is the phenomenon of modern terrorism: that revolutionaries, those rebelling against state oppression, are now willing to use weapons of terror against an innocent citizenry. In the past, revolutionaries and the theorists who espoused their causes defended their actions in terms of ridding the world of oppressive states whose leaders committed "unthinkable, barbarous acts upon the citizenry." By committing similar "unthinkable, barbarous acts upon the citizenry," revolutionaries have fundamentally altered their philosophy. It is important to understand the substance of this changed philosophy, and the reasons for the change, to understand modern terrorism.

## THE RATIONALIZATION OF VIOLENCE

The terrorist revolution is the only just form of revolution.
—Nikolai Morozov (1880)

Revolutionaries such as Morozov came to view terrorism as the only chance for successful revolution in czarist Russia. **Anarchism,** which advocated "propaganda of the deed," became increasingly committed to nonselective violence, as the possibility of forcing change within the structure of the existing state became less feasible.

Indeed, anarchism, as a theory, is less strict in its adherence to the injury of only "guilty" persons than were the revolutionaries of nineteenth-century Russia. Louis August Blanqui asserted that the transformation of society could only come about from a small, well-organized group of "terrorists" acting as the vanguard of the revolutionary process.[1] With the imperial abdication in France in 1870 and the establishment of the Paris Commune in March 1871 (composed as it was of a Blanquist majority), "a red terror once again came into being, accentuated by class division and violence."[2]

The anarchosyndicalist credo expressed by American revolutionary propagandist Emma Goldman offers another insight into the transition of revolutionary theory. Goldman advocated "direct action against the authority of the law, direct action against the invasive meddlesome authority of our moral code."[3] This rejection of our moral code as "invasive" and "meddlesome" and belonging to those in authority is certainly a shift in philosophy. Revolutionaries of previous centuries had claimed that such a code justified their actions against a clearly immoral state. This change in perception of the existing moral code will be explored shortly, in the context of discussion of the self-justification of modern terrorists.

Franz Fanon, the theoretical architect of the Algerian independence movement, also offered some changes to traditional revolutionary theory. He argued for the use of "the technique of terrorism," which, he asserted, consisted of individual and collective attempts by means of bombs or by the derailing of trains to disrupt the existing system.

Both of these theorists express a philosophy radically different from that espoused by the early Russian revolutionaries or earlier advocates of tyrannicide. The legitimate victim of violence need no longer be exclusively either the soldier or the government official. Rather, with increasing frequency, he or she is an innocent civilian third party, whose injury or death is intended to hurt or frighten the entire body politic.

In the United States, anarchist philosophy also began to engender radical demands for indiscriminate violence. Anarchist publications in the 1880s were candid in their enthusiasm for the widespread use of explosives. A letter in one extremist paper, *Alarm,* enthused:

> Dynamite! Of all the good stuff, this is the stuff. . . . Place this in the immediate vicinity of a lot of rich loafers who live by the sweat of other people's brows, and light the fuse. A most cheerful and gratifying result will follow.[4]

Anarchist violence did indeed claim innocent lives, often through the use of dynamite, during the following decades. While strains of both nonviolent socialism and violent anarchism mixed in the labor movement, unfairly tainting much of labor's legitimate attempts to organize, acts of random violence were unabashedly carried out by anarchist extremists within the movement.

On October 1, 1910, the *Los Angeles Times* building was destroyed by dynamite. Two young ironworkers eventually confessed to this crime, in which 20 innocent persons died and another 17 were injured. On September 16, 1920, an explosion on New York's Wall Street destroyed an even larger number of innocent lives. Forty people were killed in this blast, and another 300 were injured. A hitherto unknown group, calling itself the American Anarchist Fighters, claimed credit for this devastation whose victims were ordinary working people. In spite of the fact that anarchists were, in theory, committed to conflict with the "rich ruling elites," victims of its violence were in many cases *not* wealthy or powerful persons but innocent bystanders.

Violence among groups seeking to correct societal injustices has not been limited to anarchistic rationalization. In Uruguay, terrorism was justified by the Tupamaros on nationalistic and socialistic grounds. Uruguay, until the late 1950s a model of democracy and prosperity in a largely authoritarian sea of South American nations, began to falter economically in 1958. Young middle-class professionals and intellectuals, hit especially hard by the economic difficulties and moved by the wretched living and working conditions of many groups in the country, began to seek radical solutions to the nation's woes. Over the next few years, their activities ranged from the hijacking of trucks carrying food (which they subsequently distributed to needy people) to bank robbery and kidnapping for ransom.

These activities alone would not constitute terrorism, perhaps. However, the targets for the kidnapping were frequently foreign diplomats or employees of foreign companies, whose only "crime" was their presence in Uruguay. Assassinations of police officers were so common that some police officers refused, in fear, to wear their uniforms to work.

Attacks on the military are standard and largely acceptable during a time of revolution and social upheaval. Attacks on unarmed civilian personnel is neither acceptable nor readily justifiable. Socialism and nationalism in Uruguay combined to create a climate similar to that which prompted the "Macedonia for Macedonians" cry of the IMRO. The desire to drive out foreign influence and to forcibly redistribute wealth served, in this case, as the justification for terror-violence.

# REBELLION AND THE RIGHT OF SELF-DETERMINATION

The evolution of revolutionary violence into terrorism is significant. It has long been a stumbling block in the creation of effective international law concerning terrorism. Revolutions have occurred throughout history without recourse to terror-violence; an effort must be made to understand why such revolutions do not continue to occur without the use of terrorist tactics. Do they not occur, or can they not occur *successfully* without the use of terrorism?

Although rebellion cannot be separated from violence, certain types of violence have, as noted earlier, not been acceptable. Violence that is directed deliberately against innocent parties is destructive not only of law and of legal systems but also of civilized society, according to one expert on international law.[5]

As the United Nations (UN) Secretariat, in its study of the nature and causes of terrorism, concluded, "The legitimacy of a cause does not in itself legitimize the use of certain forms of violence, especially against the innocent." Paragraph ten of the study notes that this limit on the legitimate use of violence "has long been recognized, even in the customary laws of war."[6]

Two points here are worth noting. First, the community of nations regards the limits on the legitimate use of violence as being of long standing, not the product of twentieth-century governments seeking to prevent rebellions. Although many nations

have come into being during this century through both rebellion and peaceful decolo-
nization, the customary laws restraining the use of force were not created to harness
this explosion of nationalism.

Second, the community of nations, not just in the Secretariat's report but in many
documents and discussions, has agreed that there are in fact limits to the legitimate use
of violence, regardless of the justice of the cause. Moreover, these limits are acknowl-
edged to exist even in times of war. Indeed, it is *from* the laws of war that we obtain our
clearest understanding of precisely what these limits on the use of violence are.

Therefore, a condemnation of terrorism is not a denunciation of revolutionaries
or guerrillas. It is only a reiteration of the limits of violence that a civilized society is
willing to permit. It does not in any sense preclude the right to revolution, which is a
recognized and protected right under international law.

As one scholar points out, those who attack "political and military leaders . . .
will not be called terrorists at all" in international law.[7] Another knowledgeable
expert remarks that "today's revolutionaries want to be guerrillas, not terrorists," as
there is no stigma attached to the status of rebels.[8]

No pejorative status is attached to rebels and revolutionaries, but even armies
engaged in warfare must by law recognize certain limits on the use of violence. The
right to revolution and self-determination cannot be predicated on the wrongful
deaths of innocent persons, nor is it prevented in any meaningful way from other
nonprohibited activity by the condemnation of terrorist tactics.

To cite a venerable legal maxim, ***jus ex injuria non oritur,*** meaning "rights do
not arise from wrongs." Revolutions have occurred throughout history without depending for success on the use of terrorism. There seems to be no legitimate reason that they
cannot continue to occur successfully in spite of a ban on terrorist tactics. The position
of governments committed to this concept was stated in part by former U.S. secretary
of state William Rogers when he spoke at the 1972 opening of the UN General
Assembly: "[T]errorist acts are totally unacceptable attacks against the very fabric of
international order. They must be universally condemned, whether we consider the
cause a terrorist invoked noble or ignoble, legitimate or illegitimate."[9]

Not all nations, governments, or individuals agree with this assessment. Even the
nations who do, however, are not unfailingly willing to adhere to it. For instance, during World War II, Nazism was regarded as "an ultimate threat to everything decent . . .
an ideology and a practice of domination so murderous, so degrading even to those who
might survive it, that the consequences of its final victory were literally beyond calcula-
tion, immeasurably awful."[10]

But nonstrategic, random terror bombing, by those same nations who have
authored and defended the current laws against terrorism, resulted in the deaths of
thousands of German civilians. These persons were apparently sacrificed for "psychological" purposes (i.e., to create fear and chaos in an audience). Such "sacrifices"
and indiscriminate destruction of civilians today would be roundly condemned by
those same nations if they were performed by a revolutionary or guerrilla force or by
a rogue state carrying out terror-violence against its own citizens.

So the distinction between acceptable and unacceptable use of force is not always clear and is, of course, influenced by the nations responsible for making the rules. But as noted earlier, the *mores* prohibiting certain forms of violence are not of recent vintage—they have been evolving over many centuries.

One of the ingredients in the formulation of the rules that govern civilized society today that *is* new is the **right of self-determination.** The UN Charter, written in 1945, states that people have a right to determine for themselves the form of state under which they choose to live.[11] Since that time, nations and legal scholars have been trying to work out just which people have this right and how extensive a justification this right confers on individuals engaged in wars of "self-determination."

The answers to these and related questions are not readily attainable. As one scholar notes:

> [A]ccording to United Nations practice, a "people" is any group that August organization wishes to liberate from "colonial and racist regimes." Thus, the Puerto Ricans are a people but the Kurds are not; the Namibians are a people and possess their own state but the population of East Timor (or what remains of it) is without identity and without hope.[12]

Obviously, this right is not clearly defined by the concepts essential to it. Nor is it clear just how fundamental or extensive this right to self-determination is. Is it more fundamental than the right to life? If not, then the pursuit of self-determination cannot intentionally jeopardize any person's right to life. Does the right to self-determination supercede the right of a state to try to protect itself and to provide for its citizens a safe and stable system of government?

No people seeking to exercise their right to self-determination do so today in a vacuum. Their actions in the course of their struggle necessarily have an effect, often a negative one, on other persons within their community. As in any other armed struggle, there must remain limits within which their right to pursue self-determination must operate, to limit the adverse effects of such a course of action on the rights of others.

The problem that this newly articulated right to self-determination has created in terms of the limitation of armed warfare is important. This right is readily conferred on, or claimed by, many groups who do not enjoy, and probably can never gain, majority support among the indigenous population of their state. This means that many groups of disaffected persons may claim this right who have no hope of ever waging even a successful guerrilla war against an established state. The argument has, of course, been made that these groups therefore cannot reasonably be held to conventional rules of warfare, for to hold them to those rules is to condemn them to inevitable failure.

Faced with the overwhelming odds in favor of the well-established and well-armed state, many of the peoples seeking to exercise their right to self-determination have been increasingly willing to use less conventional methods and means of waging war. Lacking large popular support from the indigenous population, facing a state whose trained army and weaponry make conventional resistance a mockery, such groups are increasingly willing to use unthinkable weapons, such as terrorism, to achieve their right.

The difficulties facing such groups seeking self-determination are very real, but the problems that they create are also formidable. What happens, for example, if two peoples claim that their right to self-determination gives them the right to occupy and control the same piece of land? Who decides which group's right should prevail? Should the decision be based on which group can establish control or on which has the better legal claim to the land? Again, who or what is to make such a determination?

This is not a hypothetical situation. Such dilemmas exist at this very moment. The rival claims of the Palestinians and the Israelis to the same land have provoked decades of bloodshed and bitter fighting. Each people in this struggle claim a historic right to the land.

For more than four decades, Israel managed to secure its right to determine its own form of government and to exercise control over its own people. But it has had to do so through force and to maintain, until the late 1990s, its existence through occupation of additional land. Peace is seldom achieved, in the long term, through occupation, and Israel has begun the difficult process of pulling out of those occupied lands. But now there are Jewish settlers, who have lived in those lands for decades, whose identity and security as a people is threatened by the withdrawal and whose right to self-determination may well be lost in the peace process. As long as a people exists within or near the borders of this troubled land whose right to self-determination remains unsatisfied, terrorist acts may well continue to be a threat to peace in the region.

The assassination in late 1995 of Yitzhak Rabin, prime minister of Israel, by a Jewish student seeking to derail this withdrawal of Israel from the occupied territories, makes this threat very clear. Certainly, the satisfaction of the Palestinians' right to self-determination will be difficult to achieve in any way that is acceptable to all of the people of Israel. One Israeli military officer noted that even children, born and raised in Palestinian refugee camps, will state that they are from Jaffa and other coastal cities (of what used to be Palestine). Because this land is now an integral part of Israel, there seems to be little likelihood that the aspirations of those Palestinian adults who have fostered this sense of belonging to old homelands can ever be satisfied.

Violent actions taken during the peace process begun in 1993 have made it clear that some Palestinians do not want "independence" in the West Bank or the Gaza Strip. They want to return to, and to claim, their homeland of Palestine, including the land that is today Israel. It would appear to be impossible to satisfy their right to self-determination without infringing on Israel's right to exist. Just as the Jewish people rejected other offers of homelands around the turn of the twentieth century, insisting on their right to return to the homeland of their theological ancestors, Palestinians have found it difficult to accept alternatives that fall short of a return of *their* homeland.

On whose side does "right" rest in this conflict? The right of self-determination that the Palestinians seek to exercise is the same one for which the Hagganah fought against the British occupying forces in the 1930s and 1940s. Just as the Jewish Irgun and its radical offshoot, the Stern Gang, used terror tactics to force out an occupying power, the Palestinians have resorted to terrorist acts to rid themselves of what they perceive to be occupying powers.

This right to self-determination is, by its very lack of clarity, a dangerous justification for unlawful violence. Because neither the peoples nor the extent of the right itself appears to have any specific legal limitations, the exercise of such rights can lead to vicious spirals of violence, as rival peoples seek to claim their rights within an international system whose state of flux lends credence to first one and then the other's rights.

## TERRORIST BELIEFS AND IMAGES

Terrorism, then, has been justified by relatively sophisticated theories, such as anarchism, and by less well-defined concepts, such as that of the right of self-determination. But how do modern terrorists justify themselves, on a personal level, for their actions? Do they indeed think in terms of broad theoretical justifications, or is their belief system less complex?

The content of terrorist belief systems has not, in fact, been the subject for much systematic study, for some understandable reasons. For one thing, the study of terrorism is a relatively new field, with very little emphasis placed thus far on the worldview of terrorists.[13]

Another, more serious problem in analyzing terrorist belief systems lies in the difficulties in acquiring and interpreting data. Few if any extensive memoirs, minutes of meetings, or interviews with terrorist decision makers are available to facilitate a reconstruction of events. Much of the data that do exist are classified by governments in ways that make this information virtually inaccessible to researchers.

This does not mean that no studies exist of terrorist belief systems. Gerald A. Hopple and Miriam Steiner employed content analysis in 1984 to evaluate 12 factors as potential sources of action, applying the techniques to 46 documents from the German Red Army Faction, the Italian Red Brigades, and the Basque ETA. Their findings indicated that emphasis within belief systems changes over time and that different groups stress different motivations.[14]

From the studies that have been done, some significant components of terrorist belief systems have emerged. A brief review of these, though not sufficient to explain why *all* terrorists do what they do or what they all believe, will offer insights into the framework of logic by which a terrorist justifies his or her actions.

One of the significant components of a belief system is the **image of the enemy.** Dehumanization of the enemy is a dominant theme. The enemy is viewed in depersonalized and monolithic terms, as capitalist, communist, bourgeois, or imperialist. It is not human beings whom the terrorist fights; rather, it is this dehumanized monolith.

As one group of researchers has noted, for many terrorists, "the enemy is non-human; not good enough. He is the enemy because he is not the hero and is not friendly to the hero."[15] This rationalization is particularly prominent among right-wing terrorists, whether neofascist or vigilante. Like other right-wing theorists, such groups tend toward prejudicial stereotyping, based on class or ethnic attributes. The enemy thus might be all journalists, lawyers, students, intellectuals, or professors, who are regarded by such terrorists as leftist or communist.

It is all too easy to make war, even illegal, "unthinkable" war, on an inhuman enemy. As long as that enemy does not have a face, a spouse or child, a home, grieving parents or friends, the destruction of that enemy is a simple matter, requiring little or no justification beyond the enemy status.

Viewing the enemy in these terms also makes the depiction of the struggle in which the terrorists see themselves as engaged relatively simple. It is a struggle in which good and evil, black and white, are very obvious. The enemy is often seen as much more powerful in its monolithic strength, with many alternatives from which to choose. The terrorists, on the other hand, have no choice except to resort to terrorism in confronting this "monster," which becomes, in their view, a response to oppression, not a free choice on their parts but a duty.

Also of interest in this belief system is the terrorists' **image of themselves.** Terrorists of both the left and right tend to think of themselves as belonging to an elite. Most left-wing revolutionary terrorists view themselves as the victims rather than the aggressors in the struggle. The struggle in which they are engaged is an obligation, a duty, not a voluntary choice, because they are the enlightened in a mass of unenlightened.[16]

Like terrorists of the right, revolutionary terrorists seem to view themselves as above the prevailing morality, morally superior. Normal standards of behavior do not apply to them. They do not deem themselves in any sense bound by conventional laws or conventional morality, which they often regard as the corrupt and self-serving tool of the enemy. It would clearly be useless to condemn as "immoral" an action by terrorists, because the people embracing terrorist tactics have likely already reached the belief that the morality that would condemn their actions is inferior to their own morality.

This view of morality is integral to terrorists' view of the **nature of the conflict** in which they are engaged. Not only is this a moral struggle, in which good and evil are simplistically defined, but terrorists tend to define the struggle also in terms of elaborately idealistic terms. Terrorists seldom see what they do as murder or killing of innocent persons. Instead, they are wont to describe such actions as "executions" committed after "trials" of "traitors."

Menachem Begin offered insights into this legalistic rationalization. He noted that, in terrorist struggles, "what matters most necessary is the inner consciousness that makes what is 'legal' illegal and the 'illegal' legal and justified."[17]

Also of importance in understanding the belief system of terrorists is **the image of the victims** of the violence. If the victims are fairly easily identifiable with the enemy, then as representatives of the hostile forces, they are despised and their destruction easily justified, even if such victims have committed no clear offense against the terrorist or his group. As Michael Collins, founder of the Irish Republican Army, noted with reference to the killing of 14 men *suspected* of being British intelligence agents, such persons were "undesirables . . . by whose destruction the very air is made sweeter." This remained true, according to Collins, even though not all of the 14 were guilty of the "sins" of which they were accused.[18]

Innocent victims, persons whose only "crime" was in being in the wrong place at the wrong time, are generally dismissed as unimportant by-products of the struggle. Fate, rather than human acts, is often blamed for the deaths of such persons.

This brings up one last important point about terrorist belief systems: the predominant **theme of millenarianism.** Personal redemption through violent means is a millenarian theme found in many terrorist belief systems. Violence is often viewed as being essential to the coming of the millennium, whose coming may be hastened by the actions of believers willing to violate the rules of the old order in an effort to bring in the new order (often conceived of in terms of total liberation).

Such beliefs have led to a deliberate abandonment of restraints. Coupled with the tendency to divide the world into clear camps of good and evil, as noted earlier, this abandonment of restraints usually entails a strong conviction that no mercy can be shown to the evil that the enemy embodies. Terrorists are wrapped in an impenetrable cloak of belief in the absolute righteousness of their cause and the ultimate success that will inevitably come. If all violence brings the millennium closer, then no violence, regardless of its consequences, can be regarded as a failure. The terrorist always "wins" in this struggle.

Other elements are common to some terrorist belief systems. Some, for instance, place a premium on martyrdom, suggesting this as a desirable goal. Others suggest the desirability of Marxist revolution.

Understanding at least these few fundamental elements of terrorist beliefs may facilitate an ability to address terrorism in its many forms and to anticipate its future growth patterns. Certainly the modern terrorist appears to hold belief systems very different from those of either soldiers or criminals.

## CAUSES OF THE LEFT AND RIGHT

In addition to belief systems that help the individual to justify terrorist actions, a wide variety of causes exist for which men and women have committed terrorism. Let us briefly consider a few of the motives for modern terrorism.

## Religious Fanaticism

The Islamic Jihad has given the world ample evidence of the destructive power of individuals committed to waging "holy" war on religious principles, disciples of **religious fanaticism.** The holy war waged by Islamic fundamentalists has torn Lebanon apart, caused the death or continued captivity of numerous Western hostages, and continues to feed the flames of conflict between Iran and most of its neighbors.

In their righteous fervor, Shiite fanatics have been unrepentantly responsible for the loss of hundreds, perhaps even thousands, of lives. Planes are sabotaged, temples stormed, and unrelenting guerrilla warfare waged, all in the name of "religion." It is a war that pits Shiite Muslims against Sunni Muslims, as well as against Christians, Jews, and other religious groups. Martyrdom is a compelling lure, and self-sacrifice is valued above many other virtues, including mercy or pity. In the name of Allah, rivers of blood have flowed, and will no doubt continue to flow, for fanatics of any sort are seldom ever satisfied by any gains.

## Anarchism

Few groups still operate today that hold strictly to this cause. Over the last three decades of the twentieth century, we witnessed the growth and demise of the Weather Underground and the Symbionese Liberation Army in the United States. The Japanese Red Army is one group that, in its rhetoric, has espoused anarchistic beliefs. Such groups have tended to be small and short-lived, perhaps because their goals are somewhat nebulous, and thus they find it difficult to draw others into their ranks. Anarchism's more extreme form, nihilism, in which the destruction of *all* structure and form of society is sought, still exists as an ideology among certain Western European terrorist groups.

## Neo-Nazism/Neofascism

In recent years, a number of groups have sprung up throughout Western Europe and the United States embracing **neofascism.** In the United States, for example, the Aryan Nations, and several of its splinter groups, including the Order, the White Patriots Party, the Covenant, the Sword and the Arm of the Lord, and Bruder Sweigen Strike Force II, have been involved in armed conflict with the authorities and have been responsible for several bombings in which innocent people were killed. Indeed, one White Patriot Party leader has been indicted for helping to arm and train a paramilitary group in North Carolina. The devastating bomb blast in Oklahoma City in 1995, after which a shocked nation watched the bodies of small children carried lifeless or dying from the rubble, was carried out by a person who had been a member of a paramilitary group in Michigan.

**Neo-Nazism** has also emerged. A paramilitary, essentially neo-Nazi group, the Hoffman Sports Group, operated for a time in Germany, while Italy, in the latter twentieth century, has witnessed the resurgence of right-wing paramilitary groups, engaging in acts of terror-violence, including the bombing of a train.

## Separatism

Perhaps the best-known group embracing **separatism** is the ETA, the Basques who seek independence or at least autonomy from Spain and have used bombs and machine guns to try to force the Spanish government to accede to their demands for independence. The French-Canadian separatists, the FLQ, were less active in the 1980s but were responsible for several acts of terrorism during the previous two decades. Within the United States, Omega 7, the violent Puerto Rican independence faction, has committed many acts of violence, including the placing of bombs in New York's crowded airports and the attempted murder of U.S. officials.

## Nationalism

It is difficult to separate **nationalism** from separatism as a motivator of terrorism; the distinction is somewhat unclear in many cases. Groups whose motivation is nationalism are those who seek for their portion of society, which is sometimes but not always a minority, to gain control of the system of government and the allocation of resources within that nation-state. Such groups do not seek independence or separation from the nation. With this in mind, the Irish Republican Army, whose terrorist acts in Northern Ireland are infamous, could conceivably have been classed in this category prior to the peace process in the 1990s. Organizations such as the African National Congress, whose members from time to time have been accused of engaging in acts of terrorism, could also have fallen, at one time, in this category.

## Issue Orientation

Within the past few years, various forms of **issues orientation** have aroused such violent sentiments that adherents to one side or another have resorted to terrorist violence to enforce their beliefs. Abortion is one such issue: its opponents have actually bombed abortion clinics. Oddly enough, environmental and animal protection activists, during the latter twentieth century, have become increasingly militant in their insistence that such protection is crucial and worth fighting for. Placing spikes in trees and in paths through the woods and burning down animal testing centers have become all too common actions by such groups. Doctors have been killed to save the fetuses that those doctors may have been willing to abort. Earth Now, one militant environmental group in the United States, rationalized that, if it was necessary to kill people to save the trees, then they would be justified in killing people.

The issue of nuclear power and nuclear weapons also has provoked violence. Several modern novelists and screenwriters have created all too realistic scenarios concerning the possibility of antinuclear activists detonating a nuclear weapon to illustrate their contention that such weapons must be banned. Thus far, such an incident exists only in fiction, but the growing intensity of the debate on this issue makes such an incident uncomfortably close to reality.

## Ideological Mercenaries

The legendary Ilyich Ramirez Sanchez, known to the world as "Carlos the Jackal," and the more recent Abu Nidal have given rise to a fear of the proliferation of "terrorists for hire," or **ideological mercenaries.** While it is beyond debate that such persons do exist and cause considerable violence, little evidence suggests the development of a mercenary army of terrorists. Indeed, the arrest of Carlos, from his abode in the Sudan, and his removal for trial in France indicate that the next century may have less tolerance politically for such individuals, in a world in which nations no longer can count on a cold war to protect them from direct intervention by a stronger nation, if they harbor such a mercenary.

## Pathological Terrorists

Some persons kill and terrorize for the sheer joy of terrorizing, not for any "cause" or belief. Charles Manson was perhaps one such; those who commit "serial murders" are of the same cast. **Pathological terrorists** have no cause; they are sick and twisted individuals, whom Frederick Hacker has called "crazies."[19]

## Counterterror Terrorists

Perhaps the most frightening development toward the end of the twentieth century is the proliferation of so-called **counterterror terrorists,** the death squads that mete out summary justice to those judged by their leaders to be "terrorists." Several authoritarian states, threatened by political change, have resorted to these semiofficial troops, thereby inspiring that spiral of terror-violence discussed earlier. Several countries in Central and South America have fallen prey to the lure of counterterror tactics to control terrorism.

## CONCLUSION

Terrorism *is* different today, with many different forms and many different causes. The argument continues to be made that the justice of the cause, the nobility of the motive, in some way makes the terrorist act less heinous. To understand the cause for which one fights and the belief system in which one operates, it is said, makes it less likely that one will whole-heartedly condemn the actions taken.

But does the woman whose legs are blown off in an explosion in the supermarket understand that the bomb was placed by persons who bore her no personal grudge but were merely seeking independence or separatism for a disenfranchised minority? Will the family of a child killed in an airline explosion accept the explanation that the group responsible for the explosion had not enough weapons to fight a legitimate battle with an authoritarian government?

No cause, however just or noble, can make such actions acceptable. Understanding cannot diminish the horror of the atrocity committed against the innocent. The right of self-determination, if it must be secured by the wrong of the murder and maiming of innocents, is not worth the price in the eyes of the rest of the world.

## *Evaluation*

If a group is exercising its right to self-determination, does this give it the right to commit a wrong on other persons? To what extent is one justified in committing a wrong to secure a right? Is there ever a time in which, as some have argued, the needs of the many—to secure the right of self-determination or freedom—can be said to outweigh the needs of the few—victims of the violence?

Consider and discuss the following incidents, keeping in mind several questions: Were these acts of terrorism? For what cause were they committed? Were they in any sense justified?

1. *Assassination of Franz Ferdinand.* Ferdinand was shot to death by a man who felt, with some justice, that the rights of the minority of which he was a part were being cruelly ignored in the carving up of Europe. Ferdinand's death precipitated the events leading up to World War I. His death was, in some ways, the catalyst to that cataclysm.

2. *Assassination of Anwar Sadat.* This Egyptian president was shot by men who felt that Sadat had betrayed the Arabs by his willingness to establish a peaceful relationship with Israel. Sadat's death considerably slowed down the peace process in the Middle East. His successor, Hosni Mubarak, was understandably reluctant to take similar unpopular steps.

3. *Bombing of the U.S. Marine barracks in Lebanon.* This act was carried out by militants who regarded the U.S. military presence in Lebanon as an invasive influence in their civil war. The attack resulted in over 200 deaths and a diminishing U.S. presence in that war-torn country. Syrian and Israeli influence and presence, however, remain strong in that country's territory.

4. *Bombing of Hiroshima.* Carried out by U.S. bombers carrying atomic weapons, this attack was designed to end the devastating battles in the Pacific during World War II. It did indeed achieve this, at the cost of countless thousands of Japanese civilian dead or maimed and many more who bore disease and deformity for generations.

## Suggested Readings

Brown, Michael. "Right Wing Extremism as an Extension of American Frontier Tradition of Violence." Unpublished manuscript, Missouri State University, Academy of Criminal Justice Scientists, 1987.

Crenshaw, Martha. "Ideological and Psychological Factors in International Terrorism." Paper presented to the Defense Intelligence College Symposium on International Terrorism, Washington, D.C., December 2–3, 1985.

Hacker, Frederick J. *Crusaders, Criminals, and Crazies: Terror and Terrorism in Our Time.* New York: Bantam, 1978.

Jenkins, Brian. *The Terrorist Mindset and Terrorist Decisionmaking: Two Areas of Ignorance.* Santa Monica, CA: Rand, 1979.

Kidder, Rushworth M. "The Terrorist Mentality." *Christian Science Monitor,* May 15, 1986.

Schechterman, Bernard. "Religious Fanaticism as a Factor in Political Violence." *International Freedom Foundation* (December 1986).

"Turner Diaries: Blueprint for Right-Wing Revolution." *Law Enforcement News,* June 30, 1987.

Wright, Robin. "Holy Wars: The Ominous Side of Religion in Politics." *Christian Science Monitor,* November 12, 1987.

## Endnotes

1. R. Blackey and C. Payton, *Revolution and the Revolutionary Ideal* (New York: Pergamon, 1976), 91–93. See also B. Croce, *History of Europe in the Nineteenth Century,* trans. H. Furst (New York: Rienner, 1953).

2. Sandra Stencel, "Terrorism: An Idea Whose Time Has Come," *Skeptic: The Forum for Contemporary History* (January–February 1976): 51.

3. Emma Goldman, *Anarchism and Other Essays* (New York: Dover, 1969), 66. This is a republication of the original 1917 edition. Of particular note to the student of terrorism are Goldman's essays on the meaning of anarchism and the "psychology of political violence."

4. Quoted by Jonathan Harris in *The New Terrorism: Politics of Violence* (New York: Messner, 1983), 141.

5. Robert Friedlander, "On the Prevention of Violence," *The Catholic Lawyer* 25, no. 2 (Spring 1980): 95–105.

6. U.N. Secretariat Study, "Measures to Prevent International Terrorism" (November 2, 1973), U.N. Doc. A/C.6/418; prepared as requested by the Sixth Legal Committee of the General Assembly.

7. C. Leiser, "Terrorism, Guerrilla Warfare, and International Morality," *Stanford Journal of International Studies* (1974): 39–43.

8. J. Bowyer Bell, "Trends of Terror: Analysis of Political Violence," *World Politics* 29 (1977): 476–477.

9. For the full text of his remarks, see State Department Bulletin no. 67 (1972), 425–429.

10. Quoted by Robert Friedlander, "On the Prevention of Violence," 67.

11. The United Nations Charter entered into force on October 24, 1945.

12. Robert Friedlander, "The PLO and the Rule of Law: A Reply to Dr. Annis Kassim," *Denver Journal of International Law and Policy* 10, no. 2 (Winter 1981): 231.

13. Brian M. Jenkins, *The Terrorist Mindset and Terrorist Decisionmaking: Two Areas of Ignorance* (Santa Monica, CA: Rand, 1979), 6340.

14. Gerald W. Hopple and Miriam Steiner, *The Causal Beliefs of Terrorists: Empirical Results* (McLean, VA: Defense Systems, 1984).

15. Franco Ferracuti and Francesco Bruno, "Italy: A Systems Perspective," in *Aggression in Global Perspective,* ed. A. Goldstein and M. H. Segall (New York: Pergamon, 1983), 274.

16. Martha Crenshaw, "Ideological and Psychological Factors in International Terrorism," paper prepared for the Defense Intelligence College Symposium on International Terrorism, Washington, D.C.: December 2–3, 1985.

17. Quoted by Martha Crenshaw, "Ideological and Psychological Factors in International Terrorism," 8.

18. Rex Taylor, *Michael Collins* (London: Hutchinson, 1958), 17.

19. Frederick J. Hacker, *Crusaders, Criminals, Crazies: Terror and Terrorism in Our Time* (New York: Bantam, 1978).

# 4

# Criminals or Crusaders?

*Nothing is easier than to denounce the evil doer;*
*nothing is more difficult than to understand him.*

—Fyodor Dostoyevsky

## Key Concepts

crazies

criminals

crusaders

characteristics of a

   "successful" terrorist

fedayeen

"soldiers of the revolution"

group dynamics

trends in recruitment

trends in membership

What kind of person becomes a terrorist? Perhaps considering the dynamics of becoming a terrorist will increase our understanding of this phenomenon. As noted in the previous chapter, terrorist acts are committed for a wide variety of causes. It is also true that a wide variety of individuals and groups commit terrorist acts. Although it is not feasible to study all such persons in detail, a brief analysis of some of the important characteristics of modern terrorists might be informative.

The political world has changed a great deal in the last two decades of the twentieth century. These political changes have influenced the type of persons more likely to be recruited into terrorist groups. A study of the type of individuals known to be drawn to terrorism in the twentieth century will, perhaps, help us to predict the most probable type of twenty-first-century terrorist. This could be an extremely useful tool for governments and institutions that must plan to cope with terrorism.

## PROFILE OF A TERRORIST

Why do people become terrorists? Are they crazy? Are they thrill seekers? Are they religious fanatics? Are they ideologues? Is there any way to tell who is likely to become a terrorist?

48

This final question provides a clue as to why political scientists and government officials are particularly interested in the psychological factors relating to terrorism. If one could isolate the traits that seem to be most closely related to a willingness to use terrorist tactics, then one would be in a better position to predict, and prevent, the emergence of terrorist groups.

Unfortunately, the isolation of such traits is not easy. Just as not all violence is terrorism and not all revolutionaries are terrorists, not all persons who commit acts of terrorism are alike. Frederick Hacker has suggested three categories of persons who commit terrorism: criminals, crusaders, and crazies. He notes that one is seldom "purely" one type or the other but that each type offer some insights into why an individual will resort to terrorism.[1]

Understanding the individual who commits terrorism is vital, not only for humanitarian reasons but also to decide how best to deal with those individuals *while they are engaged in terrorist activities.* From a law enforcement perspective, for example, it is important to appreciate the difference between a criminal and a crusading terrorist involved in a hostage-taking situation. Successful resolution of such a situation often hinges on an understanding of the mind of the individuals perpetrating the crime.

Let us consider the three categories of terrorists described by Hacker. For the purposes of this study, we need to establish loose descriptions of these three types. Hacker offers some useful ideas on what is subsumed under each label. **Crazies,** he suggests, are emotionally disturbed individuals who are driven to commit terrorism "by reasons of their own that often do not make sense to anybody else."

**Criminals,** on the other hand, perform terrorist acts for reasons that are understood by most—that is, for personal gain. Such individuals transgress the laws of society knowingly and, one assumes, in full possession of their faculties. Both their motives and their goals are usually clear, if still deplorable, to most people.

Not so the **crusaders.** These individuals commit terrorism for reasons that are often unclear both to themselves and to those witnessing the acts. Their goals are frequently even less understandable. Although such individuals are usually idealistically inspired, their idealism tends to be a rather mixed bag of half-understood philosophies. Crusaders, according to Hacker, seek not personal gain but prestige and power for a collective cause. They commit terrorist acts in the belief "that they are serving a higher cause," in Hacker's assessment.

What difference does it make what kind of terrorist there is behind the machine gun or bomb? To the law enforcement individuals charged with resolving the hostage situation, it can be crucial to know what type of person is controlling the situation. Criminals, for instance, can be offered sufficient personal gains or security provisions to induce them to release the hostages. Crusaders are far less likely to be talked out of carrying out their threats by inducements of personal gains, because to do so they would have to betray, in some sense, that higher cause for which they are committing the action.

For the same reason, it is useful to security agents to know what type of individual is likely to commit a terrorist act within their province. A criminal, for example, would be more likely to try to smuggle a gun aboard an airline than a bomb, since the criminal usually anticipates living to enjoy the reward of his or her illegal activities. Crusaders, however, are more willing to blow themselves up with their victims, because their service to that "higher cause" often carries with it a promise of a reward in the life to come.

The distinction between criminals and crusaders with respect to terrorism needs some clarification. Clearly, when anyone breaks the law, as in the commission of a terrorist act, he or she becomes a criminal, regardless of the reason for the transgression. The distinction between criminal and crusader, though, is useful in understanding the differences in the motives and goals that move the person to commit the act.

The majority of the individuals and groups carrying out terrorist acts in the 1990s are crusaders. This does not mean that there are not occasional instances or individuals who, because of some real or perceived injury, decide to take a machine gun into the target of their anger or kidnap or destroy anyone in sight. Nor does it mean that there are not individual criminals and criminal organizations that do not engage in terrorist activities.

Nonetheless, the majority of individuals who commit modern terrorism are, or feel themselves to be, crusaders. According to Hacker, the typical crusading terrorist appears to be normal, no matter how crazy his cause or how criminal the means he uses for this cause may seem. He or she is neither a dummy nor a fool, neither a coward nor a weakling. Instead, the crusading terrorist is frequently a professional, well trained, well prepared, and well disciplined in the habit of blind obedience.

Table 4.1 indicates a few dramatic differences among the types of terrorist Hacker profiles. One is that crusaders are the least likely to negotiate a resolution to a crisis, both because such action can be viewed as a betrayal of a sublime cause and because there is little that the negotiator can offer, since neither personal gain nor safe passage out of the situation are particularly desired by true crusaders. Belief in the cause makes death not a penalty but a path to reward and glory; therefore, the threat of death and destruction can have little punitive value. What can a police or

**TABLE 4.1**

| Type of Terrorist | Motive/Goal | Willing to Negotiate | Expectation of Survival |
|---|---|---|---|
| Criminal | Personal gain/profit | Usually, in return for profit and/or safe passage | Strong |
| Crusader | "Higher cause" (usually a blend of religious and political) | Seldom, because to do so could be seen as a betrayal of the cause | Not substantial, because death offers reward in an afterlife |
| Crazy | Clear only to perpetrator | Possible, but only if negotiator can understand motive and offer hope/alternatives | Strong, but not based on reality |

military negotiator offer to a crusader to induce the release of hostages or the defusing of a bomb?

Similar problems exist with crazies, depending on how much in touch with reality such an individual is at the time of the incident. Negotiation is difficult, but not impossible, if the negotiator can ascertain the goal/motive of the perpetrator and offer some hope (even if it is not real) of success in the achieving of that goal by other, less destructive means. One of the critical elements is that crazies, according to Hacker's evaluation, have a limited grip on the reality that they themselves may die in the course of this action. Thus, the threat of death by a superior force carries diminished weight if the perpetrator cannot grasp the fact that he or she may die in this encounter. Just as very young children find the reality of death a difficult concept to grasp, crazies, too, offer serious difficulties for negotiators because they can often not grasp this reality.

Criminals, then, are the preferred perpetrators, because they will negotiate; their demands are quite logical (although often outrageous) and are based in terms that can be met or satisfied with rational alternatives. Criminals know that they can be killed and have a strong belief/desire that they will live to enjoy the rewards of the actions they are taking. Thus, negotiators have specific demands to be bartered, and their "clients" can be expected to recognize superior force and to respond accordingly in altering demands and resolving the incident.

These differences are critically important to those agencies entrusted with resolving situations in which hostages are held by terrorists. The type of terrorist engaged in the incident significantly impacts the successful, peaceful resolution of the situation.

How is this information useful? To political scientists, as well as to military, police, and other security and intelligence units assigned the task of coping with terrorism, an understanding of the type of person likely to commit acts of terrorism is invaluable. As our understanding of a phenomenon increases, our ability to predict its behavior with some accuracy also increases. Thus, as we try to understand who terrorists are and what they are like, we should increase our ability to anticipate their behavior patterns.

## CAN WE GENERALIZE ABOUT A "TYPICAL" TERRORIST?

What do we know about the type of individual who becomes a terrorist? About the successful terrorists we frequently know very little, in terms of personal data, because successful terrorists depend on secrecy for protection. Through the capture of those less efficient in the art of terrorist operation, we have learned some useful information, and our security and intelligence organizations have added substantially to that data pool.

Nevertheless, it remains true that to generalize about the "typical" terrorist can be very difficult with any degree of accuracy. The search for a "terrorist personality" is a legitimate exercise, but it is unlikely to produce any common denominator capable of uniting a wide variety of countries, periods of time, cultures, and political alliances. In other words, the community of nations is unable, at this point, to agree on such a profile.

Some scholars have, of course, attempted to create a profile of a typical terrorist. Their successes are mixed, at best, but do offer some ideas that help us not only to understand what a typical terrorist may be like (if such a person can be said to exist) but also to evaluate how terrorists as well as terrorism have changed in recent years.

Edgar O'Ballance offers one such critique of what he calls a "successful" terrorist (by which he appears to mean one who is neither captured nor dead). In his book *The Language of Violence,* O'Ballance suggests several essential **characteristics of a "successful" terrorist:**

1. *Dedication.* To be successful, a terrorist cannot be a casual or part-time mercenary, willing to operate only when it suits his convenience or his pocket. He must become a **fedayeen,** a "man of sacrifice." Dedication also implies absolute obedience to the leader of the political movement.

2. *Personal bravery.* As the terrorist must face the possibility of death, injury, imprisonment, or even torture if captured, O'Ballance regards this trait as important, to varying degrees, depending on one's position within the terrorist group's hierarchy.

3. *Without the human emotions of pity or remorse.* Because most of his victims will include innocent men, women, and children, whom he must be prepared to kill in cold blood, the terrorist must have the killer instinct, able to kill without hesitation on receipt of a code or signal. As this expert notes, many can kill in the heat of anger or in battle, but few, fortunately, can do so in cold blood.

4. *Fairly high standard of intelligence.* As the would-be terrorist has to collect, collate, and assess information, devise and put into effect complex plans, and evade police, security forces, and other hostile forces, intelligence would appear to be a requisite.

5. *Fairly high degree of sophistication.* This quality is essential, according to O'Ballance, for the terrorist to blend into the first-class section on airliners, stay at first-class hotels, and mix inconspicuously with the international executive set.

6. *Reasonably well educated with a fair share of general knowledge.* By this, O'Ballance means that the terrorist should be able to speak English as well as one other major language. He asserts that a university degree is almost mandatory.

O'Ballance notes that "all terrorists do not measure up to these high standards, but the leaders, planners, couriers, liaison officers, and activists must."[2] This assertion is difficult to challenge effectively, because if the terrorist is successful, then the implication is that he or she has succeeded in evading law enforcement, security, and intelligence officers, and hence the information about the individual is necessarily either scant or unconfirmed.

We could conclude, with some justice, that most of O'Ballance's assertions, like most generalizations, are at least half-true, half-false, and largely untestable. But these generalizations, with their grains of truth, are still useful in analyzing terrorism and terrorist behavior. Let us instead examine each of his suggested attributes of a terrorist to discover whether they can be substantiated by insights into contemporary behavior.

Dedication certainly appears, on the surface, to be characteristic of modern terrorists. The Palestinians involved in various groups, for example, have indicated a willingness to wait for as long as it takes them to realize their dream of a return to a nation of Palestine. They have been willing to wait as long as the Zionists waited, or longer, and many are reluctant to settle for the current peace settlements, because that decision would represent at this point less than full national independence for a nation of Palestine. Like the Zionists, they have unbounded faith in the justice of their cause and seem willing to die to achieve it.

The progress toward a comprehensive peace settlement in the Middle East in the last years of the twentieth century indicates that this tenacity may be a liability to the emerging government being established by Yasir Arafat in Gaza and parts of the West Bank, because this area represents only a portion of the land that was Palestine and does not constitute full sovereignty from Israel for the Palestinians. Anger by the Palestinian group Hamas, a radical movement supported throughout the Middle East by Iran, indicates that a significant portion of the Palestinians remain committed to full restoration of Palestine to the Palestinian people. The suicide bombings in 1994 and 1995, which claimed the lives of many innocent men, women, and children, have given credence to this absolute resolve.

Nor is such dedication limited to Palestinians. Observers in Northern Ireland have suggested that religious fanaticism is handed down from generation to generation in this region as well, carrying with it a willingness to fight and die for a cause. Schoolchildren in Northern Ireland have exhibited an intolerance and a bitterness that is too often translated into violence. Where children, preachers, and priests join in willingness to commit murder in a "holy" cause, dedication has produced countless bloody massacres and seemingly endless terrorism.

However, as is the case in the Middle East, progress is being made toward a political settlement of the problem of Northern Ireland. Like the situation of Palestine, though, the solution will probably not satisfy all of the truly dedicated terrorists. The IRA's willingness to negotiate a peace has angered absolutists in the Catholic community, and the movement of the British to negotiate with the IRA openly has raised equal anger in militant Protestant groups. If a resolution of the dispute of the British with the IRA is reached, and a merging of Northern Ireland with the Republic of Ireland planned, there is reason to fear that a similarly dedicated group of terrorists will emerge, determined to force the United Kingdom into retaining sovereignty (thus keeping Protestant control).

Such dedication is not always directed at so specific a nationalist cause. The Japanese Red Army (JRA), for instance, founded in 1969, described themselves as **"soldiers of the revolution"** and have pledged themselves to participate in all revolutions anywhere in the world through exemplary acts. This group was responsible for the massacre of 26 tourists at Lod Airport in Tel Aviv, Israel. These dedicated revolutionaries have undertaken numerous terrorist attacks, many of which, like the Lod Airport massacre, were essentially suicide missions, since escape was scarcely possible.

Personal bravery is also a characteristic often attributed to modern terrorists. There are, however, two views of the bravery with which terrorists may be said to be endowed. One might argue, with a great deal of justice, that it can scarcely be termed "brave" to use weapons mercilessly against unarmed and defenseless civilians. The men, women, and children at Lod Airport were wholly unable to defend themselves against the JRA's vicious attack. Was it "brave" of the JRA to slaughter these innocent and unarmed people?

The opposing view, which does in fact attribute bravery to those perpetrating acts of terrorism, is that to be willing to carry out missions in which one's own death or at least imprisonment are inevitable entails no small degree of personal courage. A willingness to give one's life for a cause has, throughout history, commanded at the very least a reluctant admiration, even from one's enemies.

*Bravery* is, at best, a very subjective term. One may feel oneself to be very cowardly but be perceived by others to be quite fearless. The audience for one's deeds are often able to judge one's bravery only by the commission of the deed and are unaware of the inner doubts or demons that may have driven one to the act. Nor is the individual necessarily the best judge of his or her own personal bravery, since a person's capacity for self-deception makes it so that we often do not consciously admit (or refuse to be aware of) our true motives and fears.

The question as to whether terrorists who murder innocent persons, with the knowledge that their own survival is problematic, are brave may never be answered to anyone's satisfaction. Much depends on the way in which one describes the situation.

According to O'Ballance, a successful terrorist should be without the human emotions of pity or remorse. Given the necessity of being able to kill, in cold blood, unarmed and innocent persons, this would appear to be a reasonable assumption regarding terrorist personality. Unlike the criminal who may kill to prevent someone from capturing them or to secure some coveted prize, terrorists must, by the very nature of the act that they are often called on to commit, kill persons against whom they have no specific grudge, whose life or death is not really material to their well-being or security.

Hacker states:

> Often, the terrorists do not know whom they will hurt, and they could not care less. Nothing seems important to them except they themselves and their cause. In planning and executing their deeds, the terrorists are totally oblivious to the fate of their victims. Only utter dehumanization permits the ruthless use of human beings as bargaining chips, bargaining instruments, or objects for indiscriminate aggression.[3]

This description creates a vivid portrait of a ruthless and, one would think, thoroughly unlikable killer. Yet those guilty of such acts have not always presented to the world such a vision of themselves.

Consider the following case: On July 22, 1946, an Irgun team, dressed as waiters, rolled seven milk churns full of dynamite and TNT into the empty Regency Grill of the King David Hotel in Jerusalem. At 12:37, the TNT in the milk cans exploded, creating pressure so great that it burst the hearts, lungs, and livers of the clerks working on the floors above.

Thurston Clarke gives a gruesome description of the fate of the people in the King David Hotel at that time:

> In that split second after 12:37, thirteen of those who had been alive at 12:36 disappeared without a trace. The clothes, bracelets, cufflinks, and wallets which might have identified them exploded into dust and smoke. Others were turned to charcoal, melted into chairs and desks or exploded into countless fragments. The face of a Jewish typist was ripped from her skull, blown out of a window, and smeared onto the pavement below. Miraculously it was recognizable, a two-footlong distorted death mask topped with tufts of hair.
>
> Blocks of stones, tables and desks crushed heads and snapped necks. Coat racks became deadly arrows that flew across rooms, piercing chests. Filing cabinets pinned people to walls, suffocating them. Chandeliers and ceiling fans crashed to the floor, empaling and decapitating those underneath.[4]

Ninety-one people died in that bomb blast; 28 were British, 41 were Arabs, and 17 were Jews. Another 46 were injured.

Now consider the words of the person who commanded this attack: "There is no longer any armistice between the Jewish people and the British administration of Eretz Israel which hands our brothers over to Hitler. Our people are at war with this regime—war to the end."[5] Was this bombing the deed of a fanatic, a person who could murder in cold blood many innocent people in this "war to the end"? Certainly it would seem to be the case.

And yet the perpetrator of this atrocity, the man responsible for the terrible destruction of 91 lives, was none other than Menachem Begin, who in the 1970s served as prime minister of Israel. The Irgun terrorist who plotted to destroy the hotel is the same man who, working with President Carter of the United States and President Sadat of Egypt, made significant efforts to move Israel on the road to peace with its Arab neighbors, signing the famous Camp David Accords, bringing a measure of peace between Israel and Egypt.

Is a terrorist a cold-blooded killer only at the time of the commission of his crime, or is that a trait endemic to his character? Does he, in fact, commit such acts because of a fatal flaw in his character, which makes him unable to feel pity or remorse, or is he driven by circumstances and forces to commit acts that are personally abhorrent to him?

Just as there is no safe generalization with regard to the personal bravery of terrorists, so there seem to be pitfalls in making too broad a characterization of terrorists as incapable of pity or remorse. Perhaps of all that O'Ballance has to say about this particular aspect of successful terrorists' characteristics, it is accurate only to say that they appear to have a killer instinct simply in the sense that they are willing to use lethal force.

Some may indeed kill without pity or remorse, and they may in fact be incapable of such emotions. But to say that terrorists as a whole are so constructed is a generalization for which there is insufficient data and conflicting indicators in known cases.

The characteristics of sophistication and education that O'Ballance suggests are less true of post-1970s terrorists than they were of terrorists prior to that time. Many nineteenth-century revolutionary terrorists were indeed intelligent, sophisticated, university educated, and even multilingual. Those responsible for the murder of Czar Alexander II of Russia in March 1881 were men and women who possessed a much higher level of education and sophistication than most other young people of their nation. They were led by Sophia Perovskaya, daughter of the wealthy governor-general of St. Petersburg, the empire's capital.

Similarly, the Tupamaros of Uruguay were primarily composed of young, well-educated liberal intellectuals who sought, but never fully gained, the support of the less educated masses. The Baader-Meinhof gang in West Germany, which terrorized that nation throughout the 1970s, was also made up of middle- and upper-class intellectuals. This gang's master strategist was Horst Mahler, a radical young lawyer, and it drew its membership and support system heavily from the student body of German universities.

The founder of one of Italy's first left-wing terrorist bands, the Proletarian Action Group (GAP), was Giangiacomo Feitrinelli, the heir to an immense Milanese fortune and head of one of Europe's most distinguished publishing houses. Like the Red Brigades, which would succeed this group as Italy's leading left-wing terrorist group, the GAP drew much of its initial membership from young, often wealthy, intellectuals.

Terrorists, in fact, until the 1980s tended to be recruited from college campuses. Many came from well-to-do families, so that sophistication and an ability to mix with the international set were well within their grasp. Intelligence, sophistication, education, and university training: not only the leaders but also many of the practitioners of both nineteenth-century anarchism and contemporary terrorism possessed these attributes.

But standards and modes of behavior among terrorists as we move toward the twenty-first century are changing. The French anarchists would not have abducted children and threatened to kill them unless ransom was paid. The Narodnaya Volya would not have sent parts of their victims' bodies with little notes to their relatives as the right-wing Guatemalan MANP and NOA did. Neither French nor Russian anarchists would have tormented, mutilated, raped, and castrated their victims, as too many terrorist groups have done in the latter part of the twentieth century.

As Walter Lacquer points out, "Not all terrorist movements have made a fetish of brutality; some have behaved more humanely than others. But what was once a rare exception has become a frequent occurrence in our time."[6] According to Lacquer, the character of terrorism has undergone a profound change. Intellectuals, he contends, have made "the cult of violence respectable." In spite of the violence that characterized their movement, he asserts that no such cult existed among the Russian terrorists, a difficult claim to either prove or disprove.

Nevertheless, Lacquer is correct in his assertion that the terror of recent decades is different—that much has already been established in preceding chapters. It is also true that modern terrorists are significantly different and that the difference in the type of person becoming a terrorist today has a great deal to do with the difference in terrorism.

# TERRORISM *IS* DIFFERENT TODAY

## Motivation

Part of the difference lies in the motives that drive individuals to embrace terrorism. Again Lacquer sums up the situation very well:

> Whatever their motives may be, the "ardent love of other" which Emma Goldman observed is not among them. The driving force is hate not love, ethical considerations are a matter of indifference to them and their dreams of freedom, of national and social liberation are suspect. Nineteenth-century nationalist terrorists were fighting for freedom from foreign domination. More recently, appetites have grown, the Basques have designs on Galicia, the Palestinians not only want the West Bank but also intend to destroy the Jewish state, and the IRA would like to bomb the Protestants into a united Ireland. The aims of terrorism, in brief, have changed, and so have the terrorists.[7]

A less than clear political purpose seems to be involved in much of the terrorism perpetrated today. Moreover, the motives of individuals involved in a struggle against a cruel oppressor are surely significantly different from those of persons rebelling against a democratically elected government. While idealism, a social conscience, or hatred of foreign oppression can serve to drive one to commit acts of terrorism, so can boredom, mental confusion, and what psychologists term "free-floating aggression."

Certainly religious fanaticism is today as strong a motivator for the commission of terrorism as it has been in previous centuries. The holy war waged by Muslims on Christians and fellow Muslims is no less violent than that waged during the Middle Ages. The mixture of political and religious fanaticism has always been a volatile and often violent combination.

What difference does it make whether terrorism is committed by social idealists or persons suffering from free-floating aggression? We could speculate that a social conscience would be more likely to inhibit the perpetrator from the use of indiscriminate violence against the unprotected masses. Perhaps "mental confusion" contributes to an inability to recognize limits on the use of terror-violence.

## Group Dynamics

These are, at best, only suppositions as to why modern terrorists, if they are indeed idealistic, are more brutal than their predecessors. Before considering demographic information that might help to substantiate and explain this difference, let us first consider the impact of the terrorist *group* on the terrorist. If **group dynamics** help to shape terrorist thought and action, then its impact must certainly be understood to comprehend the contemporary terrorist.

Modern terrorists are, for the most part, fanatics whose sense of reality is distorted. They operate under the assumption that they, and they alone, know the truth and are therefore the sole arbiters of what is right and what is wrong. They believe themselves to be moralists, to whom ordinary law does not apply, because the existing law has been created by immoral persons for immoral purposes.

They are not, of course, consistent in their logic. For example, they demand that governments that capture terrorists treat them as prisoners of war, as they are involved in a war against either a specific government or society in general. However, they vehemently deny the state's right to treat them as war criminals for their indiscriminate killing of civilians. In other words, they invoke the laws of war only in so far as it serves their purposes but reject any aspect of such laws that limit their ability to kill at will.

Two other points should be made with respect to understanding the contemporary terrorist. The first point is relatively simple and involves what seems like a truism: The less clear the political purpose that motivates terrorism, the greater its appeal is likely to be to unbalanced persons. A rational individual will be more likely to require a clear purpose for the commission of an extraordinary act. Thus, an act whose motivation is unclear is more likely to appeal to an irrational mind.

As already noted, contemporary terrorism has significantly less clear political purpose than that of earlier centuries. Therefore, it seems fair to say that a larger proportion of contemporary terrorists may well be unbalanced persons, the crazies that Hacker described.

The second point relates to what psychologists term *group dynamics.* If it is true that a terrorist's sense of reality is distorted, as asserted earlier, then the greater the association the terrorist enjoys with his or her group of fellow terrorists, the greater that distortion will be. The more, in other words, an individual perceives his or her identity in terms of the group of fellow terrorists, the less will be that person's ability to see the world as it really is. For the terrorist who is a member of a close-knit organization, reality is defined by the group. Remember, too, that this group rejects the reality of laws as they currently exist and morality, as it is defined by anyone except themselves.

Thus, conventional moral and legal constraints have little meaning to an individual who is deeply involved in a terrorist group. The group determines for itself what is moral and what is legal. An individual who has just joined the group may be able to perceive the difference between what the group declares to be morally or legally justified. The longer he or she remains with the group, or the stronger the identification with the norms of the group the individual adopts, the less able the individual becomes to see the difference between reality and "reality" as it is defined by the group.

The strength of the individual's acceptance of the group's definition of reality is particularly evident in situations in which terrorism has been a significant part of the culture for several generations. In Northern Ireland, for instance, young people have been "brought up to think of democracy as part of everyday humdrum existence, but of recourse to violence as something existing on a superior plane, not merely glorious but even sacred."[8]

***Religion as a Factor in Group Dynamics.*** Consider the case of the individual who commits terrorism as a member of a fanatic religious group. Religions, as a rule, offer to some extent their own versions of reality, as well as a promise of reward for conformity to the norms of that reality. The reward is usually promised for a future time, when the present reality has passed away.

Thus, the religious zealot committing an act of terrorism is assured by his or her religion and its leaders that those acts are acceptable to a "higher morality" than may currently exist. He or she is reinforced in their belief that what they are doing is right by the approval of their fellow zealots. Further, the religious fanatic is assured of immortality and a suitable "reward" therein if he or she should die in the commission of a terrorist act.

It would be difficult if not impossible to dissuade such a person of his or her beliefs by reasonable arguments. There is little that could be offered to such a person as an inducement for discontinuing the act of terrorism. What reward can compete with the promise of immortality, approval by one's peers, and religious sanctification?

Obviously, the dynamics of some groups are much more powerful than those of others whose reward system and expensive spiritual support system is less organized or persuasive. Certain types of terrorists are thus much more difficult to deal with on a rational basis, because of this ability of a group to distort reality.

## TRENDS IN TERRORIST RECRUITMENT AND MEMBERSHIP

So groups have an impact on modern terrorist behavior; some groups have more than others. Motivation has some effect on the type of individual involved in contemporary terrorism. Yet we have not established what a modern terrorist is really like, beyond a few generalizations. Is it, in fact, possible to be more specific about a typical terrorist personality?

It is unlikely that this search for a terrorist personality could be successful in creating a set of common denominators that could span several continents, time periods, cultures, and political configurations. All that most experts seem to agree on regarding terrorists today is that they are primarily young people. There are, it seems, very few old terrorists.

Some demographic **trends** in modern terrorist affiliations, however, do offer some clues as to who is currently becoming a terrorist. Although this approach falls short of providing a profile of a modern terrorist, it does yield insights into not only who modern terrorists are but also the impact of such a demographic configuration on contemporary terrorism.

## Age

Terrorism is not only a pursuit of the young; it became in the late 1970s and 1980s a pursuit of the *very* young. While terrorists during the time of the Russian anarchists tended to be at least in their midtwenties, during these two decades, the average age steadily decreased. During the turbulent 1960s, many terrorists were recruited from college campuses throughout the Western world. This brought the average age down to about 20, give or take a year, since the leaders were several years older, often in their early thirties.

Research in 1977 indicated that the usual urban terrorist was between 22 and 25 years of age. Among the Tupamaros, the average age of arrested terrorists was about 24.1, while in Brazil and Argentina, the average was 23 and 24, respectively. These figures remained true for the ETA, the IRA, and groups in Iran and Turkey during that time.

As early as the spring of 1976, however, evidence of a change in the age level of terrorists began to emerge. Arrests of Spanish ETA-V members revealed a number of youths in their teens. In Northern Ireland, some of the terrorists apprehended were as young as 12 to 14.[9]

Today, however, while the majority of active terrorists are in their twenties, there has been a tendency, particularly among the Arab and Iranian groups, to recruit children of 14 or 15 years of age. These children are used for dangerous, frequently suicidal missions, partly because their youth makes them less likely to question their orders and partly because their extreme youth makes them less likely to attract the attention of the authorities.

One explanation of this phenomenon is that the anarchistic-revolutionary philosophy that had begun to infiltrate the province of the university students has begun to infiltrate the secondary school level. Another explanation may lie in the number of children growing up in cultures in which violence is indeed a way of life. In the Middle East and in Northern Ireland, for instance, children growing up in violent community struggles could easily become a part of terrorist activities that span successive generations within the same family. Children were thus recruited not by philosophy learned at university or secondary school but by the dogma and lifestyles of their parents, facilitating a potentially more comprehensive assimilation into the terrorist group.

However, by the 1990s, this trend began to reverse, as peace within those two regions came closer to reality. Religious fanaticism is less likely to be the motivating factor compelling a 12-year-old into terrorism; instead, as Hamas membership indicates, most members are closer in age to the early 1970s terrorist profile. The individuals responsible for the bombing of the Pan Am flight over Lockerbie and those involved in the bombing of the World Trade Center in New York City were certainly not 12 or 13 years of age!

## Sex

During the earlier part of the twentieth century, while the leaders of terrorist cadres included some women among their numbers, the rank and file were usually predominantly male. In many such groups, women were assigned the less life-threatening roles of intelligence collection, courier, nurse or medical personnel, and maintenance of safe houses for terrorists on the run.

Terrorism of the late twentieth century, however, has been an equal opportunity employer. The commander of the JRA for years, Shigenobu Fusako, was a woman, and of the 14 most wanted West German terrorists in 1981, 10 were women. Moreover, studies have shown that female members of terrorist groups have proved to be tougher, more fanatical, more loyal, and possessors of a greater capacity for suffering. Women have also, in some terrorist groups, tended to remain a member longer than men, on the average.

One example serves to demonstrate the difference in the roles played by women in terrorism today. It was a pregnant woman who was given the task of carrying a suitcase loaded with explosives aboard an airplane in the 1980s. Only a few decades ago, she would have been, at best, allowed to provide a safe haven for the man entrusted with that task. This illustration is *not* to suggest that this is in any way "progress," but it does indicate a marked difference in the role women now play in terrorism.

## Education

Until the mid-1970s, most of the individuals involved in terrorism were quite well educated. Almost two-thirds of the people identified as terrorists were persons with some university training, university graduates, or postgraduate students. Among the Tupamaros, for example, about 75 percent of their membership were very well educated, and of the Baader-Meinhof organization in West Germany, the figure reached almost 80 percent.

In the Palestinian groups, most members were university students or graduates, frequently those who had, by virtue of their middle-class wealth, been able to study at foreign universities. By 1969, several thousand Palestinians were studying abroad at universities, particularly in Europe, where they were exposed to anarchistic-Marxist ideas. This group became an important recruiting pool for the Popular Front for the Liberation of Palestine (PFLP). Indeed, the chief for decades of the PFLP, George Habbash, was a medical doctor who had obtained his degree abroad.

But the level of education of the average terrorist is declining today, partly because of the trend in recruitment age of the latter twentieth century already noted. If young people are being recruited out of secondary school rather than out of college, then the number of individuals in terrorist groups with college education will necessarily decline as well.

This trend brings with it another important decline: a diminishing of the understanding by the rank and file among terrorists of the political philosophies that have supposedly motivated the groups to adopt terrorist activities. Elementary school children are clearly unable, as a rule, to grasp the impetus of Marxist philosophy toward social revolution. Unlike the college students of the 1960s who studied and at least half-understood the radical political philosophies, today's new terrorist recruits are fed watered-down versions of Marx and Lenin by leaders whose own understanding of these philosophers is certainly suspect.

This downward trend in education and understanding of political philosophy is exhibited by terrorist leadership figures as well as by the cadres' rank-and-file memberships. The notorious terrorist, Abu Nidal, leader of the group bearing his name, only attended college in Cairo for two years. Contrary to his claim in subsequent years, he never obtained an engineering degree, or indeed any other degree. He dropped out and went home to teach in the local school in Nablus.

The rising age level of recruits does not, apparently, signify a return to highly educated cadres. The individuals responsible for most of the recent bombings and overt attacks have been, for the most part, no better educated than Nidal, at best having acquired part of a college degree. Thus, whereas age level appears to be rising, education level does not.

## Economic Status

During the 1960s, many young people joined terrorist organizations as a way of rejecting their parents' comfortable, middle-class values. They were often children of parents who could afford to send them to private colleges, and they were rejecting the comparative wealth of their surroundings to fight for "justice" for those less fortunate.

Today's terrorists tend to be drawn more from the less fortunate than from comfortable, middle-class homes. Although some come from families who have had wealth but lost it through revolution or confiscation, most are from absolute destitution, for whom terrorism represents the only way to lash out at society's injustices. In the terrorist group, these individuals find a collective wealth and ability to improve one's financial situation that is enormously appealing to the impoverished.

Again, Abu Nidal provides insight into the change in the economic circumstances of the type of person who becomes a terrorist today, in many parts of the world. Nidal, born Sabri al-Banna, was the son of wealthy Palestinian parents who lost everything. From the lap of luxury, his family moved into the extreme poverty of refugee camps. The bitterness and frustration of this life of endless poverty and state-lessness may well have produced the catalyst for the terrorist he was to become.

## Socialization toward Violence

As noted earlier, intellectuals have, during the past few decades, helped to make the cult of violence "respectable." But today's terrorists have been socialized toward vio-lence in ways never experienced before in civilized society. Intellectual terrorists of the 1960s were, for the most part, first-generation terrorists. Today we see an increas-ing number of third- and even fourth-generation terrorists. Young people recruited in such circumstances have been socialized to accept violence as a normal pattern of life. Peace, as much of the rest of the world knows it, has no meaning for them, and the related values of a civilized society have equally little relevance in their lives.

In Northern Ireland and parts of the Middle East, until the peace efforts of the 1990s, this pattern of successive generations of terrorism has produced terrorists who have no understanding of the kind of limits on the use of violence that much of the rest of the world regards as customary. Violence is not only a normal pattern of life; it is a means of survival, and its successful use offers a means of security and enhance-ment of one's own, and one's family's, life.

This role of violence is made vividly clear by remarks made by the Reverend Benjamin Weir, a former U.S. hostage held by terrorists in Lebanon. He suggested that, for many Lebanese youths, the only employment open to them that offered both an income and some form of security for their families was with one of the warring militia factions. College was for decades either unavailable or unaffordable, and alternative employment in a nation whose economy was in shambles was unlikely. Life as a terrorist was, in some respects, the *only* alternative for many young people in that war-torn country.

## CASE STUDY: ABU NIDAL

In recent years, Sabri al-Banna has become notorious as one of the greatest terrorists of our time. As the architect of the massacres of tourists at the Rome and Vienna air-ports in December 1985, as well as the mastermind of countless other atrocities, he makes a fascinating subject for study in modern terrorism.

Al-Banna was born in May 1937 in Jaffa. His father, Khalil, was one of the wealthiest men in Palestine, with homes in Marseilles, France; Iskenderum, Turkey; Syria; and several houses in Palestine itself.

All of the al-Banna land was confiscated by the Israeli government in 1948 and acquired by the Jewish state. Sabri's father was dead by this time, and his family was forced to flee, first to their house near Majdal, then to the al-Burj refugee camp in the Gaza Strip. In early 1949, they moved to Nablus, on the West Bank.

From incredible wealth, Sabri saw his family reduced to life in the teeming refugee camps by age 12. From private schools and tutors, he moved to government school, graduating from the city high school in 1955. Although he entered Cairo University, he returned to Nablus two years later without having completed his degree.

Through his brother, Zakariya, he obtained a job as an electrician's assistant with a construction company in Saudi Arabia. While there, he became involved in the illegal Ba'ath party (which later stood him in good stead with the Iraqi regime). His involvement was noted by his employers and the Saudi regime. He was fired and later imprisoned, tortured, and expelled from the country.

Sabri returned to Nablus a few months before Israeli tanks rolled in, during the 1967 Six-Day War. Although he had been a passive member of Fatah for years, he became an active member after this traumatic experience. Again a refugee, he moved to Amman, where he chose the nom de guerre Abu Nidal (which can be translated to mean "father of the struggle").

Of his career since that time, no single account exists, though many stories of his exploits abound. Suffice it to say that he broke with the PLO leadership of Yasir Arafat, contending that its policy of accommodation and moderation was "selling out the Palestinians." He has established ties with several former communist nations, as well as with some Arab states, between which he has traveled with impunity.

In addition to the attacks on the Rome and Vienna airports, he directed assaults on a group of British invalids in an Athens hotel, on the Israeli ambassador to Great Britain, and on his own nephew's family. He reportedly recruited only Palestinians to his group, whose motivations are similar to his own. He had them trained in Iraq and Syria and deployed them throughout the world, primarily against civilian targets.

Although he has been reported to be "seriously ill" several times and was, at the end of the summer in 1998, said to be "detained" in Egypt, Nidal remains at large. Like Carlos the Jackal, he has become a legendary figure in the world of terrorism and one whose life offers interesting insights into the "why" question of modern terrorism.

## *Evaluation*

The modern terrorist *is* different. The requisites suggested by O'Ballance are met less frequently, even by terrorist leaders, and the trends in terrorist recruitment suggest an increasing deviation from those norms.

Taking Abu Nidal as an example of a modern terrorist leader, try to resolve the following questions:

1. To what extent does Nidal meet, or fail to meet, the criteria suggested by O'Ballance?
2. To what extent does Nidal exemplify the trends discussed (toward youthful recruitment, education, etc.)?
3. If Nidal is a "typical" modern terrorist, what does that suggest about terrorist acts today (more cruel, more indiscriminate)?
4. Are there other leaders who are more typical of modern terrorists?

5. Judging by the demographic trends, from what areas or groups are terrorist recruits more likely to come?

6. Do the individuals who committed the World Trade Center bombings or the Oklahoma City bombing fit the "typical" pattern suggested here?

7. What does this discussion suggest for those who seek to diminish the incidence of terrorism in today's world?

## Suggested Readings

Clarke, Thurston. *By Blood and Fire: The Attack on the King David Hotel.* New York: Putnam, 1981.

Hacker, Frederick J. *Crusaders, Criminals, Crazies: Terror and Terrorism in Our Time.* New York: Norton, 1976.

"Identity Movement Quietly Grows Underground; Bonds Together Far-Right Extremists." *Crime Control Digest* (July 29, 1987), 32–56.

Lacquer, Walter. *The Age of Terrorism.* Boston: Little, Brown, 1987.

O'Ballance, Edgar O. *The Language of Violence: The Blood Politics of Terrorism.* San Rafael, CA: Presidio, 1979.

Russell, Charles, and Bowman Miller. "Profile of a Terrorist." *Terrorism: An International Journal* 1, no. 1 (1977), 42–59.

Weinberg, Leonard, and William Lee Eubank. "Recruitment of Italian Political Terrorists." In *Multidimensional Terrorism,* ed. M. Slann and B. Schechterman. Boulder, CO: Rienner, 1987, 78–94.

## Endnotes

1. Frederick J. Hacker, *Crusaders, Criminals, Crazies: Terror and Terrorism in Our Time* (New York: Norton, 1976), 8–9.

2. Edgar O'Ballance, *The Language of Violence: The Blood Politics of Terrorism* (San Rafael, CA: Presidio Press, 1979), 300–301.

3. Hacker, *Crusaders,* 105.

4. Thurston Clarke, *By Blood and Fire: The Attack on the King David Hotel* (New York: Putnam, 1981), 45.

5. Quoted by Milton Meltzer, *The Terrorists* (New York: Harper & Row, 1983), 111.

6. Walter Lacquer, *The Age of Terrorism* (Boston: Little, Brown, 1987), 92.

7. Ibid., 93.

8. Connon Cruise O'Brien, "Reflecting on Terrorism," *New York Review of Books* (September 16, 1976): 44–48.

9. Charles Russell and Bowman Miller, "Profile of a Terrorist," *Terrorism: An International Journal* 1, no. 1 (1977): 20.

# 5

# Terrorism by the State

*Terror is an outstanding mode of conflict in localized primitive wars; and unilateral violence has been used to subdue satellite countries, occupied countries or dissident groups within a dictatorship.*

—Thomas Schelling (1966)

## Key Concepts

internal terrorism
external terrorism
coerced conversion
genocide
intimidation
covert terrorism

state-sponsored terrorism
state-supported terrorism
surrogate terrorism
"fishing in troubled waters"
silent partners

Individuals and groups are not the only perpetrators of terrorism. Political leaders have used terrorism as an instrument of both domestic and foreign policy for centuries. From the time when centralized governments were first organized, rulers have resorted to the use of terror tactics to subdue their subjects and to spread confusion and chaos among their enemies. Today, a ruthless state uses terrorism primarily for those two purposes.

**Internal terrorism,** practiced by a state against its own people, has produced some of the most flagrant violations of human rights that the world has ever known. **External terrorism,** practiced by one state against citizens of another, is less often cited as a form of state terrorism. Its perpetrators tend, as a rule, to try to conceal their roles as the instigators or supporters of the terrorists.

## INTERNAL TERRORISM: THE BEAST THAT LURKS WITHIN

No matter how chilling the atrocities committed by individuals or groups, these crimes pale into insignificance beside the terror inflicted by a state on its own people. Because governments have a much greater array of power, they are capable of inflicting a much greater degree of terror on their citizenry.

66

A look at casualty figures gives some perspective on the magnitude of the harm states can inflict on their people, compared with the damage caused by nonstate terrorists. In the decade between 1968 and 1978, about 10,000 people were killed worldwide by terrorist groups. In just *one* of those years, 1976–1977, the new military dictatorship in Argentina was responsible for almost that same number of deaths.

Throughout history states have used terrorist acts of violence to subdue groups or individuals. States have from time to time used such violence to create a climate of fear in which citizens will do whatever the government wants.

The history of state terrorism stretches back at least into the legacy of ancient Rome. The Roman emperor Nero ruled by fear. He ordered the deaths of anyone who either opposed him or, in his mind, constituted a threat to his rule, including members of his own family. He was responsible for the slaughter of many of the nobility and for the burning of Rome in A.D. 64. To him, everyone was an enemy, and with his power he made them all victims of his terrorism.[1]

What a state does to its own people was, until very recently, strictly its own business. Neither the rulers nor concerned citizens in other countries usually interfered with what a sovereign government chose to do with its citizens. Even today such interference is largely limited to diplomatic or economic pressures and to the problematic effects of an informed world opinion.

At least three levels of internal state terrorism have been identified as useful gradations in understanding the scope of terrorism practiced by the state. The first is **intimidation,** in which the government tries to anticipate and discourage opposition and dissent, frequently through control of the media and prolific use of police force. This form of state terrorism has existed in almost every nation-state at some point in its history, most often during times of war. Chile, Argentina, South Africa, and Uganda offered, at several points in the twentieth century, excellent examples of this type of internal state terrorism. **Coerced conversion,** involving government efforts to create a complete change in a national lifestyle, is not unusual in the aftermath of a revolution, as the Soviet Union experienced in the early twentieth century and Iran in the 1980s.

Nations in the twentieth century have also practiced the third level of internal state terrorism, **genocide,** the deliberate extermination of an entire class or an entire ethnic or religious group of people, for ideological reasons, while the rest of the "civilized world watched in horror, disbelief, or studied indifference."[2] Nor was this destruction of innocent persons confined to Nazi Germany or Stalin's Soviet Union. Certain tribes in African nations were all but obliterated by rival tribal leaders who grasped the reins of government. In the mid-1990s, Rwanda experienced at least one wave of this form of terror. Bosnia in the early 1990s was the scene of mass slaughter of people of one ethnic group by leaders of another. In Argentina, thousands of persons "disappeared" during an oppressive regime.

Let us look at some of these examples of state terrorism in a little more depth, to better gauge a comparison between their destructiveness and the destructiveness of terrorist groups. State terrorism during the twentieth century was not confined to one nation or one continent. While history is sprinkled with examples of gross state terrorism, such as that practiced by Nero or the Jacobins in the French Revolution, many modern nations must share the "honors" as terrorist states today.

One of the nations that comes most readily to most people's minds when one refers to a modern terrorist state is Nazi Germany (1933–1945). Adolf Hitler moved swiftly after he rose to power to create an authoritarian regime. He suspended all civil rights, eliminated the non-Nazi press, and banned all demonstrations. The Gestapo, his secret police, was given the power to arrest and even to execute any "suspicious person."

In the beginning thousands of people were imprisoned, beaten, or tortured to death. But this did not end Hitler's terrorism of the remaining population. Instead, borrowing the idea of concentration camps from Russia, he created such camps in Germany and in occupied nations, and he gave the Gestapo the power to send anyone they wanted to these camps, without trial or hope of appeal.

These camps became the instruments for Hitler's "final solution" for ridding himself of all his "enemies." It is estimated that during his 12-year rule of terror, between 10 and 12 million people died. Some were gassed, others hung; some faced firing squads; and countless others died by other equally violent and vicious means. In 12 years, one state murdered between 10 and 12 *million* innocent people and was responsible, through the war that it initiated, for the deaths of countless more. It is a record of terror almost unparalleled in modern history, even by the most vicious terrorist.

But it is only *almost* unparalleled: the Soviet Union under Stalin was responsible for millions of deaths as well. Only estimates have been given for the number of people who fell victim to Stalin's totalitarian society. By the time of Stalin's death in 1953, scholars have estimated that between 40 and 50 million people were sent to Soviet jails or slave labor camps. Of these, somewhere between 15 and 25 million died there, by execution, hunger, or disease.

Dictators, as a whole, have found it easier to commit terrorism without world censure than have individuals, for state terrorism is generally committed in secret. The shadowy world of state terrorism is thus less susceptible to the pressures of world opinion than the activities of terrorist groups, who actively seek this spotlight of global attention.

Cambodia, under the rule of the Khmer Rouge, illustrates this point. During its rule of less than four years, this systematic terrorism was responsible for over 1 million deaths. When one notes that only about 7 million people lived in that land, the magnitude of the terror becomes evident. This regime committed genocide against its own people.

Africa has had its share of state terrorism, too. Colonial powers used terrorism, often in the form of summary imprisonment and execution, to suppress national liberation movements. Uganda, under Idi Amin, was clearly a terrorist state. Between 1971 and 1979, over 100,000 Ugandans lost their lives to his barbaric terrorism.

Latin America, too, continues to have regimes that practice terror on their people. Argentina, Bolivia, Chile, Paraguay, and Uruguay have suffered under cruel and repressive regimes. In Uruguay, the terrorism instigated by the leftist Tupac Amaru has been repaid 100-fold by the repressive military regime that came to power in the wake of the collapse of what was, at the time, South America's only democracy.

Argentina suffered under the yoke of a brutally repressive military regime, which finally ended in 1983. Leftist terrorism in that nation provoked a right-wing military-backed response so savage that it staggered the imagination. For a time the press reported the appearance of bodies in ditches and mutilated corpses on garbage heaps and in burned-out vehicles. People "disappeared" by the thousands, abducted by armed men claiming to be members of "security forces." Although the "disappearances" became less frequent as the nation moved toward democracy, the legacy of brutality continues to burden the government in its quest for legitimacy and acceptance.

In the wake of discovering just how ruthless some rulers could be in dealing with their subjects, leaders of victorious nations after World War II tried to create international laws that would restrict the ability of governments to use terrorism against their citizens. Attempts to create such laws by consensus were only marginally successful.

On December 10, 1948, the UN General Assembly adopted the Universal Declaration of Human Rights without dissent. This document states that "everyone has the right to life, liberty, and security of person" and that these rights may not be taken away by any institution, state, or individual. According to this declaration, it is not acceptable for states to administer collective punishment or to punish any person for a crime that he or she did not personally commit. It also emphasizes the necessity of fair trials and equal justice before the law. Because terrorism by a state often involves the summary punishment of individuals not for any specific crime but because their deaths or incarceration will result in a climate of fear among other citizens, this declaration would appear to be significant in the effort to curb state terrorism. However, it has no binding effect in international law.

The problem is largely a political one. States do not openly interfere in the domestic affairs of other states, because such interference would leave them open to similar intrusions. Conventions such as those protecting human rights are often viewed as dangerous, even by states with relatively clean records in terms of state terrorism, in that these conventions open avenues for hostile governments to interfere with the internal affairs of the nation.

Kren and Rappoport argue that

within certain limits set by political and military power considerations, the modern state may do anything it wishes to those under its control. There is no moral-ethical limit which the state cannot transcend if it wished to do so, because there is no moral-ethical power higher than the state. Moreover, it seems apparent that no modern state will ever seriously interfere with the internal activities of another solely for moral-ethical reasons.[3]

Most interference in the internal affairs of a sovereign state are based on national security rather than ethical or moral grounds. Although the Nuremberg trials offered some evidence that the principle of nonintervention was being challenged by nations motivated by moral-ethical concern, since that time few nations have indicated that "crimes against humanity" undertaken within a nation's own borders are a basis for international intervention. Even evidence of "ethnic cleansing" in Bosnia during the early 1990s, although generating the formation of an international criminal tribunal, did not produce on the part of nations a willingness to subject indicted criminals to the justice process at The Hague.

The linkage between revolution and violence has already been discussed. A similar relationship exists with respect to the right of a state to protect itself from revolutionary violence. Most modern states have experienced a period of revolutionary violence. During and after such periods, however, the right of a state to protect itself remains restricted by even more rules than those that apply to its revolutionary enemies. In addition to abiding by the laws of warfare, states are entrusted with the responsibility for preserving and protecting human rights and freedoms.

A state has an abiding obligation to restrain its use of violence against its citizens. Whether at war or at peace, a state is supposed to recognize a legal commitment toward the preservation of the rights of the individual. If it is true that insurgent terrorists frequently try to provoke government repression in the hopes of generating greater sympathy and support for the terrorists' cause, then it is obviously extremely important that governments *not* respond in kind.

This does not mean that governments are or should be held to be impotent in the face of flagrant attacks on law and order. Certainly a state is responsible for protecting its citizens from violence. But the means used to ensure law and order must be carefully balanced against the responsibility of the government to guarantee the maximum protection of civil rights and liberties. Too great a willingness to sacrifice the latter in order to preserve stability within a state not only would be giving terrorists the impetus for their cause but would also be placing the state in the invidious position of breaking international law to stop someone else from breaking it.

A state that violates international law by committing acts of genocide, violently suppressing fundamental freedoms, or breaking the laws of war or the Geneva Convention on the treatment of prisoners of war and civilians can be considered guilty of "state terrorism."[4] If terrorism is defined to include acts of political violence perpetrated without regard to the safety of innocent persons in an effort to evoke a mood of fear and confusion in a target audience, then surely states have been as guilty of such acts as have individuals and groups.

Indeed, it is useful to remember that the word *terror* derives from the actions of a government—the Jacobin government of revolutionary France. In fact, terrorist regimes have been far more deadly than group or individual actors in this century, even after World War II.[5] The word *totalitarian* has become part of the political lexicon as a result of state terrorism in Nazi Germany and Stalinist Russia. Both systems relied on organized, systematized discriminate terror to create a bondage of the mind as well as of the body.[6]

If, as Hannah Arendt suggests, "lawlessness is the essence of tyranny, then terror is the essence of totalitarian domination." In her essay "On Violence," she notes that "terror is not the same as violence; it is, rather, the form of government that comes into being when violence, having destroyed all power, does not abdicate but, on the contrary, remains in full control."[7] State terrorism, thus described, is the quintessential form of terrorism.

State terrorism is frequently a nasty combination of personality and ideology. "Nazism and Stalinism were personifications of the evil genius of their leaders, but they could not have succeeded without a disoriented, terrorized citizenry," according to one expert.[8]

Totalitarianism and state terrorism aim not only at the transmutation of society but at the fundamental change in human nature itself. The basic goal of terrorist states is mass disorientation and inescapable anxiety. Modern governments whose actions have earned for themselves the soubriquet terrorist, such as Indonesia in the 1960s or Chile in the 1970s, have employed terror-violence as an integral part of the governing process.[9]

Governments have been, and continue to be, as likely to commit terrorist acts as individuals and groups. Moreover, it is probably true that, "as violence breeds violence, so terrorism begets counter-terrorism, which in turn leads to more terrorism in an ever-increasing spiral."[10] So state domestic terrorism not only transgresses international law but also often creates the political, economic, and social milieu that precipitates acts of individual and group terrorism. It is thus a causal factor in the perpetration of further terrorism.

## HOW REAL IS STATE TERRORISM?

Dozens of nations today use terrorism as (unofficial) government policy to secure and ensure control over their citizens. The use of murder, slavery, and terror to subjugate people taints the history of almost every modern nation. Other weapons used by the state in terrorism include arrest (usually in the dead of night to maximize the psychological impact), summary deportation of dissidents or "subversives," incarceration without trial for indefinite lengths of time, and, of course, torture. Torture is the ultimate weapon of state terrorism.

Amnesty International reports that foreign "experts" in torture have been sent from country to country. Schools of torture teach and demonstrate methods to government officials, particularly electroshock techniques, because they are the easiest and most commonly used form of scientific torture. Modern torture equipment is exported regularly. Some of the shock machines used by governments to torture their citizens are made in the United States.[11]

Amnesty International's *Report on Terrorism,* published in 1975, provides horrifying details of state torture and terror, including the following description of torture in Chile:

> Many people were tortured to death by means of endless whipping as well as beating with fists, feet and rifle butts. Prisoners were beaten on all parts of the body, including the head and sexual organs. . . . There were many cases of burning (with acid or cigarettes), of electricity, of psychological threats including simulated executions and threats the families of the prisoners would be tortured. At times the brutalities reached animalistic levels.[12]

The report goes on to tell of rape, sexual depravities, abortions forced by rifle butts, force-feeding of excrement, immersion in icy water or tanks of gasoline, and countless other atrocities too horrible to recount. They sicken the reader—but they are true, and they are happening now. Such bestiality did not stop with the death of Hitler or Stalin. There still exist many governments today with so little regard for human life and dignity that they are willing to perpetrate such acts of terror on their citizens.

Even the United States has experienced forms of state terrorism. The U.S. history of violence in the labor movement provides several examples of abuse of government power. The events in Ludlow, Colorado, offer a poignant vignette of state terrorism. On Easter night in 1914, members of the Colorado National Guard, aided by the company police of Colorado Fuel and Iron Company (owned by John D. Rockefeller, Sr.), poured oil on the tent city of miners and set them ablaze. The miners, who had been on strike and evicted from their homes in the company town, had dug a cave under the largest tent and placed the children there for safety. Even so, 11 children and one pregnant mother burned to death, while 5 men and 1 boy were shot to death as they tried to run to safety.

Similar blots on U.S. history also exist in the treatment of African Americans. Slavery was enforced by government law and police power for decades. Even with its official end, through the Thirteenth Amendment to the Constitution, unofficial persecution of black citizens continued unchecked. The Ku Klux Klan and similar groups murdered, lynched, beat, and raped, in a concerted effort to terrorize blacks after the Civil War and Reconstruction. While such groups were not in any sense arms of the state, they were allowed until the 1960s to carry out their terror campaigns relatively unhampered by a sympathetic or uncaring government.

But terrorism in the United States fades in comparison to that practiced by totalitarian states. In the former Soviet Union under Stalin, millions of dissenters were murdered or sent to camps in Siberia, where they died. Among these millions were intellectuals, artists, writers, army officers, and small farmers who opposed Stalin's collectivization of farms. Few survived to tell the tales of their afflictions.

# TERRORISM AS AN INSTRUMENT OF FOREIGN POLICY

Terrorism has been used by national leaders as an instrument of foreign policy, particularly in the waging of irregular warfare. This has usually taken the form of **covert terrorism,** because the acts are generally expected to be committed without the state being openly involved.

This state form of terrorist behavior usually falls into one of two categories: **state-sponsored terrorism** and **state-supported terrorism.** In state-sponsored terrorism, there is more involvement by the state, sometimes as direct as decision making and control of the group's activities. In state-supported terrorism, the state usually aids or abets existing terrorist groups that have varying degrees of independence.[13] In both types of state terror, the state utilizes groups engaged in terrorist acts to enhance state goals in other countries. Unlike the internal coercive diplomacy (which may be obvious to all observers, whether or not they are willing to label it as such), clandestine operations are, by their very nature, conducted in secrecy and consequently they are very difficult to discern. Thus, there is often little verifiable data that can be used to study this phenomenon. This makes the use of terrorism an attractive, but potentially dangerous, weapon for states seeking to carry out hostile acts without initiating a war.

State-supported and state-sponsored forms of terrorism are primarily used to produce fear and chaos within potentially unfriendly or hostile states—for example, to weaken the resistance or diminish the intransigence of states, as the cost of such antagonism is made plain. Such activities are also designed to demonstrate the weaknesses and vulnerabilities of opponents, in an effort to make such adversaries more willing to bargain.

Such activities have been described as attempts to "destabilize" unfriendly regimes. CIA efforts in Chile in the early 1970s took this form. Not only was this organization involved in clandestine efforts, including the assassination of Rene Schneider, the commander-in-chief of the Chilean Army who refused to approve plans to remove Salvador Allende from office, but it was also involved in numerous other efforts to remove Allende. Records indicate that at least $7 million were authorized by the United States for CIA use in destabilizing Chilean society, including the financing of opposition groups and right-wing terrorist paramilitary groups.

Similar clandestine efforts in Nicaragua provoked a great deal of undersirable (from the U.S. government's point of view) attention. Efforts to destabilize the Sandinista regime supposedly came to an official halt in 1982, when the U.S. House of Representatives voted to halt covert activities abroad by the CIA for the purpose of overthrowing the government of Nicaragua.[14] But, as the Iran-*contra* affair indicated, efforts to conduct clandestine terrorist operations did not cease with the passage of that law. Instead, such activities became one step *more* covert.

Claire Sterling has researched the networks of support and sponsorship that terrorist organizations enjoy. According to Sterling, nations such as the former Soviet

Union were heavily involved in sponsoring terrorism: "Direct control of the terrorist groups was never the Soviet intention. All were indigenous to their countries. All began as offshoots of relatively non-violent movements that expressed particular political, economic, religious or ethnic grievances."[15]

States have chosen to sponsor terrorism abroad either directly or, more often, indirectly. Let us consider at least one compelling reason for indirectly sponsoring terrorism. It may be that such sponsorship offers a low-risk avenue for redressing an international grievance. For example, some Arab states chose to sponsor Palestinian groups engaged in terrorist acts as a less risky method of redressing the Palestinian problem—less risky than provoking another war with Israel.

## WAGING WAR BY PROXY: SURROGATE TERRORISM

Other states have found a third form of state terrorism to be a more useful tool in the exporting of a revolution: **surrogate terrorism.** Such terrorism involves assistance to another state or terrorist organization that makes it possible for that actor to improve its capability for terrorism either at home or abroad.

Certainly Iran, under the Ayatollah Khomeini, engaged in this practice throughout the Middle East. Some nations within the former communist bloc have also offered support to terrorist groups in the form of equipment and training camps, purportedly as a way of exporting the communist revolution or perhaps as a means for weakening an adversary state (a reason often cited to explain Arab support for terrorist activities against Israel).

Libya has used terrorism as an instrument to help the state track down and eradicate exiled dissidents (or intimidate them into silence). It has also offered sanctuary and assistance to the Abu Nidal Organization and a variety of other Palestinian resistance groups. Moreover, Libya has used terrorism to redress a particular international grievance.

Again we can turn to Sterling's assessment of the former Soviet Union's reasons for becoming involved in surrogate terrorism. She suggests that "[T]he heart of the Russian's strategy is to provide the network with the goods and services necessary to undermine the industrialized democracies of the West."[16]

Even in the light of information unearthed by Sterling and other journalists who have sought to uncover the support network by which terrorist organizations operate, there is a significant lack of verifiable data to link states thought to have logical policy reasons for supporting such groups with actual instances of substantive support. While few would dispute the evidence of relatively low-level support (providing of safe houses, travel documents, and similar assistance), we lack hard evidence as to any "control" exercised by the Soviets or other states or participation by those states in any hostile events.

Although most researchers recognize that the Soviets had an interest in actions that would spread fear and chaos in the Western world, many are unprepared to go further than that assessment. What is often referred to as **"fishing in troubled waters"**—that is, assisting those already engaged in opposition to states that are one's enemies—is not an unusual policy, nor is it necessarily illicit. Does such "fishing" make the state giving the assistance culpable for the offenses committed by those receiving the assistance?

Sterling suggests that "the Soviet Union had simply laid a loaded gun on the table, leaving others to get on with it."[17] By inference, the issue of whether the Soviets directed or merely benefited from terrorist actions carried out with that "loaded gun" is less significant, while the linkage to the Soviet Union and its state policy is clear. Activities carried out by groups provided with Soviet aid are nonetheless instruments of state-supported terrorism.

Other scholars also stress the degree to which the Soviet Union was involved in surrogate warfare through terrorism. Cline and Alexander, in 1984, noted:

> In the 1970's terrorism, whether backed directly or indirectly by the Soviet Union or independently initiated, appeared to have become an indispensable tactical and strategic tool in the Soviet struggle for power and influence within and among nations. In relying on this instrument, Moscow seems to aim in the 1980's at achieving strategic ends in circumstances where the use of conventional armed forces is deemed inappropriate, ineffective, too risky or too difficult.[18]

These authors also claim that "it is obvious from the PLO documents that there exists a carefully developed international terrorist infrastructure that serves Moscow's foreign policy objectives of destabilizing non-communist governments."[19]

But did the Palestinians commit terrorism only or even specifically at the behest of Moscow? There is little evidence to support such a claim. Moreover, many other state and nonstate actors offer support to Palestinian groups. Are they instruments of *all* of their supporters' foreign policies? Perhaps it would be more accurate to say that they act at times in ways that are beneficial to a particular state's interests, and in recognition of that confluence of interest, they receive support. This still does not clarify the degree of control that the supporting state has over this policy "instrument." It does, however, suggest that this approach can be a hazardous and uncertain foreign policy operation.

One scholar sums up the evaluation of the Soviet's support of terrorist organizations as a foreign policy tool in this manner:

> Let us be clear about what we do not know. We do not know the extent, if any, to which the Soviets direct any terrorist organization. Moscow seems to have had great influence over the Popular Front for the Liberation of Palestine (PFLP) but less over other factors within the Palestinian Liberation Organization (PLO). Most of the money for many terrorist groups probably comes, not from the Soviet Union, but from wealthy Arab nations and from criminal activities.[20]

In fact, governments may engage in terrorism for a variety of reasons, which become blurred even in their own minds and are often indistinguishable in the eyes of horrified observers. One cause may be the principal motivator for a particular act, but it may have numerous desirable side effects, which become in time prime motivators, too. A state may, for example, decide to assist an organization carrying out terrorist acts or field an organization of its own, to try to redress a particular international grievance. In the course of events, the state may discover that the terrorism has helped to weaken an adversary state against which it would not ordinarily have had the strength to wage a regular war. After a time, it becomes difficult for the state to decide which is the most important reason for its decision to engage in terrorism by proxy.

Among the states who support terrorist groups or nations, there are no villains in black hats. Usually the state is at pains to conceal the linkage or to rationalize its necessity. Even more often, the links are hidden through many channels and transfers of equipment and assistance.

## RELUCTANT BEDFELLOWS: THE ARMS BAZAAR

Let us briefly examine the booming sale of arms to individuals, groups, and nations (e.g., Iran and Libya) engaging in terrorist acts, who make no secret of their propagation of terrorism. Even among the Western allies, who on paper oppose these regimes and groups, there remain strong support channels. Through these channels, with the state's knowledge and support, many companies circumvent national law in selling arms to hostile or warring nations or groups.

France sold to Libya dozens of Exocet antiship missiles, which were subsequently used by Qadhafi on the U.S. Sixth Fleet. Germans traveled to Iran to work out details on a contract for the sale of four diesel submarines, which would presumably be added to the armada with which Iran has threatened the shipping lanes in the Persian Gulf. Austria officially condemned Iraq's use of gas in the Iran-Iraq war, offering the use of its hospitals for the treatment of Iraqi victims of gas attacks. Yet Austria exported the chemicals used to make the poisonous gas—to Iraq! From the former West Germany, via Greek suppliers, Iran obtained optics and range-finding equipment. Iran also procures the G-3 assault rifle, its standard infantry weapon, from Germany.

Nor is it only Iran and Iraq who have benefited from industrial nations' desires to cash in on the arms market. Libya, which made little secret of its support for and commitment to groups and individuals engaging in terrorism against the West, has received considerable European assistance, only a part of which took the form of arms sales. The former West Germany, for instance, opposed sanctions against states supporting terrorism each time such sanctions were proposed. It may be fair to assume that part of that opposition stemmed from the fact that West Germany bought 191,000 barrels of oil from Libya in 1985.

Italy, too, has a strong trade relationship with Libya, averaging approximately $5 billion per year. Libya owned 15 percent of FIAT Corporation. In May 1986, the former chief of the Italian intelligence service admitted that his service had helped Qadhafi get arms and assisted him on intelligence matters. Italy also sold a wide variety of arms to Libya, including Augusta antitank helicopters, Assad-class missile corvettes, self-propelled howitzers, Otomat missiles, and acoustic mines and torpedoes. Many of these weapons have subsequently found their way into the hands of terrorists.

Athens, the cradle of democracy, has for years been the intermediary through which transactions from the West are channeled to various protagonists in the Middle East and North Africa. Members of the Islamic Jihad, Abu Nidal's organization, and Abbu Abbas have operated freely through Greek borders. Athens itself has been the starting point for airline sabotage and hijacking (as in the June 14, 1985, TWA Flight 847, and the November 1985 Egypt Air bombing in which 60 persons were killed). It has also been the site of heinous massacres, such as the one perpetrated at the El Al service counter, which resulted in the deaths of innocent children and holiday travelers in 1985.

Cooperation between governments in the sales of arms has certainly resulted in some strange bedfellows. None is perhaps stranger that the relationship between Israel and Iran in the 1980s. Israel was one of Iran's biggest suppliers of armaments. In 1984, for example, Israel sold 20 F-4 jet engines to Iran, routing the transaction through Greece to Teheran. In January 1985, Israel offered to sell (via telexes to brokers, including those in Iran) 150 U.S. Sidewinder air-to-air missiles.

Some defenders of such sales argue that the nations or groups would purchase such arms anyway, so why should Western nations not make the profit that is to be made in these "inevitable" transactions? Such an argument is, of course, merely a rationalization of an economic reality that contravenes political policy.

Unfortunately, the economic ties forged by such transactions make it difficult for nations to take firm stands against terrorism or terrorist groups sponsored by the recipient nations. The stronger the economic linkage is, the weaker is a government's response to restrict terrorism. The uneasy relationship between these buyers and sellers of arms clouds the issue of each nation's policy on terrorism. The seller nations, the purveyors of arms, find themselves in the dubious position of appearing to sponsor terrorism, indirectly, which is an allegation they cannot completely dismiss.

## SILENT PARTNERS: SYRIA, IRAN, LIBYA, AND SUDAN WAGE SUBTLE WAR

While few states can politically or legally afford to openly support terrorism, some are **silent partners,** in that they are states that covertly or at least discreetly enter into "partnerships" of common interest with groups engaging in terrorism. Examining a few of these silent partners in terror will illustrate the complexity of the problem.

### Syria

Syrian president Hafez al-Assad has long sought to become the dominant power broker in the Middle East, and until the fall of 1986, he came close to achieving that objective. Until that time Assad contrived to mask his support for terrorists beneath a cloak of state secrecy. By distancing himself from the terrorists, he managed to preserve deniability; and when it seemed strategically expedient, he renewed his credit with the West by intervening on behalf of Western hostages.

Assad's secure power base at home and close ties with Moscow made diplomats hesitant to criticize him openly. In the absence of evidence to the contrary, some observers have even assumed that he was a "helpful partner" in Middle East negotiations concerning Lebanon.

Evidence of his duplicity has, of course, come to light, particularly since the demise of the Soviet Union. As *U.S. News & World Report* noted, "even in the diplomatic world of studied indirection and strategic dissembling, the evidence has become impossible to ignore, and it points straight at Syrian strong man Hafez Assad."[21] Former secretary of state George Schultz noted that the case of Nezar Hindawi's unsuccessful attempt to blow up an El Al jetliner in London provided "clear evidence" of Syrian involvement in terrorism. Ariel Merari, director of the Tel Aviv University Project on Terrorism, suggested that "there is no doubt that the general policy of sponsoring terrorist activity in Western Europe is done with Assad's approval and probably his initiative." The same report contained one expert's comments that

> [f]or years, Libya's Muammar Qadhafi has been the international outlaw, condemned for his wide-ranging support of terrorism. But now it is clear that Qadhafi is an erratic bumbler compared with Assad, a hard-eyed strategist who uses terror as an essential tool of statecraft.[22]

Assad's preferred tool of persuasion was terror, according to some Middle East experts. During the early 1980s, he began exporting his deadly product, by increasingly indirect means. The CIA made public evidence that the Syrian intelligence services gave logistical support to the individuals who bombed the U.S. Marine barracks in Lebanon. After the attack, the National Security Agency also intercepted messages showing payments were sent through Damascus to the Iranian-sponsored terrorist group responsible for the bombing.

Nor were these the only evidences of Assad's involvement in terrorism. *U.S. News & World Report* published what it termed a "bill of particulars" concerning Syria's links to terrorist events in the early 1980s.[23] Because these events were also noted in the U.S. State Department's annual report on global terrorism, there is little reason to doubt the link to terrorism that the "bill" implies belongs to Syria. The following are a few of the incidents detailed during that period:

- *September 8–16, 1986, Paris*—Ten persons are killed and more than 160 are injured in bombings. An obscure Middle Eastern group, thought to be a cover for the Syria-linked Lebanese Armed Revolutionary Faction, claims responsibility. The series of bombings are carried out by brothers of jailed terrorist Georges Ibrahim Abdallah, held in French prison.

- *September 6, 1986, Istanbul*—Arab terrorists fire on Jewish worshipers at a synagogue, killing 22, wounding 3. Experts claim the Syrian-backed Abu Nidal group was responsible. (Abu Nidal himself, architect of the Rome and Vienna airport massacres, lived at the time in a heavily guarded apartment building on the outskirts of Damascus.)
- *September 5, 1986, Karachi*—Twenty-one are killed, more than 100 wounded in a massacre aboard a hijacked jet. Four gunmen, later linked to Syria, are seized after commandos stormed the plane.
- *November 23, 1985, Malta*—An Egyptian jetliner is hijacked; 60 people are killed, 2 by the terrorists and 58 by Egyptian commandos who stormed the plane. The Syrian-backed Abu Nidal group claims responsibility.
- *April 12, 1985, Madrid*—A restaurant bombing kills 18 and injures 82. Islamic Jihad, backed by Syria, is among the groups claiming responsibility.
- *September 20, 1984, Beirut*—Fourteen are killed and 70 are injured when a car bomb explodes at the U.S. Embassy. Islamic Jihad claims responsibility.
- *April 18, 1983, Beirut*—Fifty-seven persons are killed and 120 are injured in a suicide bomb attack on the U.S. Embassy. Responsibility is claimed by Islamic Jihad.

This is by no means an exhaustive summary of Syria's dealings in terrorism. There were, for instance, 5 bases near Damascus and at least 20 other Syrian-controlled camps where instruction in the techniques of terrorism was provided. Yarmouk, in Damascus, was the camp most often used for advanced terrorist training. Skills acquired at these camps were tested in Lebanon's Bekaa Valley, which Syria controlled.

General Mohammed Khouli, at one time head of the Syrian Air Force (which was Assad's personal intelligence service and base of power), directed most of these training operations. One of his deputies, Col. Haitham Sayeed, was also the intelligence coordinator for Abu Nidal. Khouli and Sayeed, according to Western intelligence agents, directed the Hindawi case.

Yet Assad managed to maintain relatively cordial relations with Western nations. Part of his ability to continue to be acceptable (or at least difficult to condemn) lay in the care with which he distanced himself from actual terrorist attacks. He also won approval by helping in hostage crises. Indeed, he became a master at the strategy of helping groups to take hostages with one hand and gaining favor with the West by aiding in their release with the other hand. Until the Hindawi case, no one could prove that what to the West seemed to be the "helping" hand knew what the terrorist hand was doing.

Unlike Libya's Qadhafi, Assad seemed to prefer secrecy to the spotlight of international attention in the drama of terrorist involvement. Assad relied on sporadic, preferably untraceable attacks, which allowed him to avoid retribution. Qadhafi, in the 1980s, treated terrorism like a banner to be waved before the troops; for Assad, it was instead as quick and silent as an assassin's bullet.

Assad had no wish to make himself an obvious target for retribution in a terrorist incident, as Qadhafi has done. He did not underestimate the desire for revenge of a nation whose citizens have been attacked, and he clearly did not wish to make himself or his country a tempting target. He preferred to wage a hit-and-run war, in which it was hard to find the guys wearing the black hats. He was, at heart, a pragmatic politician, a survivor.

One expert at the Foreign Policy Research Institute has summed up sponsors of terrorism during the 1970s and early 1980s in this manner:

> Of the four major sponsors of terrorism—the PLO, Libya, Iran and Syria—the first two get all the attention. But it's the other two we should be watching, and particularly Syria. It is quiet and deadly in its effectiveness, and until this slipup with Hindawi, it has always managed to stay in the shadows.[24]

The end of the cold war in the 1990s changed Syria's position significantly. Losing the Soviet Union as an ally, capable of support and willing to protect, appears to have strengthened Assad's determination not to be directly involved in planning or executing terrorist attacks. As the 1997 U.S. State Department's *Global Terrorism* report notes, there has been no evidence that Syrian officials have been directly involved in planning or executing terrorist attacks since 1986.[25] It is true, however, that Syria continues to provide safe haven and support for several groups that engage in such attacks. Ahmad Jibril's Popular Front for the Liberation of Palestine–General Command (PFLP-GC) and the Palestinian Islamic Jihad (PIJ) have their headquarters in Damascus, and a wide variety of groups (including but not limited to Hamas, the PFLP-GC, and the PIJ) are based or have refuge in areas of Lebanon's Bekaa Valley under Syrian control.

It should be noted that, in the wake of the Gulf War, Syria began to distance itself from its role as a sponsor of terrorism. Seeking to improve its relations with the Western nations, Syria moved away from obvious links with various Middle Eastern groups engaging in terrorism. Whether this move was permanent or only a feint designed to deflect Western criticism remains unclear. The situation in Lebanon has not yet stabilized, and the groups have not yet been forced to leave that country to seek sanctuary and assistance elsewhere. The Middle East peace process tests Syria's willingness to cooperate in the control of violence against Israel by refusing to provide shelter and assistance to such groups.

## Iran

By 1993, Iran was clearly the most active state sponsor of terrorism, being implicated in terrorist attacks in Italy, Turkey, Germany, France, Switzerland, Argentina, and Pakistan. Iran's policy makers viewed terrorism as a valid tool to accomplish their political objectives, and acts of terrorism were approved at the highest level of the Iranian government. Iran was also a preeminent sponsor of extremist Islamic and Palestinian groups, providing funds, weapons, and training. The Lebanese Hizballah, Iran's most important "client," was responsible for some of the most lethal acts of the

1980s and early 1990s, including the 1983 suicide truck bombing of the U.S. Embassy and U.S. Marine barracks in Beirut, the hijacking of TWA flight 847 in 1985, the 1992 car bombing of the Israeli embassy in Argentina, and rocket attacks on civilians in northern Israel.

Iran has openly supported many other radical organizations that have resorted to terrorism, including the PIJ, the PFLP-GC, and Hamas. The last group was particularly active during the 1994–1996 portion of the peace process, with numerous car and suicide bombings carried out in Israel, the West Bank, and the Gaza Strip.

Iran's support to terrorism has been open, unlike Syria's more covert assistance. This has made it easier to link the state to the terrorist acts but difficult to prevent such support, because the government appeared unconcerned with international disapproval or condemnation. Iran, in some respects, has been a crusader in state terrorism, willing to accept death for a cause in the confident expectation of eternal reward. Moreover, Iran's strong position as an oil-producing nation made many nations unwilling to support direct action against Iran in retaliation for such support.

Teheran conducted at least 13 assassinations in 1997, according to the U.S. State Department's *Global Report on Terrorism,* the majority of which were carried out in northern Iraq. The targets of Iran's attacks were usually members of the state's main opposition groups, such as the Kurdish Democratic Party of Iran (KDPI) and the Mujahedin-e Khalq (MEK).

Perhaps the most compelling evidence of Iran's involvement in terrorism was reviewed in the trial in Germany of an Iranian and four Lebanese for the 1992 killing of Iranian Kurdish dissidents in Berlin's Mykonos restaurant. Finding the four guilty of murder, the court stated that the government of Iran had followed a deliberate policy of assassination of enemies of the regime living outside of Iran. The judge noted further that the Mykonos murders were approved at the most senior levels of the Iranian government, by an extralegal committee that included the president, the foreign minister, the supreme leader, and the minister of intelligence and security.

Iran continues to provide support (training, money, and/or weapons) to several groups engaged in terrorism, including those mentioned earlier. The government has encouraged the violent rejection of the Middle East peace process. Indeed, in the fall of 1997, Teheran hosted a conference of "Liberation Movements," whose participants included Hamas, Lebanese Hizballah, the PIJ, and Egypt's al-Gama'at al-Islamiya. At this conference, open discussion of the Jihad and greater coordination between certain groups took place.

Elections in May 1997 could be indicative of a move in a more moderate direction. Iran's new foreign minister publically condemned the attack by Egypt's al-Gama'at al-Islamiya on tourists in Luxor, Egypt, in November. In a CNN interview on January 7, 1998, President Khatemi agreed that terrorist attacks against noncombatants, including Israeli women and children, should be condemned. These are encouraging signs of change in what the State Department's report continues to characterize as the most active state sponsor of terrorism.

# Libya

Libya has been less obvious in its support for terrorism since 1985, when linkage to a terrorist act in West Germany evoked a bombing attack on Tripoli by the United States. Indeed, Libya's support for acts of terrorism continued to cause economic and political penalties during the 1990s, following the bombing of Pan Am Flight 103 in 1988 over Scotland. The UN Security Council passed Resolution 731, which demanded that Libya take steps to end its state-sponsored terrorism, including extraditing two Libyan intelligence agents indicted by the United States and the United Kingdom for their role in that bombing. The resolution also required that Libya accept responsibility for the bombing, disclose all evidence related to it, pay appropriate compensation, satisfy French demands regarding Libya's alleged role in bombing UTA Flight 772 in 1989, and cease all forms of terrorism.

In 1992, the UN Security Council adopted Resolution 748, imposing an arms and civil aviation embargo on Libya. This resolution demanded that Libyan Arab Airlines offices be closed and that all states reduce Libya's diplomatic presence abroad. When these measures failed to elicit full compliance from Libya, the Security Council adopted Resolution 883 in 1993, imposing a limited assets freeze and oil technology embargo on Libya and strengthening existing sanctions against that nation.

By mid-1998, Libya had not yet complied in full with the Security Council sanctions. Qadhafi continued to refuse to turn over for trial in the United States or Scotland the two Libyan agents indicted in the Pan Am bombing. French officials completed in January 1998 their investigation of the 1989 UTA bombing, concluding that the Libyan intelligence service was responsible, naming Qadhafi's brother-in-law, Muhammad al-Sanusi, as the mastermind of the attack. The six Libyan suspects remain at large.

Germany in November 1997 began the trial of five defendants in the 1986 La Belle discotheque bombing in Berlin, which killed 3 and seriously injured more than 200. The German prosecutor said the bombing was "definitely an act of assassination commissioned by the Libyan state."[26]

Libya continued, through mid-1998, to support a variety of Palestinian groups, including the Abu Nidal Organization (ANO), the PIJ, and the PFLP-GC. In fact, the leader of the ANO, Sabri al-Banna, lives in Libya, working through the organization's headquarters.

Since the beginning of this UN intervention, the regime in Libya largely avoided open association with acts of terrorism and terrorist groups. While Qadhafi offered public support for radical Palestinian groups opposed to the PLO's Gaza-Jericho accord with Israel in 1993 and openly threatened to support extremist Islamic groups in neighboring Algeria and Tunisia, the level of practical open support by Libya for terrorism decreased substantially.

# Sudan

Although Sudan has taken some positive steps on terrorism, including allowing the French to arrest "Carlos the Jackal," it has not complied with Security Council resolutions demanding an end to Sudanese support for terrorism, specifically a rendering up of the three suspects involved in the 1995 assassination attempt against President Mubarak of Egypt in Addis Ababa. It continued, through 1997, to serve as a haven, meeting place, and training coordinator for several international groups engaged in terrorism. Members of Lebanese Hizballah, the PIJ, the ANO, and Hamas enjoy facilities in this nation, with some of their members receiving paramilitary training, indoctrination, money, travel documents, safe passage, and refuge in Sudan.

Although Sudan has made efforts to distance itself somewhat from terrorism, including ordering the departure of terrorist financier Osama bin Laden, it remains connected in significant fashion to several violent organizations. Its failure to comply with Security Council resolutions and its unwillingness to accept any responsibility in the attempted assassination case leave it on the list of states supporting terrorism. Thus, whereas Syria has begun to close some of its doors to terrorism, Sudan is emerging as a significant sponsor of state terrorism in the region.

Indeed, Sudan's willingness to offer safe haven to the resources and recruits of Osama bin Laden made the nation's role in terrorism a significant topic in August 1998. The United States, objecting to the relationship that it believed existed between bin Laden and a pharmaceutical company in Khartoum, launched cruise missiles to destroy the plant after bin Laden's group was implicated in the bombing of the U.S. embassies in Kenya and Tanzania. Sudan is perhaps not so "silent" a partner in this network at present.

# CONCLUSION

State terrorism, whether internal or external, offers a real threat to international peace and security. Internal terrorism breeds resistance movements, which often resort to terrorist tactics. This cycle of terror-violence can result in a whirlwind that will destroy all within its reach, innocent and guilty.

External terror, as practiced by some states, has resulted in the proliferation of terror worldwide. States whose policy specifically rejects the use of terror have been guilty of giving aid, often clandestinely, to states or groups that promote terrorism. With the exception of a few states such as Iran and Libya, most states have sought to keep their dealings with terrorists a secret.

Few states have been as successful as Syria in keeping a foot on both sides of the terrorism issue. Western nations regarded President Assad as perhaps the only one with whom they could deal in attempts to bring peace to Lebanon. These states, to some extent, turned a blind eye to his obvious dealings in the training and equipping of terrorists. They were equally reluctant to take him to task, as they had Qadhafi, over the extent to which he and his military offered intelligence and direction to terrorist attack teams.

## *Evaluation*

Is terrorism becoming the accepted method of warfare for the future? Given states' willingness to support terrorism as a form of covert warfare and as an instrument of foreign policy, this is a critical question. To assess this possibility, consider the assets of terror as an instrument of war:

1. *Low cost, financially.* It offers a relatively inexpensive method of operation for insurgent groups who lack the money, human resources, and the armament to take on a powerful army. It also offers states a fairly inexpensive way to wage war, openly or clandestinely, on a hostile state whose resources make a full-scale war undesirable.

2. *Low cost, politically.* For states, particularly those who engage in clandestine support for terrorist groups, the political cost can be quite low, while the profit in, for example, arms sales, can be temptingly high. As long as the support is not too blatant, as it was in Libya's case, the leaders of other nations have shown a tendency to look the other way.

3. *High yield, financially.* States engaged in arms sales to terrorists can profit quite handsomely, while suffering little if any political or economic reprisals. Assad's involvement in the Hindawi affair, for instance, resulted in the recall of a couple of ambassadors but not the complete rupture of any diplomatic or trade relations.

4. *High yield, politically.* For freedom fighters who engage in terrorism, the yields can indeed be significant. Government reaction or overreaction can lead to a weakening or even the fall of a regime. Major concessions or changes can also be "bought" at the price of a successful terrorist incident.

5. *Low risk (usually), politically and financially.* Because the cost of financing these operations is considerably less than that required for a fully equipped and trained army, the loss of the individuals carrying it out is minor. If an operation succeeds, the rewards can be enormous. If it fails, the loss is usually minimal, unless the failure is a openly linked to a state. Since the end of the cold war, such linkage has become increasingly costly, both in financial and political terms, as Sudan discovered in 1998.

What, then, is to deter individuals and nations from engaging in this high-profit, low-risk form of warfare? If nuclear warfare is unthinkable and unconventional warfare is expensive and often unwinnable, as both Vietnam and Afghanistan illustrated, will individuals and nations turn more often to this unpleasant alternative?

## Suggested Readings

Gurr, Ted. *Why Men Rebel*. Princeton, NJ: Princeton University Press, 1970.

Harris, Jonathan. *The New Terrorism: Politics of Violence*. New York: Messner, 1983.

Kidder, Rushworth M. "Unmasking State-Sponsored Terrorism." *Christian Science Monitor,* May 14, 1986.

Kittrie, Nicholas. "Response: Looking at the World Realistically." *Case Western Journal of International Law* 13, no. 2 (spring 1981).

Liston, Robert A. *Terrorism*. New York: Elsevier/Nelson, 1977.

Meltzer, Milton. *The Terrorists*. New York: Harper & Row, 1983.

"More on State Sponsored International Terrorism." *Contemporary Mideast Backgrounder* 240 (September 29, 1987).

Norland, Rob, and Ray Wilkinson. "Inside Terror, Inc." *Newsweek,* April 7, 1986.

U.S. Department of State. *1997 Global Terrorism Report*. Washington, D.C.: Government Printing Office, January 1998.

U.S. Department of State, Bureau of Public Affairs. "Iran's Use of International Terrorism." *Special Report no. 170,* October 27, 1987.

## Endnotes

1. Milton Metzer, *The Terrorists* (New York: Harper & Row, 1983), 193.

2. Martin Slann, "The State as Terrorist," *Annual Editions: Violence and Terrorism 91/92.* (Guilford, CT: Dushkin, 1991), 69.

3. This declaration was adopted with 48 states voting in favor, none against, and 8 abstentions (including Saudi Arabia, the Union of South Africa, the Union of Soviet Socialist Republics, and Yugoslavia). For a full copy of the text of this declaration, see Louis Henkin, Richard Pugh, Oscar Schachter, and Hans Smit, *International Law: Cases and Materials* (St. Paul, MN: West, 1980), 320.

4. International Covenant on Civil and Political Rights, 21 U.N. GAOR, Supp. (no. 16), 52, U.N. Doc. A/6316 (1966). Entered into force March 23, 1976.

5. George Kren and Leon Rappoport, *The Holocaust and the Crisis of Human Behavior* (New York: Holmes and Meier, 1980), 130.

6. See Nicholas Kittrie, "Response: Looking at the World Realistically," *Case Western Journal of International Law,* 13, no. 2 (Spring 1981): 311–313.

7. See, for further documentation of this trend, the Annual Reports by Amnesty International, as well as that organization's *Report on Torture* (1975).

8. Carl J. Friedrich, "Opposition and Government Violence," *Government and Opposition* 7 (1972): 3–19.

9. Hannah Arendt, *The Origins of Totalitarianism* (New York: Harcourt, Brace & World, 1973), 464.

10. See Erich Fromm, *The Anatomy of Human Destructiveness* (New York: Rinehart & Winston, 1973), 285–288.

11. Ted Gurr, *Why Men Rebel* (Princeton, NJ: Princeton University Press, 1970), 213.

12. United Nations Secretariat Study, "Measures to Prevent International Terrorism," U.N. Doc. A/C.6/418 (November 2, 1973). Prepared as requested by the Sixth Legal Committee of the General Assembly.

13. Robert A. Liston, *Terrorism* (New York: Elsevier/Nelson, 1977), 79.

14. *Report on Terrorism,* Amnesty International (New York: Farrar, Straus, and Giroux, 1975), 27.

15. Claire Sterling, "Terrorism: Tracing the International Network," *New York Times Magazine,* March 1, 1981, 19.

16. Ibid., 54.

17. Claire Sterling, *The Terror Network* (New York: Holt, Rinehart and Winston, 1981), 293.

18. Ibid., 295.

19. Ibid., 297.

20. Ray Cline and Yonah Alexander, *Terrorism: The Soviet Connection* (New York: Crane and Russak, 1984), 6.

21. Ibid., 55.

22. James Q. Wilson, "Thinking about Terrorism," *Contemporary Review,* 186 (April 1981), 36.

23. "The Unmasking of Assad," *U.S. News & World Report,* November 10, 1986, 27.

24. Ibid., 26.

25. Ibid., 29.

26. U.S. Department of State, *1997 Global Terrorism Report* (Washington, D.C.: Government Printing Office, 1998), 24.

# Terrorism, Inc.

*The greatest change in recent decades is that terrorism is by no means militants'
only strategy. The many-branched Muslim Brotherhood, the Palestinian Hamas,
the IRA, . . . the ETA, . . . and many other groups . . . have had political as well
as terrorist wings.*

—Walter Laqueur (1997)

## *Key Concepts*

networking
international terrorism
  congress
strategic planning
revolutionary taxes
bonuses
Libyan connection

fedayeen
fighting fund
Hizballah
NORAID
internationalize
narcoterrorism
unholy triangle

## NETWORKING

The three Japanese who disembarked from Air France Flight 132 at Lod International
Airport in Tel Aviv, Israel, in May 1972 appeared no different from the other tourists
bound for the Holy Land. Chatting pleasantly to the other passengers, they made
their way swiftly to the luggage conveyor belt, where they retrieved their bags.

Opening one suitcase, they extracted a lightweight Czech-made submachine gun and a few hand grenades. They then opened fire on the crowd of disem-
barking passengers and visitors, using their weapons to strafe the airport lounge from
side to side. From time to time they lobbed the grenades into the groups of terrified
people.

In this attack, 26 people died. At least six of them were decapitated. One child
of about seven was cut in half twice by the barrage of bullets. More than half of the

87

dead were Puerto Ricans on a tour of the Holy Land. An additional 78 persons were wounded, many of them dismembered. The entire episode was over in seconds.

As an example of the **networking** of international terrorists, in the creation of an interconnected system linking groups with common goals, this incident excels. Here Japanese members of the JRA killed Puerto Ricans on behalf of Palestinian Arabs who sought to punish Israelis.

Cooperation between terrorist groups with, if not a common cause, at least a shared hatred, has occurred with alarming frequency. Anti-NATO sentiment, for example, drew several European groups into cooperative action. A communiqué on January 15, 1986, declared that the Red Army Faction (RAF) of West Germany and Action Direct (AD) of France would together attack the multinational structures of NATO. Shortly thereafter, assassins killed the general in charge of French arms sales and a West German defense industrialist. On August 8, 1985, two Americans were killed in a bomb blast at a U.S. air base in Frankfurt, West Germany. The RAF and AD claimed joint responsibility for this attack. This attack was followed by the bombing of a U.S. antiaircraft missile site.

These French and German terrorists used explosives stolen from a Belgian quarry, which suggests a connection with Belgium's Fighting Communist Cells. This latter group bombed NATO pipelines and defense-related companies. Portuguese and Greek terrorists have also attacked NATO targets in their homelands, although evidence of collaboration in these countries is less clear.

Linkage between terrorist groups *does* exist, however. It appears in the form of shared members, training camps, weaponry, and tactics. It is obvious in the propaganda being disseminated by the groups.

Study of contemporary terrorist groups suggests that terrorists in the latter part of the twentieth century shared intelligence information, weapons, supplies, training facilities and instructors, sponsors, and even membership. Such frequent ad hoc sharing does not necessarily constitute an organized "network of terror," as some have suggested. But the dimensions of cooperation between groups with unrelated or even opposing ideological bases offer useful insights to police, military, intelligence, and academic personnel who understand the web that does from time to time link terrorists.

That web is tenuous for the most part, constructed in a pragmatic fashion to meet common needs for relatively scarce resources. This characteristic does not, of course, diminish the potential for serious damage posed by such linkages. It simply makes the danger more difficult to assess, as the linkages not only are usually covert but also appear to be in an almost constant state of flux.

Let us examine, then, some of those linkages as they have been shown to exist (usually after the fact in a terrorist event or confrontation). It is not necessary to study *all* of the available data on such linkages to establish that such connections exist. A brief survey of some of the evidence of cooperation or collusion will suffice to illustrate both the reality and the hazards of this insidious merging of terrorist interests and assets.

## SHARED STRATEGIC PLANNING

In 1975 French police learned that the international terrorist known as "Carlos the Jackal" was running a clearinghouse for terrorist movements. His clients included the Tupamaros, the Quebec Liberation Front, the IRA, the Baader-Meinhof gang from West Germany, Yugoslavia's Croatian separatists, the Turkish People's Liberation Army, and the Palestinians.[1]

An **international terrorist congress,** a meeting of terrorists from all over the world to work out agendas and to organize cooperative efforts, took place in Frankfurt, Germany, in 1986, reportedly attended by no less than 500 people. Meeting under the slogan "The armed struggle as a strategic and tactical necessity in the fight for revolution," it proclaimed the U.S. armed forces in Europe to be the main enemy.[2] Attendees decided that the correct strategy was to kill individual soldiers to demoralize their colleagues and lower their collective capacity to kill.

Among those represented at this congress, or present as guests, were German, French, Belgian, Spanish, and Portuguese terrorists, as well as the PLO, the PLFP, the African National Congress, the IRA, the Tupamaros, the Italian Red Brigades, and the ETA (Basque separatists). Most of the manifestos issued by this congress were basically Marxist-Leninist in style. The congress was financed largely by Libya.

Reports that surfaced in May 1987 tell of Khomeini making the following offer to Nicaragua: Teheran would raise its $100 million in annual economic and military aid by 50 percent if Nicaragua would help recruit Latin American immigrants in the United States to join Iranian expatriates in forming joint terror squads. The mission of these squads: to strike back if the Americans made any attack on Iran.[3]

Some evidence indicates that attempts at coordinating activities have been made by various terrorist groups, but concrete proof of shared strategies suggesting a "terrorist conspiracy" perhaps manipulated by a common hand—such as Qadhafi— is insufficient. One prominent expert, James Adams, suggests instead that terrorist groups act more like a "multi-national corporation with different divisions dotted around the world, all of which act in an essentially independent manner."[4]

In his book *The Financing of Terror,* Adams illustrates his analogy by suggesting that these "independent divisions" offer to the head of another operation, when he comes to town, the use of the company apartment, an advance against expenses, and perhaps access to local equipment. In a similar manner, terrorist groups carrying out an operation in a foreign country may be granted such assistance by the host country's terrorist groups.

This analogy between different divisions in a multinational corporation and terrorist groups is more credible than that of a "conspiracy," based on the fragmentary and often subjective nature of the evidence brought forth as "proof" of a true conspiracy among terrorist groups. The cooperation in terms of **strategic planning** that has been authenticated to date between terrorist groups has been (1) ad hoc, focused on the planning of just one particular operation between groups whose other contacts remain fragmentary, and/or (2) bombastic, consisting primarily in the issuing of declarations by "congresses" or transient alliances between groups briefly united against a perceived common target.

But contact between various terrorist groups does exist, and it has been documented.[5] Moreover, Western intelligence believes that, between 1970 and 1984, 28 meetings involving different terrorist groups have been held around the world. While these meetings were generally called to discuss cooperation rather than coordination of revolutionary activities, it is difficult to establish precisely what plans and agreements have emerged from these contacts.

## TERRORISM *IS* BIG BUSINESS

If the PLO were an American corporation, it would have been on the list of Fortune 500 companies. What was the PLO worth in the mid-1980s? British journalist James Adams calculated the organization's financial empire at $5 billion. Return on investments was the group's largest source of income at that time, bringing in about $1 billion per year.

Let us take a look at the financial headquarters of this group, as James Adams describes it:

> Just off Shah Bander Square in downtown Damascus is a five-story building of light brown cement. It looks more like the office of a low-level government department, unpainted since the colonials departed, than the headquarters of one of the wealthiest multinational corporations in the world.[6]

On the top floor of this building were banks of Honeywell computers, which were tended by white-coated young Palestinians. Most of these computer experts have been trained in the United States, some at MIT and some at Harvard. From this world of high technology and superefficiency, the Palestinian National Fund managed investments that generated a total annual income greater than the total budget of some third world countries, an income that made the PLO the richest and most powerful terrorist group in the world.

Almost all of the PLO's assets were held indirectly through private individuals and in numbered bank accounts in Switzerland, West Germany, Mexico, and the Cayman Islands. Its primary banking institution was the Palestinian-owned Arab Bank, Ltd., headquartered in Amman, Jordan. The chairman of the Palestine National Fund at that time, Jawaeed al-Ghussein, administered the PLO finances.

PLO financiers invested money in the European market, as well as a few blue-chip stocks on Wall Street. The PLO also held large amounts of lucrative money certificates in the United States. These and other investments were said to provide as much as 20 percent of all of the group's revenues.

The PLO, like many multinational corporations, was also involved in a wide variety of business ventures, not all of which generated a monetary profit. Some were primarily political, made to win friends for the PLO. PLO money flowed covertly, through dummy corporations established in such places as Liechtenstein and Luxembourg, into investments in third world countries. Much of this investment money passed through the Arab Bank for Economic Development in Africa and the Arab African Bank.

The PLO owned dairy and poultry farms and cattle ranches in the Sudan, Somalia, Uganda, and Guinea. It reportedly purchased a duty-free shop in Tanzania's Dares Salaam International Airport and then negotiated for similar shops in Mozambique and Zimbabwe.

The point is, not only did the PLO have cash assets of staggering proportions; it succeeded in investing them for capital, political, and strategic gains. Its stock and bond investments were exemplary and brought in considerable revenue, its investment in third world ventures brought it considerable support and goodwill from many nations, and its ventures into such operations as duty-free airport concessions provided it with security-proof access through which to transfer materials from country to country. The PLO not only had money—it learned how to use much of it wisely.[7]

Not all groups carrying out terrorist acts are so well endowed. Most have to depend on the largess of patrons or on their own success in staging robberies and ransom situations. The ETA, which had close ties with the IRA and the PLO, adopted one of the PLO's less publicized methods of raising money. Funds for this group, which received training and support from Libya and the PLO, were generated through **revolutionary taxes** levied on Basque businessmen. The PLO levied such a tax against the wages of Palestinians working abroad throughout the Arab world.

Of the financial patrons of contemporary terrorist groups, two deserve special attention. Libya and Iran have been responsible for the training and arming of countless terrorist teams during the latter part of the twentieth century. Under their aegis, international terrorism took on a truly international flavor.

## CASE STUDY 1: LIBYAN PROTECTOR

Under Qadhafi, Libyan agents dispersed huge amounts of aid during the 1970s and 1980s to various terrorist groups. That this dispersal appeared to depend greatly on whim, and consequently caused a great deal of frustration among terrorists dependent on Qadhafi's support, does not detract from the substantial contributions he made to the financing of terrorism worldwide.

Qadhafi supported Palestinian groups, including the PFLP, the DFLP, and the PFLP-GC, with donations of as much as $100 million a year. He also assissted the IRA, the ETA, the Baader-Meinhof gang, the JRA, the Red Brigade, the Tupamaros, and the Moros (in the Philippines).

His assistance was not confined to the financing of the terrorist operation itself. Israeli intelligence suggested that Qadhafi paid a $5 billion bonus to the Black September terrorists who were responsible for the Munich massacre in 1972. Western intelligence also believed that Qadhafi paid Carlos the Jackal a large bonus, about $2 billion, for his role in the seizure of the OPEC oil ministers in Vienna in December 1975.

**Bonuses** were given for success, such as that paid to Carlos, and for "injury or death on the job." By the 1990s, these significantly decreased in amount. Qadhafi reportedly paid only between $10,000 and $30,000 to the families of terrorists killed in action in the late 1980s, down considerably from the $100,000 reportedly paid to a terrorist injured in the OPEC incident in 1972.

So Qadhafi has given money to support terrorist groups, and he has furnished monetary incentives for participating in terrorist events. Other leaders throughout history have supported dissident groups and provided for the survivors of their military or quasi-military activities, but Qadhafi has taken his support of terrorists to greater lengths. When the United States carried out air raids on Libya on April 15, 1986, Qadhafi was, of course, furious. He offered to *buy* an American hostage in Lebanon, so that he could have him killed. On April 17, Peter Kilburn, a 62-year-old librarian at American University who had been kidnapped on December 3, 1984, was executed after Qadhafi paid $1 million to the group holding him.

Declining oil revenues, particularly due to UN sanctions, have diminished Libya's role today in financing terrorism. In six years, this income fell from $22 billion to about $5.5 billion, seriously reducing Qadhafi's ability to bankroll terrorism. Although he remained after this loss involved in the training of terrorists, his role as "godfather" of terrorism decreased dramatically during the last decade of the twentieth century, making it difficult to predict his role for the twenty-first century.

Libya's role has decreased but not ended. This became obvious when, after having been expelled from both Iraq and Syria, Abu Nidal, the Palestinian master terrorist who planned the *Achille Lauro* hijacking, was given refuge in Tripoli. Western sources fear that, under Libya's protection, Nidal could repay Qadhafi by striking at more American targets.

Moreover, Libya developed a strong "connection" in Central and South America through its ties to Nicaragua. The Sandinista government of Nicaragua was, until the early 1990s, the **Libyan connection** in this region, supplying arms, training, and logistical support to revolutionary groups in that region. Long before they came to power in 1979, Sandinista leaders had been training in PLO camps in Libya and Lebanon. When the Sandinistas finally seized power, Qadhafi promised political and financial aid, promises that he indeed kept over the years.

In the early years, the Sandinistas received a $100 million "loan" from Libya. In 1983, Brazilian authorities inspecting four Libyan planes bound for Nicaragua discovered that crates marked "medical supplies" actually contained some 84 tons of military equipment. This "military assistance" included missiles, bombs, cannons, and two unassembled fighter planes!

In Managua, leaders from Germany's Baader-Meinhof gang, Spain's ETA, Colombia's M19, Peru's Sendero Luminoso, and El Salvador's FMLN met with Libya and the PLO. Through Nicaragua, Libya was able to funnel arms to many of these groups.

M19's attack on Colombia's supreme court, in which more than 100 were killed, was carried out with arms supplied through Nicaragua, by Libya. Many of the guns captured in that raid were linked to Libya, some of which reached M19 through conduits in Vietnam, Cuba, and, of course, Nicaragua.

Nicaragua's Libyan connection highlights the continuing spiral of terror funded by Qadhafi. Libya supported a revolutionary terrorist group with money and arms, and when it had managed to seize control of Nicaragua, Libya used that government as a conduit to funnel arms and support to other terrorist groups engaged in similar struggles throughout Central and South America.

The peaceful end of the Sandinista regime, through democratic elections, brought to an end this "Libyan connection." With Libya's declining profile in supporting terrorist groups in the 1990s, this transition has left several groups without a sponsor or support system. Some have begun to link with the illicit drug cartels in Colombia, providing "security" for drug lords and the shipment of their goods. This has diminished, to some degree, the revolutionary focus of such groups but has helped to fill the gap left by the loss of Libyan patronage.

## CASE STUDY 2: IRANIAN FEDAYEEN

As James Adams noted, when one prime supporter falls away, another tends to rise to take its place. Ayatollah Ruhollah Khomeini was able, to a large degree, to take Qadhafi's place as the leading patron of terrorism in the Middle East, Europe, and America.

To understand Iran's commitment to terrorism, one can look back 900 years to the time of al-Hassan ibn-Sabbah. Sabbah, a leader of the dissident Muslim Ismaili group (which in turn is one of the two divisions of the Shiite sect) was the founder of the previously mentioned Brotherhood of Assassins, the hashish-smoking terrorists who terrorized the Persian Gulf region in the twelth century. Sabbah called his followers **fedayeen**—meaning "adventurers" or "men of sacrifice"—a name adopted by many terrorists today.

Iran is the home of the Shiite branch of Islam, which has been in conflict with the majority Sunni branch for many centuries. When Khomeini came to power after the fall of the shah, he began to rally Shiites all over the world to this ancient conflict. In March 1982, clergy and leaders of Shiite revolutionary movements from all over the world came to Teheran. At this meeting, in addition to agreeing to establish a number of training camps for terrorists in Iran, it was agreed that $100 million would be immediately allocated as a **"fighting fund"** to support worldwide terrorism.

Moreover, an additional $50 million was projected to be spent each year for an indefinite period of time to bankroll specific acts of terrorism.[8]

From this capital outlay has come a variety of terrorist activities. Several powerful groups operating in Lebanon were financed by Iran during the last two decades of the twentieth century. Bomb attacks on moderate Arab states, including Kuwait, Saudi Arabia, and Egypt, have caused serious personal and monetary damage. Islamic fundamentalism has risen rapidly in southern Asia, supported by substantial cash infusions. Hit squads have been dispatched throughout Europe to eliminate "enemies" of Shiite Islam. And a global network of clergy-dominated religious groups has been formed, whose purpose is to mastermind further terrorism and recruit new assassins to serve in Iran's holy war.

The French authorities fear a renewal of the bombing waves that hit Paris in recent years, first from Palestinian groups and then from Algerian fundmentalist Islamic fighters. Terrorists struck twice in September 1987 at two Arab-owned banks, one Saudi, the other Kuwaiti. Both incidents were believed to be the work of pro-Iranian terrorists seeking vengeance for the deaths of Iranian pilgrims in Mecca and for Kuwait's pro-Iraq stance in the Iran-Iraq war. In the mid-1990s, France was once again a target of attacks, this time from Algerians angry for France's support for the military regime that had prevented the strong Islamic fundamentalist parties from winning the election in Algeria. Attacks in this case included a hijacking and numerous bomb attacks, including attacks on the subways and monuments in Paris.

Faced with the threat of continuing Iranian-sponsored terrorist bombings and hijackings, some wealthy Kuwaiti citizens began taking extended vacations during the late 1980s in other Arab states and Western Europe. The Kuwaiti government naturally was concerned that too large an exodus of such persons could set off panic among Egyptians, Palestinians, Pakistanis, and other guest workers, who made up 70 percent of the Kuwaiti workforce. Accordingly, Kuwait was forced to moderate its antagonism toward Iran, fearing that Iran's terrorist retaliation might cripple the Kuwait economy beyond repair. In light of Iraq's subsequent invasion of Kuwait, this move to placate Iran by not appearing to favor Iraq too much in the previous conflict appears quite ironic.

Saudi Arabia, which has also been a victim of Iranian-directed terrorism, was also very cautious in taking public stands in the Iran-Iraq conflict. Although many Saudi officials, including Prince Bandar ibn Sultan, the Saudi ambassador to the United States in the 1980s, urged a tough stance toward Teheran, King Fahd maintained an extremely cautious approach. Remembering the violence of the Iranian-provoked riot in Mecca in July 1987, which left more than 400 dead, the Saudis have been careful not to deliberately antagonize the terrorist state of Iran. The bombing in late 1995 of the building used as U.S. military training headquarters for years in Riyad indicated that such caution may not have been sufficient.

Months before a bloody street battle on July 31, 1987, between Iranian pilgrims and Saudi security forces, Saudi intelligence knew that a specialist unit of Iran's Revolutionary Guards had been training for a major sabotage action during the pilgrimage season in Mecca. Unable, as custodians of Islam's holiest shrines, to ban Iranian pilgrims, they could only respond to the violence instigated by the pilgrims, in a debacle that left 400 dead.

Even in light of the Saudi political wariness, however, terrorism continues to pour from Iran in an unpredictable flow that encompasses friend and foe alike in the Arab world. Kuwait Airways Flight 422 was hijacked on April 5, 1988, in a plot hatched four months earlier in Teheran by Shiite radicals from Bahrain, Lebanon, and Iran. The mastermind of the plot was apparently Immad Mughniye, a Shiite religious fanatic responsible for planning bombings of the U.S. Embassy and the U.S. Marine headquarters in Lebanon five years earlier.

The world, with the exception of Iran, watched in horror as the bodies of innocent persons were thrown from the plane by the terrorists, whose demands for the release of other terrorists held in Kuwaiti prisons the Kuwaiti government steadfastly refused to meet. Those imprisoned terrorists were responsible for Iranian-directed bombings of the U.S. and French Embassies in Kuwait.

Intelligence sources have indicated that a dozen terrorists drawn from **Hizballah**—the Iranian-backed Party of God—and the Bahrain Front, also led from Teheran, were sent for training in the Bekaa Valley of Lebanon in March of 1988. At the same time, Iranian agents checked Bangkok airport for security weaknesses that could be exploited in the hijack. So blatant was Iran's involvement in this terrorist episode that, when the plane reached Mashad Airport in Iran, after the hijacking was in progress, the Iranians allowed the hijackers a "crew change." It is also thought that the Iranians allowed the hijackers to take aboard at this point sophisticated two-way radios, giving them a link to the persons directing the hijack during the subsequent negotiations in Cyprus and Algeria.

Iran has indeed been willing to carry its terrorism into all parts of the world. Banks, embassies, airports, even temples are under increasingly violent attacks, organized and supported by this nation.

# NORAID: The U.S. Terror Connection

According to James Adams:

> From the onset of modern terrorism in Northern Ireland in 1969, the United States has played a key role in its support. The enormous Irish-American population has always felt a strong sentimental attachment to "the old country," and this has been translated into a steady stream of cash and guns to the IRA, which has, in part, enabled them to survive.[9]

Irish Northern Aid, generally known as **NORAID,** was established in 1969 by Michael Flannery, a former IRA member living in New York. Its purpose was to facilitate the giving of assistance to the IRA. Headquarters were established at 273 East 194th Street in the Bronx, New York City.

Conflicting reports are offered about the importance of NORAID for the IRA (now known as the Provisional IRA or PIRA, after the 1969 split in the IRA leadership) during the last three decades of the twentieth century. Certainly in the early 1970s, NORAID could be termed crucial to the PIRA's survival, because it supplied over 50 percent of the cash needed by the PIRA. By the end of the twentieth century, however, the PIRA could expect to receive less that $200,000 of their estimated $7 million budget from NORAID.

During the late 1980s, NORAID no longer supplied only cash to the PIRA. Instead, cash raised at traditional annual dinners was frequently used to purchase arms, which were then smuggled to Ireland. Because each dinner was expected to raise between $20,000 and $30,000, and such dinners were held in cities throughout the United States, the supply of arms that could be purchased and smuggled was substantial.

Following the murder of 79-year-old Lord Mountbatten and other members of his family, including his 14-year-old grandson, by the IRA in 1979, U.S. intelligence agencies, including the FBI, began to cooperate with the British in attempting to stem the flow of arms from NORAID to the IRA. Although initial successes in this effort were few, by 1984 the cooperation yielded significant results. In early September of that year, for instance, an 80-foot trawler, registered in Ipswich, Massachusetts, left Boston bound for Ireland. In its cargo were rockets, grenades made in Korea, 100 German automatic rifles, 51 pistols and revolvers, shotguns, and a .50-caliber heavy machine gun. A CIA surveillance satellite tracked the trawler to its rendezvous with an Irish trawler. A report on this cargo and its transfer was made to the Irish government, which subsequently seized the ship and confiscated its $500,000 cargo of illegal arms.

NORAID was crippled in the last two decades of the twentieth century by more than the stepped-up scrutiny and cooperation between intelligence services of the United States and Britain. In chapter 11 on methods of combating terrorism, more details will be given. Suffice it to say at this point that court challenges to NORAID members in the United States, based on claims for injuries incurred by victims of the weapons purchased by NORAID money, have substantially drained NORAID coffers, making the donation of cash and the purchase of arms difficult, if not completely impossible. Moreover, the peace process, begun in the mid-1990s, has helped to make the transfer of this type of aid to the IRA much less politically acceptable in the United States.

# TRAINING AND EQUIPPING THE TERRORISTS

Not all of the networking among terrorists involves outright financing of terrorist operations, as NORAID's activities have shown us. The fact that the former Soviet Union was often not listed as a major sponsor of terrorism can be explained in light of these alternative methods of support, methods not involving simply bankrolling terrorist groups, for terrorism worldwide. For example, Pres. Fidel Castro of Cuba has operated camps for training terrorists since 1961. Recruits were accepted at first from Latin America and Africa. Later recruits from Palestine, Europe, and North America were allowed to attend these special camps. By 1967, more than a dozen training camps for terrorists and guerrillas from all over the world had been established in Cuba. These camps were under the direction of Col. Vadim Kotchergin of the Soviet security services (or KGB) during the 1960s and 1970s. Among those trained there were Weather Underground members Bernadine Dohrn and Mark Rudd.

The Soviet Union, according to intelligence reports at the time, operated training camps that taught techniques of guerrilla warfare and other skills that are useful for groups engaged in terror-violence. Such skills included the use of explosives, mining techniques, commando field tactics, urban guerrilla tactics, and the use of shoulder-fired rockets. Several camps of this type were located in the Soviet Union itself. Other camps with Soviet instructors were located in Eastern Europe, Cuba, and several Middle Eastern states, including Syria. Alumni of these camps include the infamous Carlos the Jackal, leaders of the Italian Red Brigade, and more than a thousand Palestinians.

The Soviet Union and several Eastern European states supplied arms directly to groups that engaged in terrorism, including the PLO and Turkish leftists. Evidence also suggests that such aid was given to the Basque ETA and to the PIRA. This supplying of arms to groups engaged in terrorism changed dramatically with the demise of the Soviet Union. While Russia and several other former Soviet states still sell arms prolifically, by the mid-1990s neither Russia nor most of the European states who had foremerly been part of the training network could afford, financially or politically, to openly operate training camps or supply weapons to terrorist groups.

However, the Soviet Union used other pro-terrorist states, such as Libya, as conduits in the supplying of arms and training for terrorists. Soviet-manufactured weapons given to Libya, for example, found their way into the hands of the Baader-Meinhof gang and its successor, the RAF. These weapons still appear in the hands of many terrorist groups, but they appear now to be sold, not given, through conduit states.

As disturbing as the provision of arms and training is the willingness of states to offer safe harbor and freedom of movement to known international terrorists. According to Claire Sterling, author of *The Terror Network,* known terrorists were able to travel freely through Eastern Europe. In that region, she notes, these persons received medical care for injuries received on missions and acquired false passports and documents that enabled them again to penetrate the Western nations. For a time, top Italian terrorists were practically commuting to Prague.[10] Although this situation is clearly no longer the case, it is unclear to what extent states within that region have begun to exercise control over the transit and accommodation of terrorists.

Unlike Iran and Libya, the Soviets were more discreet in their support of terrorism itself, instead arguing that they were providing training only for people involved in legitimate struggles for national liberation. Because the United States also, in its School for the Americas, offers training in the use of weapons of violence to leaders and groups engaged in "legitimate" struggles within their nations, it is difficult to establish beyond doubt that such support is, in fact, a form of state support for a terrorist network. Like Syria in recent years, Russia and the United States have tried to distance themselves from the actual training of terrorists.

There is little evidence to suggest that Russia exercises any form of centralized control over an international terrorist network, in spite of editorial commentary that regularly suggests such a premise. Publicly, neither the Americans nor the Russians sanction all of the actions committed by the groups trained or equipped by their military. Nor is there any reason to feel that terrorism would vanish without such support. But we may reasonably assume that terrorism is changing dramatically in its patterns of support since the end of the cold war.

## THE INTERNATIONALIZATION OF TERRORISM: AN RAF CASE STUDY

The RAF is the oldest and most ruthlessly violent left-wing terrorist movement in Germany in the late twentieth century. Emerging from a small residue of left-wing extremists from the student protests of the late 1960s, it was responsible for half a dozen bombing attacks in 1972. Although it suffered large defeats in 1977 and again in 1982 (owing to the arrest of many of its original leaders), it continued to successfully regroup and reemerge as a violent political force until Germany was reunited in the early 1990s.

Early generations of the RAF were to some degree international in the struggle that they waged against imperialism. In 1977, the RAF carried out a PFLP plan to hijack a Lufthansa aircraft to Mogadishu. The PFLP plan was designed to capitalize on the Schleyer kidnapping. Two members of the RAF, Hans-Joachim Klein and Gabriele Krocher-Tiedemann, were recruited by Carlos the Jackal to assist in the raid on the Vienna OPEC conference in 1975. Another two members of the RAF, Wilfred B'o'se and Brigitte Kuhlmann, participated in the 1976 hijack to Entebbe.

But in July 1984, West German police found documents indicating that the RAF planned to further **internationalize** their struggle by uniting with other terrorist groups in attacks on the "representatives of repression," specifically NATO allies. This anti-imperialism brotherhood of bombers and assassins began to wage war throughout Europe in the 1980s.

German, French, and Belgian radicals assassinated prominent members of Europe's defense establishment and set off explosives at such targets as a U.S. air base, military pipelines, and a variety of other NATO installations. Nor have the targets remained specifically military. A Berlin nightclub filled with off-duty soldiers and German civilians was bombed in 1984, allegedly by this terrorist alliance.

One source close to the German underground noted, "From the Red Army Faction point of view, the only opportunity to fight NATO suppression around the world is to organize a kind of illegal guerrilla war and get in contact with more and more people."[11] This transformation apparently took concrete form first in 1981.

Italian counterterrorist forces revealed that in that year, exiles from the RAF, the Italian Red Brigades, and other groups met in Paris. From this meeting, the order went out to kidnap James L. Dozier, a U.S. Army brigadier general stationed in Rome. From being indigenous terrorist groups, operating primarily on their own soil for essentially nationalistic purposes, these groups began to focus their attention and activities against an international enemy: NATO.

Working together, these European terrorists created an informal network that enables them to strike at a variety of NATO targets throughout that region. With relatively open borders among nations in the European Union, these terrorists have managed to operate in a manner that makes it difficult for law enforcement officials to predict and prevent their attacks or to capture them after the events. Evidence suggests that they share personnel, resources (explosives and weapons), and safe houses, as well as the low-level support system involved in such activities as the production of travel documents.

## NARCOTERRORISM

Terrorists of the future may be even less dependent than those of the present on the sponsorship of patron states. A new source of revenue has come into the hands of terrorist groups in the last decades of the twentieth century, prompting some experts to decry the existence of what they call "**narcoterrorism**," a networking of the trade in drugs and terrorism. *U.S. News & World Report* called this "the unholiest of alliances, a malevolent marriage between two of the most feared and destructive forces plaguing modern society—terror and drugs."[12]

The use of drugs to underwrite the costs of terrorism adds a new dimension to law enforcement efforts to combat both drugs and terrorism. The drug trade offers vast profits, too, for nations that, although they want to continue to sponsor terrorist groups, find their coffers seriously depleted in recent years. Syria, for example, and more recently Iran have engaged in international drug smuggling to help finance their support for terrorist groups.

The netherworld of narcoterrorism has three main players: the terrorist groups such as the Tamils, the ETA, or the Sikhs; the government officials and intelligence services of nations such as Iran and Cuba, whose foreign policy includes the exporting of revolution; and the narcotic-dealing gangsters, such as Juan Mata Ballesteros, who also deal in political violence and terror. Through a complex network of contacts, these narcoterrorists deal in weapons, launder money, share intelligence information, trade false passports, share safe havens, and offer other forms of assistance.

It is a loose global alliance of two elements of the criminal world. Those who deal in drugs have long become inured to dealing in death and find little incongruent in their relationship with terrorists. In spite of the apparent callousness in such groups as the PLO toward the taking of human life, these groups are very sensitive to charges that they deal in drugs. Indeed, PLO treasurer Jaweed al-Ghussein vehemently repudiated such charges. "We are fighting for our homeland. We are not drug smugglers. That is against our values."[13]

Regardless of such denials, it is true that in war-torn Lebanon, the annual 1,500-ton hashish trade (recently supplemented by opium and heroin) has supported terrorists of many ideologies for years. "Lebanese hashish helps to pay for everything from hijacking and bombing spectaculars in Europe and the Middle East to a simmering revolt by Moslem insurgents in the Philippines."[14]

It is certain that Syria would be unable to conduct its assistance to insurgent groups without the infusion of millions of dollars in drug profits. Without such profits, the Syrian economy would be even more threadbare than it has become in the years since the collapse of the Soviet Union. Intelligence agencies suggest that Syrian government involvement in the drugs-for-terrorism trade involves persons at high levels of the Syrian government, through the activities of Rifat Assad, the president's brother.

Nor is the Middle East alone in experiencing the impact of narcoterrorism. In Peru, the coca growers and drug traffickers are in a working alliance with the Sendero Luminoso, or Shining Path. While the ultimate ends sought by each group is different, their alliance does benefit each significantly, and the stability and legitimacy of the Peruvian government is constantly sabotaged. Because this destabilization is a shared goal (as well as the shared desire to make a profit) and because all members of this network want "liberation" from interference by the police and the military, there is a strong network of cooperation in Peru in narcoterror.

The Sendero Luminoso is one of the best-armed militia in the region. Peru's police and military were, until recently, viewed as underequipped in comparison. The successful resolution of the takeover of the Japanese Embassy in Lima in 1997 changed international perception of the capabilities of Peruvian counterterror forces. But the situation with the drug traffickers and Shining Path remains unresolved. Few economic enterprises can command the market power and earning potential that the contemporary narcotics trade commands today. As the expert providing much of this picture on the situation in Peru notes:

> Narcoterrorism is a growing movement. The police and the military have not been able to solve the problems of the Peruvian people; the Senderos provide a solution, however risky it might be. The Senderos have literally taken over hundreds of towns, usually welcomed in because they provide order and freedom to produce coca.[15]

## CONCLUSION

Terrorism today is big businesss. No one country is wholly responsible for terrorism's scope, nor is any single country so essential to the existence of terrorism that the withdrawal of its support would seriously diminish terrorism's spread. The continuation of terrorist attacks in Europe, the Middle East, and now the United States after the collapse of the Soviet Union has made it clear that no one state's support is essestial to the survival of international terrorism. States such as the former Soviet Union made it *easier* for terrorists to network, but such support, while no longer available, is clearly not critical to the survival or the networking of many groups.

Moreover, evidence indicates that terrorist groups are becoming increasingly self-sufficient. The PLO blossomed from a group that hijacked planes in the 1960s into a sophisticated multinational corporation that used both terrorism and sound investments to achieve its goals. Unlike its earlier years, when its ability to operate depended on substantial contributions from sympathetic Arab states, the PLO by the 1990s obtained about five-sixths of its annual expenditures of $600 million from its own operations.

Organizations such as the PLO and the IRA have become increasingly entrenched, both in the communities in which their followers live and in the governments that do business with them. The PLO, for instance, has invested in farms, factories, the import-export business, and real estate. These investments provide revenues and jobs; they helped to integrate the PLO into the local economy, and they provided members of the organization with valuable experience as managers of both personnel and money, all of which should benefit the Palestinians as they begin self-government in the West Bank and the Gaza Strip.

Furthermore, governments in Europe now have bureaus that have been created to deal with these groups. The PLO now has a mission to the United Nations in New York, and it has begun to operate as a government over a population and territory. Even before the peace accords in the 1990s, the PLO was able, owing to its structure and resources, to act more as a government in exile than a terrorist operation. This does not suggest that it automatically abandoned its terrorist operations when it secured funds and investments, just that it, like the government of Syria, began trying to distance itself from the use of terrorist tactics.

Many terrorist organizations, however, still depend heavily on the support of "patron" states. It is more frequently these groups that commit the small-scale acts of terror, such as hostage taking in Turkey or Burma, to prove to their patrons that they are capable of operating efficiently and are worthy of support. Such groups have also been responsible for bomb attacks—a low-cost but lethal operation.

When terrorists strike, countries such as Libya or Iran applaud—and quickly deny that they had anything to do with the attack. All of the major Middle Eastern terrorist groups maintain offices in Tripoli and Teheran. Training camps for terrorists operate openly in the Bekaa Valley of Lebanon, an area controlled primarily by the Syrians.

Two final points need to be made with regard to this concept of a terror network. The first has to do with the transition of terrorist organizations into "corporations." As such groups become institutionalized, in terms of formalized government contacts and offices, entrenched in the local economies of many nations, and independent of a need for sponsor financing, they become increasingly difficult to destroy.

Their adherents begin to include government bureaucrats whose offices regularly deal with them, businesses that share joint economic interests, and communities whose livelihood depend on the network's employment.

The other point is that, with the increasing contact and sharing of support among terrorists, there is a potential for greater sophistication in the carrying out of terrorist acts. Terrorists operating in a foreign country, if they are able to avail themselves of the local expertise of indigenous groups, can carry out more efficient operations.

Thus far, evidence of this increase in expertise is limited. Indeed, there has been evidence that terrorists operating on foreign soil are still receiving inadequate or incorrect intelligence information about their targets and intended victims. On September 3, 1985, for instance, the Palestine Popular Struggle Front, a small PLO faction, carried out what it supposed was an attack on a hotel swimming pool in Athens, Greece, frequented by American military personnel. Instead, the two grenades that this group tossed over the wall killed 2 and wounded 13 disabled British tourists. Bungling such as this increases, rather than decreases, the work of security forces charged with combating terrorism, of course, because the selection of victims is not just arbitrary but illogical. Ironically, cooperative assistance may increase the ability of a group to select an appropriate target. But such cooperation also increases the likelihood that the group can in fact penetrate that target, as local expertise is added to fanatical commitment. Sharing information, arms, and training, terrorists of the twenty-first century can brandish a stronger, if still not coordinated, array of daggers at the throat of the civilized world.

## *Evaluation*

Consider these examples of narcoterrorism's lethal harvest:

1. There was evidence of Soviet influence in the operation of Kintex, the state import-export trading organization of Bulgaria. Through this organization, heroin and hashish were funneled into Western Europe, concealed among legitimate cargoes. Profits from the sales of the drugs were used to purchase weapons, which were then shipped to various European and Middle Eastern terrorist groups and to Kurdish and Armenian rebels in Turkey. Bulgaria acquired hard currency, terrorists got weapons, and NATO nations were further destabilized by the influx of drugs.

2. In April 1987, more than 150 people were killed in Sri Lanka when a powerful car bomb, set by Tamil rebels, exploded at a bus terminal in Colombo, destroying at least six buses filled with homebound commuters. The Tamils, an ethnic minority that has been seeking a separate homeland, have been financing their terrorist campaign through heroin sales in Canada, Germany, and France, where authorities arrested almost 200 Tamil drug couriers in the late 1980s. Earlier that same month, Tamil militants killed 145 civilians in a similar massacre.

3. In 1984, when Indian troops stormed the Golden Temple in Amritsar in an attempt to crush Sikh militants, reports surfaced that the soldiers found "huge quantities" of heroin

and hashish. This cache was reputedly planned to be sold to finance arms purchases, just as the Tamils in nearby Sri Lanka had done.[16]

4. At a secret meeting in Bogotá, Colombia, Cuba's ambassador offered Colombian drug barons safe passage through the territorial waters of Cuba—for the modest price of $800,000 per drug boat! A modest 25-ton hashish shipment smuggled into Florida or the Bahamas could be worth $12 million. Weapons for insurgents in Guatemala, El Salvador, and (until the mid-1990s) Nicaragua were loaded in Havana for the return trip of the drug boats.

5. Lebanon remains a primary source of hashish for the international market, and both production and trafficking occur with either the permission or the collusion of a number of terrorist organizations and Syrian military officers in the occupying forces. Nearly all of the militant groups in the area obtain revenue from the drug industry, either directly or by protecting the contraband as it is transported through their area of influence. This "industry" generates an estimated $1 billion per year, most of which is used to finance the activities of terrorist groups and sponsoring states.[17]

5. Iran, in the late 1980s, began establishing its own smuggling routes from Lebanon's Syrian-controlled Bekaa Valley into Europe. The 4,000-strong pro-Iranian Shiite militia, at Teheran's direction, began to carve out for Iran a portion of that lucrative trade. Iran used the money to offset the costs of its war with Iraq and to enable it to continue to export terrorism worldwide.

What are the implications of this new source of financial independence for terrorist groups and states? Is this alliance of drugs and terror a result of temporary coincidence of needs, or does it have longer-term, broader, more strategic aims? It has been said that drugs could destroy the Western world. Is the **unholy triangle** of drug traffickers, terrorists, and state officials committed to the destruction of that world just a mischance, or is it of deliberate design? How will this affect the way nations deal with drug traffic? Will there be any attempts to effect cooperation between agencies charged with combating drugs and those pledged to combating terrorism, similar to that attempted between Mexico and the United States in the mid-1990s?

## *Suggested Readings*

Adams, James. *The Financing of Terror.* New York: Simon & Schuster, 1986.

Friedman, Thomas L. "Loose-linked Network of Terror: Separate Acts, Ideological Bonds."

Laqueur, Walter. *The Age of Terrorism.* Boston: Little, Brown, 1987.

McCormick, Gordon H. *The Shining Path and Peruvian Terrorism.* Santa Monica, CA: Rand, 1987.

———. *The Shining Path and the Future of Peru.* Santa Monica, CA: Rand, 1990.

———. *From the Sierra to the Cities.* Santa Monica, CA: Rand, 1992.

Raynor, Thomas P. *Terrorism.* New York: Franklin Watts, 1982.

Rosewitz, Barbara, and Gerald F. Seib. "Big Business: Aside from Being a Movement, the PLO Is a Financial Giant." *Wall Street Journal,* July 21, 1986, A28.

Scott, Marvin. "What Is the PLO Worth?" *Parade Magazine,* September 21, 1986, 17–28.

Segaller, Stephen. *Invisible Armies: Terrorism in the 1990s.* New York: Harcourt, Brace
    Janovich, 1987.

Wardlaw, Grant. "Linkages between the Illegal Drugs Traffic and Terrorism." Paper presented
    at the Conference on International Drugs: Threat and Response, Defense and
    Intelligence College, Washington, D.C., June 2–3, 1987.

## *Endnotes*

1. When French police moved in to capture Carlos at his headquarters, he escaped in a spectacular shoot-out, during which he killed two French police officers. For further information and commentary, see *Terrorism,* by Thomas P. Raynor (New York: Franklin Watts, 1982).

2. Walter Laqueur, *The Age of Terrorism* (Boston: Little, Brown, 1987), 290. Laqueur describes both the participants and the agenda of this congress in some detail.

3. "Iran's Offer," *U.S. News & World Report,* May 25, 1987, 17.

4. James Adams, *The Financing of Terrorism* (New York: Simon & Schuster, 1986), 16.

5. See, for example, Thomas L. Friedman, "Network of Terror," *New York Times,* April 27, 1987, A12.

6. Adams, *The Financing of Terrorism,* 107.

7. Marvin Scott, "What Is the PLO Worth?" *Parade Magazine,* September 21, 1986, 17.

8. Adams, *The Financing of Terrorism,* 73.

9. Ibid., 134.

10. Claire Sterling, "Terrorism: Tracing the International Network," *New York Times Magazine,* March 1, 1981, 20.

11. Charles J. Hanley, "Reborn Terrorist 'Armies' Target NATO," *Winston-Salem Journal,* April 9, 1986, 1.

12. *U.S. News & World Report,* May 4, 1987.

13. Scott, "What Is the PLO Worth?" 18.

14. "Narcotics: Terror's New Ally," *U.S. News & World Report,* May 4, 1987, 36–37.

15. Rebecca Knickerbocker, "Narcoterrorism," in *Sendero Luminoso and the Threat of Narco-terrorism,* Center for Strategic and International Studies, Washington, D.C. (The Washington Papers), 1990.

16. "Narcotics," 32.

17. Grant Wardlaw, "Linkages between the Illegal Drugs Traffic and Terrorism," paper presented at the Conference on International Drugs: Threat and Response, Defense Intelligence College, Washington, D.C., June 2–3, 1987.

# How Do They Operate?

*So in the Libyan fable it is told*
*That once an eagle, stricken with a dart,*
*Said, when he saw the fashioning of the shaft,*
*"With our own feathers, not by others' hands,*
*Are we now smitten."*

—Aeschylus

## *Key Concepts*

| | |
|---|---|
| explosive bombs | OPEC |
| incendiary bombs | shaped-charge principle |
| disguise techniques and | automatic weapons |
| clandestine travel | "little brother" |
| recruitment | precision-guided munitions (PGMs) |
| communication | organophosphates |
| intelligence gathering | botulinal toxins |
| counterintelligence | threat-hoax |

Thus far we have noted who is likely to become a terrorist, who trains a person to become a terrorist, and some of the purposes for which a person might resort to terrorism. We have, in part, attempted to answer the "who" question and some of the "why" questions. Part of the "where" questions—relating to where terrorists operate and are trained—have also been discussed.

Now we will discuss the important "how" questions. How are they trained—at what sites and on what topics? How are they equipped, in terms of weapons available to them? How do they tend to operate; that is, what tactics do they choose and why do they choose to use or not use certain weapons?

Some of these questions can be answered by briefly listing the important points. Others, such as those relating to the type of weaponry available to contemporary

**TABLE 7.1**

| Nation | Location of Training Camp(s) |
| --- | --- |
| Bulgaria | Varna |
| Cuba | Camp Matanzos |
| Czechoslovakia | Ostrova and Karlovt Varv*$ |
| East Germany | Pankow*$@& |
| Hungary | Lake Belaton |
| Lebanon | Boalbok |
| Libya | Res Hilal*$& |
| | Misurata |
| | Sirte |
| | Tameona |
| | Focra |
| North Korea | Three major centers (names not available at this time) |
| South Yemen | Khayat*$ |
| Syria | Bekaa Valley (area under Syrian control in Lebanon)*$& |

**Note:** Four symbols have been used in this list to indicate additional assistance given at and through these camps to terrorists: * indicates that terrorists are also provided with arms at these camps; $ denotes that money is channeled to terrorists from the host country, usually through these training facilities; @ indicates that the host country shares its personnel with the terrorist in the training camp; & signifies that the host country provides intelligence information to terrorists at the camp.

terrorists, require considerable explanation. None need to be answered in depth here, for two reasons. First, this book is, at best, a cursory look at terrorism, a brief sketch of only the minimum points relating to this confusing topic. Second, just as terrorism itself is in considerable flux today, so the lists of training sites and topics of today's terrorists may well be inadequate for understanding and predicting the actions of tomorrow's terrorist. The training topics and tactics are unlikely to become obsolete, but the list may well be expanded in the twenty-first century.

## TRAINING SITES

Until the 1990s, more than a dozen nations offered training camps for terrorists worldwide. Some of these camps were specifically for terrorists, whereas others were camps used by the host country for military or intelligence training, as well as by terrorists.

Table 7.1, though not comprehensive, details most of the major training facilities used for terrorist training until the end of the Soviet Union. Sites are listed by country, rather than by size or affiliation with particular terrorists organizations, to demonstrate the geographic distribution of these camps.

A number of countries during the 1960s through the 1980s operated training facilities within the structure of their own military services. Names for these terrorist training facilities are still not readily available, but a list of training sites would be inadequate without including at least the names of such countries:

- *Iran.* In addition to providing training to terrorists, Iran also offers funding (already discussed in the previous chapter), a safe haven for terrorists on the run, and passport and diplomatic assistance.

- *Iraq.* In spite of the drain on its resources made by its war with Iran and its subsequent invasion of Kuwait, Iraq still provides some training for terrorists, as well as arms, funding, a safe haven, and diplomatic and passport assistance. This aid did not end with Iraq's defeat in the Gulf War.

- *Sudan.* By offering safe haven to Osama bin Laden and encouraging his investment and recruitment efforts, Sudan began to allow both training and arming of terrorists during the early 1990s.

This is not, of course, a comprehensive list of all locations at which terrorists received training during the latter part of the twentieth century. Some nations were more discreet than others in the training that they provided. Moreover, information concerning such camps necessarily came from some national intelligence service, meaning that the information was certainly biased according to how that nation defined terrorism. It is unlikely, for instance, that the intelligence assessment of a particular nation would list "friendly" nations as hosts for terrorist camps. Instead, such assessments would cite such camps as training sources for legitimate insurgent or revolutionary groups.

Moreover, the dramatic changes that occurred in the world in the early 1990s have seriously impacted the ability of the listed states to offer training, arms, or specific support to terrorist groups. Of the states on this list, only a few still offered significant levels of training and support in the 1990s. Iran remained a major supporter, providing weapons, funds, and training primarily to Hizballah, but also to the Palestinian Islamic Jihad, Ahmad Jibril's Popular Front for the Liberation of Palestine–General Command, the Kurdistan Workers' Party, and, of course, Hamas. Iraq, too, continued to defy international concern, as articulated through UN resolutions, and offered training facilities and safe havens to several groups, such as the Palestine Liberation Front (Abu Abbas's organization), the ANO, and the Arab Liberation Front.

Cuba, however, could no longer financially or politically afford to flout Western censure by openly offering training to terrorist groups. While it continued in the 1990s to offer safe haven to members of the ETA (Basque separatists) and to members of the Manuel Rodriguez Patriotic Front (a Chilean insurgent group), as well as to the FARC and the National Liberation Army (from Colombia), Cuba could no longer provide weapons or training on the scale that had been available before the fall of its sponsor, the Soviet Union.

Nations such as Syria and North Korea became similarly unable or unwilling to openly offer terrorist training and support after 1987. While Syria continued to offer safe haven to the PFLP-GC, Hamas, the PIJ, the JRA, and other groups, the training assistance and access to weapons was no longer made freely available. The political costs, lacking the shelter of the Soviet superpower, were simply too high.

Perhaps one of the most dramatic highlights of the diminishing role of states involved in providing sanctuary to terrorists came in August 1994, when the Sudanese government handed over notorious terrorist Ilyich Ramirez Sanchez (a.k.a. "Carlos the Jackal"). Carlos had been given sanctuary in the Sudan in 1993 but was peacefully handed over to French authorities one year later. Open sanctuary to internationally known terrorists was obviously a less attractive policy option as the century neared its end.

# TRAINING TOPICS: WHAT DO THEY LEARN AT CAMP?

In June 1967 a Venezuelan, Manuel Carrasquel, told an investigating committee of the Organization of American States about the training his group had received in various subjects. They included tactics, weapons training, bomb making (particularly how to blow up oil pipelines), map reading, cryptology, photography, the falsification of documents, and disguise.[1]

Terrorists do not go to training camps just to acquire arms, intelligence information, or funding. They undergo, at most such camps, a rigorous program of activities, gaining proficiency in a wide variety of skills. A brief review of some of the topics taught at these training camps provides useful insights into the type of tactics that terrorists employ in their ventures. It also yields a better understanding of the depth and breadth of the training available to terrorists today. It is surprising to note that many terrorists are more highly trained in a wider variety of tactics than the police in the nations combating terrorism.

Again, it should be noted that the following sketch of training topics is not exhaustive. It is merely meant to offer a rudimentary understanding of the scope of training available today, with the intent of making one more aware of the potential array of tactics from which contemporary terrorists may choose.

## Arson and Bombs

Because about 50 percent of all terrorist incidents involve bombings, this ranks as one of the most prevalent and most popular training topics. Terrorists are, as a rule, taught how to make and use two types of bombs: explosive and incendiary. **Explosive bombs** are generally of either fragmentation or blast type. The most commonly used fragmentation bomb at these camps is the pipe bomb, usually employing gunpowder as the explosive agent. Terrorists are taught how to use commercial or military-type dynamite with a blasting cap for detonation in the creation and usage of blast-type bombs.

Terrorists also learn how to create and use **incendiary bombs,** as such bombs are quickly and easily constructed. These are simply fire bombs, generating extensive fire damage. They are also inexpensive. Terrorists are often taught, for instance, how to make a simple fire bomb, consisting of a glass bottle filled with an inflammable mixture, to which a fuse is attached. Fire bombs can vary in sophistication from time-delay fused and barometric bombs to fertilizer mixed with fuel oil. The bomb blast in Oklahoma City in 1995 was clearly the latter type of incendiary bomb, simple in construction but incredibly destructive.

Not every training camp offers instruction on all such bombs, nor is every trainee instructed in the construction and use of all bomb types. But the array of weapons of destruction from just instruction in arson and bomb usage is of great use to every terrorist recruit.

## Assassination and Ambush Techniques

Terrorists are usually taught how to penetrate personal security systems to kill at close hand. They are instructed in the proficient use of handguns and silencers. Methods of clandestine approach, disguise, and escape are generally incorporated into this part of every terrorist's training. Increasingly, modern terrorists are being instructed in the commission of flamboyant, execution-style assassinations, instead of the unobtrusive gunman-in-a-crowd techniques favored by the anarchists of earlier years.

## Raising Money

Contemporary training courses for terrorists often now include information on how to raise money for indigent terrorist groups. Part of the curriculum is information on how to conduct bank and armored car robberies and how to extort money from wealthy sources, usually the families or employers of kidnap victims. In the 1970s, the latter technique was a source of considerable wealth, particularly for groups operating in Central and South Ameria. United States firms in these areas were at first willing to pay large sums for the safe return of their kidnapped executives. However, during the 1980s, businesses began making it a formal part of their policy *not* to submit to ransom demands. As a result, kidnapping for ransom money has become a less profitable enterprise.

In the 1980s, terrorists were trained in the use of kidnap victims for the extortion of *political* rewards or concessions as well as money. Although many governments have a state policy of not conceding to terrorist extortion demands, most have from time to time found it expedient to yield rather than allow a kidnap situation to drag on indefinitely or to end disastrously. Events in Lebanon give credence to the credible and profitable use by terrorist groups of this tactic.

## Disguise Techniques, Clandestine Travel, Recruitment, and Communications

Terrorists today are trained in many of the same techniques that the counterintelligence services use. They are taught methods of **disguise techniques and clandestine travel,** including how to travel inconspicuously (contrary to popular belief, an

Arab engaged in a terrorist attack does not routinely wear a burnous, nor does he or she travel by camel). Instruction is also given in the procuring of false passport and identification papers and altering one's appearance to permit one to slip through surveillance nets.

Most terrorists are also trained in the techniques of **recruitment,** as all terrorist groups require transfusions of new members but must constantly beware of the dangers of counterintelligence penetration. The screening and selection of potential recruits is thus a vital talent for every successful terrorist group.

Terrorists are also trained in sophisticated methods of **communication.** Recognizing the importance of reliable and secure means of communicating during a terrorist incident, leaders of terrorist organizations are having larger numbers of their recruits trained in the advanced technology of communication. Not for the modern terrorists are the simple two-way radios still favored by many police forces.

## Intelligence Collection and Counterintelligence

Not surprisingly, many modern terrorists are more skilled at gathering intelligence information than are many members of the intelligence organizations of some nations. Terrorists now receive comprehensive training not only in the techniques of intelligence gathering but also in the equally important methods of counterintelligence operations.

**Intelligence gathering** means that terrorists are currently being taught how to infiltrate target areas, gather relevant data, and return that information to headquarters. The use of codes and the translation of intelligence data bits into comprehensible information are basic to the education of today's terrorist.

Terrorists are also being taught methods of **counterintelligence,** including how to disseminate misinformation designed to confuse their enemies. Such instruction generally includes information on how to protect the organization from infiltration by police, military, and governmental intelligence operatives.

This does not mean, of course, that all terrorists are trained in all of these methods. Most organizations can usually afford to train only a carefully selected number in these sophisticated techniques. But the ability of most terrorist organizations to have at least a few such skilled recruits is becoming a matter of survival. Lack of information or misinformation can seriously cripple an organization's ability to carry out a successful operation. So the extent to which a terrorist group can field operatives skilled in intelligence matters is crucial to that group's success today.

## Weapons

This last item is by no means the least important in the repertoire acquired by terrorists in training facilities. The number and variety of weapons available to terrorists through the different training camps over time certainly has varied considerably, which makes generalizations difficult. Without detailing all of the weapons available to modern terrorists (which is covered in the following section), we can briefly note here the types of weapons for which terrorists are being trained.

In addition to being trained in the use of small firearms, including pistols, rifles, and sawed-off shotguns, terrorists are currently being trained in the use of automatic and semiautomatic weapons. Training is regularly given in the use of machine guns and machine pistols, particularly those manufactured in the former Soviet Union and several other countries in Eastern Europe, including Poland and the Czech Republic.

Training is also available in light-tank antirocket launchers, principally the Soviet-made RPG-7 and the U.S. LAW. Use of the French Strim F-1 has also been taught at some camps. Such weapons are portable and easy to conceal. Surface-to-air missiles, known to be in the hands of terrorists, are also a part of some training programs, including those led by the United States.

There is no available evidence of training being given to terrorists in the use of some of the more exotic weapons, such as chemical or biological agents. Although the use of such weapons remains relatively infrequent today, the use of sarin gas by terrorists in Japan on the subway in the mid-1990s presented the spectre of appalling destruction. Although the twentieth century escaped without many serious successful attempts by groups to utilize chemical or biological weapons, their use may well be significant in the twenty-first century. Moreover, it should be noted that *states* in the twentieth century have been distressingly willing to use such weapons on a dissident population, as the Iraqis did on the Kurds in the 1980s.

The training process appears to be quite comprehensive, even formidable in its potential for turning out proficient terrorists. Let us consider one operation carried out in the 1970s, when training camps were far less organized and their "graduates" perhaps less sophisticated than they later became.

## CASE STUDY: OPEC KIDNAPPING IN VIENNA

Carlos the Jackal, who was a graduate of training camps in Cuba and, arguably, the former Soviet Union, masterminded this terrorist act. Together with a hand-picked assault team, composed of Arabs and members of the German Red Army Faction, Carlos and his five confederates walked into the **OPEC** (Oil Producing and Exporting Countries) conference meeting in Vienna, Austria, in December 1975. They carried sports duffel bags, in which they concealed their weapons and equipment.

As Sheik Yamani, a hostage at the conference, described the situation, "There is no doubt that Carlos and his group had made very careful plans. We could tell at once that they knew every detail about the building. They knew exactly where to go, and each member of the gang knew precisely what to do."[2]

These terrorists carried out their plan of attack with ruthless efficiency. Hans-Joachim Klein destroyed the switchboard, preventing a telephone warning from being issued. Gabriele Krocher-Tiedemann calmly shot two men who tried to resist the gang's entrance. A third man, a member of the Libyan delegation, was shot by

Carlos as he attempted to disarm the terrorist leader. Order was restored quickly, and the terrorists were in clear control before the Austrian police teams arrived.

The terrorists had a clear and simple list of demands that they gave the negotiators. Carlos, on his way to Austria, had arranged for sympathizers to send his demands to radio stations anyway, even if his mission failed—a back-up plan that has become common among terrorists today. When the Austrian government agreed, with very little argument, to those demands, Carlos moved his group and their hostages into a well-planned escape route.

This whole operation demonstrated to the world that terrorists were indeed capable of carefully planned and brilliantly executed attacks. Reconnaissance, timing, and planning were clearly techniques with which terrorists were becoming increasingly familiar. In a few years, an increasingly sophisticated arsenal of weapons would make such an attack many times more lethal.

## POTENTIAL FOR DESTRUCTION: THE TERRORIST'S ARSENAL

Before examining the tactics chosen by trained terrorists, let us look briefly at the arsenal of weapons available to the terrorist today. From contact in training camps, certain weapons have become favored by some terrorist groups. Other weapons have gained popularity because of their proven effectiveness or their relative availability.

### Explosives

Terrorists worldwide continue to use explosives, frequently in the form of homemade devices. These are most often blast rather than fragmentation bombs. Explosives, as Kupperman and Trent have pointed out, "offer many advantages to a terrorist: they are available everywhere and crude bombs can be fabricated locally; they are concealable and can be readily disguised so that X-ray and magnometer inspections are ineffective defenses."[3]

The destructive quality of bombs does not depend necessarily on the sophistication of their construction. Trucks packed with forms of TNT have created substantial damage and caused innumerable deaths. One truck laden with fertilizer and gasoline in Oklahoma City in 1995 destroyed a federal building and left hundreds of casualties, dead or injured.

But the ability of a small amount of explosive to create a large amount of damage has been enhanced by terrorists, using the **shaped-charge principle,** which focuses the force of the explosion in a desired direction. Terrorists have shown themselves to be proficient in the use of both conical or "beehive" bombs, which increase the charge's penetration, and linear bombs, which have a "cutting" effect.

# Small Arms

In recent years, terrorists have continued to use pistols, rifles, and such crude weapons as the sawed-off shotgun. The supply of such weapons is vast, the cost relatively small, and the training for their use fairly simple, making these popular weapons for small or underfinanced terrorist groups.

Handguns continue to be the weapon of the political assassin, but more importantly in terms of modern terrorism, they are often the preferred weapons of those taking hostages. Moreover, unlike the automatic weapon, laws limiting the sale and possession of handguns are either very lax or nonexistent in many countries.

# Automatic Weapons

While the automatic weapon is essentially an antipersonnel weapon, it has also been used by terrorists to assault cars and even airplanes. It is a favorite weapon of terrorist groups for several reasons: its availability, concealability, high rate of fire, and, perhaps most important, its psychological impact on unarmed civilians or lightly armed security forces.

There are two basic types of **automatic weapons:** the assault rifle and the submachine gun.[4] Both are easily obtained through arms dealers or the military of various nations, particularly since the demise of the Soviet Union. The Russian AK-7 is one of the most popular weapons of terrorists today, owing to its accessibility as well as to its performance record. Assault rifles can be obtained in either their military form, such as the AK-7 assault rifle, or in their semiautomatic commercial version.

In recent years, the **"little brother"** of the submachine gun, the machine pistol, has become popular among terrorist groups and police forces. This is particularly true of European terrorists, where such weapons can be easily procured.

# Portable Rockets

In recent years, training of terrorists in the use of **precision-guided munitions (PGMs)**—devices that can launch missiles whose trajectories can be corrected in flight—has increased dramatically. Most, but not all, PGMs are portable, meaning that they are fairly lightweight and can be carried and operated by one or perhaps two persons. Such weapons are designed to destroy aircraft and, on the battlefield, tanks. There are documented incidents, to date, in which terrorists have attempted to use a weapon such as the Soviet-made SA-7 (code-named Strela) against aircraft. In 1973, for instance, a Palestinian group planned to use two SA-7s to shoot down an El Al airliner near Rome, but the attempt was foiled. A similar plot in Kenya in 1975 also failed, but by 1978 the SA-7 was apparently used successfully against a commercial airliner.[5]

Of the surface-to-air rocket systems currently available, the most popular appear to be those of the United States, Russia, and the United Kingdom. The U.S.-made

Stinger (the successor of the Redeye), the aforementioned Russian-made SA-7, and the British Blowpipe have achieved a considerable degree of popularity among contemporary terrorists. Most such rockets employ infrared devices, heat-seeking sensors that, as a rule, serve to guide the missile to a heat source, presumably the aircraft engine. They generally weigh between 30 and 40 pounds, with an effective range of at least several kilometers. Worst of all, from a security standpoint, such weapons are becoming all too readily available to terrorist organizations. It is interesting to note the observations made by Rand Corporation's terrorist expert, Brian Jenkins, two decades ago, with regard to the proliferation of these weapons:

> First-generation PGMs such as the Strela and the Redeye will be available to 30 or 40 countries in the Third World. It is not realistic to expect that all of these countries will maintain strict security measures; some may find it in their interest to make these weapons available to nongovernmental groups. If we postulate a conservative loss rate worldwide, by theft or diversion, of one-tenth of one percent over the next five years, then man-portable PGMs will be "loose" in the hundreds by the beginning of the 1980s.[6]

Such weapons *were* loose in at least the hundreds if not the thousands in the 1980s. Not only did third world nations allow and even assist in their dissemination, but Western nations whose laws forbade the "sharing" of such weaponry were guilty of allowing these missile systems to come into the hands of terrorists.

Less sophisticated but about as lethal are the light antitank rocket launchers, such as the U.S. Viper and the Russian RPG-7, which have been used with increasing frequency by terrorists. Such systems are compact, self-contained, lightweight, and easily transported (once dismantled) in a suitcase. Terrorists could use such weapons with devastating effect against limousines, aircraft, transformer banks, vehicles transporting radioactive wastes, and oil or natural gas pipelines.

## "SCIENCE FICTION" WEAPONS

Robert Kupperman, in a report prepared for the Department of Justice in October 1977, made a useful analysis of the devastation that could be wrought by chemical, biological, and radiological weapons and nuclear explosives:

> In terms of fatalities, conventional weapons such as machine guns and small bombs constitute the least threat. They can produce tens or hundreds of casualties in a single incident. Chemical weapons such as nerve agents constitute a substantially greater threat, being capable of producing hundreds to thousands of fatalities. A small nuclear bomb could produce a hundred thousand casualties, but biological agents—both toxins and living organisms—can rival thermonuclear weapons, providing the possibility of producing hundreds of thousands to several millions of casualties in a single incident.[7]

Let us first consider the possibilities (for as yet they remain primarily possibilities, with only a few attempted usages, fortunately) of a terrorist groups using chemical or biological agents of mass destruction. That most groups have not yet done so is less a factor of the difficulties and dangers involved in producing such weapons than in the problems in effectively disseminating the toxic material.

There are tens of thousands of highly toxic chemicals, some of which are available to the general public in the form of, for instance, rodenticides. **Organophosphates,** the so-called nerve agents, could be synthesized by a moderately competent chemist, with limited laboratory facilities. Indeed, for terrorist groups lacking even such a chemist and laboratory, some forms of these agents, such as TEPP (tetrathylpyrophosphate), are available commercially as insecticides.

The use of an organophosphate by a group in Japan in 1995 demonstrated both the effectiveness of the agent and the vulnerability of major urban centers to such attacks. The injury to thousands, generated by a relatively small amount of substance, makes clear that Kupperman's assessment was distressingly accurate.

But the dissemination of such agents of destruction is not simple. Aerosol dispersal would be a difficult and risky in some areas, although subways, trains, planes, and buses make inviting targets. Contamination of a large water supply is normally inhibited by such factors as hydrolysis, chlorination, and the required minimum quantity of toxic material per gallon of water for effectiveness.

Similar problems inhibit the dissemination, if not the production, of even more lethal **botulinal toxins,** highly toxic nerve agents created by anerobic bacterium, often found in spoiled or ill-prepared food. Although compared with the most toxic nerve agent, botulinal toxin is at least a thousand times more dangerous, similar problems arise in the dissemination of botulinal toxins. Dissemination through the food supply is an obvious route, one that concerns the food industries considerably.

Unfortunately, botulinal toxins are easily produced. There is a vast array of literature on their growth, serological typing for virulence, the techniques for continuous culturing, separation, and purification of the toxin. The toxin that causes botulism is produced by the organism *Clautridium botulinium,* which is found almost everywhere.

Kupperman produced a useful data set for the comparison of the lethality of such weapons with more conventional (and better-understood) weapons. It would seem, from his data, that while it would take *320 million grams* of fuel air explosives (e.g., such as the crude truck load of fertilizer and gasoline used in Oklahoma City) to produce heavy casualties within a square-mile area, it would take only *8 grams* of anthrax spores to produce the same approximate casualty count. Although his data set postulates "ideal" conditions (including requirements for dissemination), making his projections somewhat suspect, it nevertheless highlights how powerful these small but toxic agents are.[8]

This comparison makes it clear that certain chemical and biological weapons are even more potentially lethal than even a relatively small nuclear weapon. It is startling to note that, according to Kupperman's information, anthrax is *100,000 times more effective* as an agent of destruction than is a highly toxic nerve gas, such as the one used in Japan. The pneumonia-like illness caused by *Bacillus anthracis* is apparently almost 100 percent fatal if untreated (which it usually is, since by the time the symptoms appear, antibiotic therapy is no longer useful).

Many chemical and biological agents are fairly readily produced or obtained, often through legitimate sources. They are also incredibly deadly, capable of killing thousands, even hundreds of thousands, of people. Thus far, the difficult step of dissemination may be one of the only remaining reasons why contemporary terrorists have not yet used these agents of mass destruction. The success of the use of such an agent in Japan in 1995 may well encourage other groups to begin to utilize these "science fiction" weapons.

Jenkins, in 1975, suggested another reason that might inhibit terrorists' use of such weapons. According to his understanding of terrorism at that time:

> Incidents in which terrorists have deliberately tried to kill large numbers of people or cause widespread damage are relative rare. Terrorists want a lot of people watching, not a lot of people dead—which may explain why, apart from the technical difficulties involved, they have not already used chemical or bacteriological weapons, or conventional explosives in ways that would produce mass casualties.[9]

However, it is no longer true that all modern terrorists eschew mass violence. Bombs have been placed aboard airliners, such as the Pan Am flight over Lockerbie, Scotland, killing hundreds. Explosives have been used in vast quantities, as in Oklahoma City and New York City, resulting in hundreds of injured and dead. Hundreds have been injured on subways with toxic materials.

It seems, then, that Jenkins's premise regarding terrorists' reluctance to use weapons of mass destruction is less accurate as the century draws to a close. It may well be that the reason that few groups have yet used such weapons rests on the difficulty in disseminating the toxic substance in sufficient quantities. That is, surely, a frail defense for those nations that may find themselves the target of such attacks.

## Nuclear Weapons

For years modern nations have tried both to secure the materials necessary for the production of nuclear weapons and to remain secure in their belief that, even if some small portions of such materials should fall into terrorist hands, the terrorists would lack the technical skill to manufacture such weapons. The former is a manifestly false premise, particularly since the breakup of the former Soviet Union, and the latter is, at the very least, an arguable premise.

Experts have estimated that, to produce a crude nuclear weapon, terrorists would have to have perhaps a half-dozen technologically trained individuals (with training in subjects such as nuclear chemistry, physics, metallurgy, electronics, and perhaps the handling of high explosives) and considerable time, space, and money.

Let us consider each of these requisites to determine whether such a weapon does in fact lie within the realm of possibility for some terrorists today.

The financial resources of terrorists has already been discussed in some detail. Oil revenues (which had enabled patron states to be generous in their support) and, more recently, drugs have served to swell the coffers of many terrorist groups. An organization such as, for instance, the RAF could well afford the necessary funds to procure the materials, trained technicians, and facilities necessary to the building of such a weapon.

For small, poorly financed groups, a lack of time as well as money could well inhibit the production of a nuclear weapon. Such groups are compelled to produce results at once if they are to obtain the funding and support from the patron states that they require to survive. They cannot afford to wait while technicians are either trained or recruited and suitable facilities are constructed.

Well-financed groups can, however, afford to wait while personnel are put into place in an adequately constructed facility. With their contacts among friendly governments, they might even be able to secure a safe testing ground for the weapon, prior to its use, although such a step would not be essential to its use. Military experts are concerned with such matters as high reliability and predictability yield. All terrorists need be concerned with is that the bomb produces a sufficiently audible "bang" and visible mushroom cloud.

The requirement of space, too, is one that well-established and funded groups can manage. Because there are considerable hazards attendant upon working with radioactive materials, it would be necessary to build or obtain the use of a laboratory of fairly substantial size, equipped with specialized equipment. Like the fissionable materials, the acquisition of such facilities is increasingly within the grasp of some groups today. If they can gain access to military training facilities, as described earlier, then the possibility exists that terrorists can also gain access to the use of suitable research and development facilities.

Trained personnel are also obtainable for groups and states that can afford market prices for such personnel, after the demise of the Soviet Union. According to one study, about one-third of individuals identified as terrorists were persons with some university training, university graduates, or postgraduate students. In some groups, such as the Tupamaros (Uruguay), the Argentine Revolutionary People's Army, and the Monteneros, the figure was nearly 75 percent in the 1970s. Even in Turkey and Iran, university-trained terrorists were the rule rather than the exception, according to this study. In Turkey and Iran, too, the fields of study tended to be the more exact sciences such as engineering. Yasir Arafat is a graduate engineer.[10]

In the Sudan in 1998, the United States stated that a pharmaceutical plant in Khartoum was producing a chemical whose sole market value was as a percusor for VX toxin. Here, the space and the technologically trained individuals were apparently available through a plant that had, according to U.S. information, ties to Osama bin Laden's terrorist university. Thus, several of the key elements necessary for the completion of a lethal, nontraditional weapon may have been available to individuals engaged in terrorism.

Thus, while it might not be feasible to train a recruit with only grade school or even high school education in the technology necessary for the construction of nuclear weapons, terrorists have a large pool of university graduates from which to select, as well as a large number of trained scientists seeking employment following the crash of the Soviet system.

But it is important to note that those terrorists who may possess or be able to obtain the necessary resources to construct a crude nuclear weapon are often those who are least likely to benefit from the commission of such a barbarous act. Well-established terrorist organizations have tended to try to distance themselves from acts of barbarity, as did the group leadership in Japan following the use of gas on the subways. The reasons for such distancing is obvious: these organizations have attachable assets and fixed locations and personnel on which retribution could be meted.

Arafat, for instance, would have been extremely reluctant to use the PLO's resources for the construction and subsequent detonation of a nuclear device. To do so, even before the peace process began in the 1990s, would have irreparably damaged his credibility with the United Nations and would have played into the hands of his enemies, giving them good reason for condemning him as a murderer of unparalleled proportions.

Two forms of nuclear terrorism remain feasible, however. One is the **threat/ hoax** by which leaders are frightened or blackmailed into acceding to terrorist demands, based on the threat of detonating a hidden nuclear device in a crowded area, such as a city. While it sounds more like the stuff of which science fiction is created, such threats have in fact already been made. Leaders in several nations, including the United States, have already had to deal with such threats.

To date that is all they have been: threats/hoaxes. But the time may well be at hand when leaders may no longer be so confident that terrorists do not truly possess a nuclear device that they are prepared to detonate. The increasing willingness of some terrorists to commit carnage on a large scale must surely give pause to those who would claim that the devastation wrought by a nuclear device would be on too large a scale for contemporary terrorists. As terrorism continues to become more violent, nuclear terrorism becomes more of a possibility.

The greatest potential for a nuclear disaster, and one that has concerned governments more, is the possibility of either a takeover/hostage situation at an existing nuclear facility or sabotage of such a facility. With the growing number, both of nuclear power plants inside countries that have for some years produced nuclear power and weapons, and of nuclear facilities in previously nonnuclear states, the possibility of these types of situations has dramatically increased.

In either case, great damage could be done, without the expenditure of a great deal of time, money, or personnel recruitment and training. In other words, such an action is well within the reach of most contemporary terrorists. Security protections at such facilities, while gradually increasing, are at present inadequate to prevent a

determined and well-planned assault. Such an assault could be carried out by indigenous or foreign groups, as long as sufficient intelligence-gathering and reconnaissance measures had been taken.

The "science fiction" terrorism of earlier years, then, is rapidly becoming part
of the potential pattern of terrorism today and tomorrow. Chemical, biological, and
nuclear terrorism is technically within some terrorists' grasp today. That they have,
for the most part, not chosen to pursue such tactics—yet—is a subject for conjecture.
It would be unwise to rely, however, on the terrorists' need for popular approval or
goodwill as an indefinite defense against an attack with weapons of this kind.

## TERRORIST TACTICS

It may be useful at this point to briefly review what we do know about the tactics used
by contemporary terrorists. Already we have discussed how they are trained and what
kind of weapons they use. The tactics chosen, given these variables of training and
weapons, should prove illuminating in discerning patterns of contemporary terrorist
tactics and perhaps enable us to predict more accurately patterns of terrorist acts in
the twenty-first century.

Described here are various types of terrorist tactics reported worldwide, together
with a few brief remarks about their usage. Although not an exhaustive list, it features
most of the major tactics employed by terrorists to date.

### Bombing

Bombs are the most common tool of contemporary terrorists, accounting for about
50 percent of all terrorist incidents. Most recent trends in the use of this tactic include
efforts to maximize the casualties, the use of secondary explosives, and the use of
highly sophisticated devices. The letter bomb of earlier years has in large measure
been replaced (except in the case of the U.S. Unabomber) by vehicle bombs, which
can carry a larger charge.

Review of a few examples of the use of bombs by terrorist groups indicates that
the use of such weapons is becoming common throughout the world and that such
attacks are extremely lethal. These examples were selected to give a sense of the
scope, in terms of geography and variety (of groups involved and types of bombs
used), as well as lethality.

- *April 1983, Beirut*—A car bomb is detonated in front of the U.S. Embassy, killing 63
  and wounding over 100.
- *April 1985, Madrid*—A bomb explodes at a restaurant outside the city frequented by
  U.S. soldiers. Eighteen Spaniards are killed and 82 people wounded.
- *September 1985, Athens*—Two grenades are thrown into the lobby of a Greek hotel,
  wounding 18 British tourists.

- *December 1988, Lockerbie*—Pan Am Flight 103 explodes from a bomb, killing over 200 people. Responsibility for planning and support for bombing are traced to Libya, Iran, and Syria.
- *March 1991, Sri Lanka*—State Minister for Defense Wijeratne is killed in a car bombing in Colombo along with 50 other victims. The LTTE is responsible.
- *June 1991, Honduras*—The Morazanist Patriotic Front launches an RPG-7 rocket at the UN Observer Group headquarters in Tegucigalpa.
- *February 1993, New York*—An explosion of a massive van bomb in an underground parking garage below the World Trade Center kills 6 and wounds over 1,000. Islamic extremists are convicted.
- *June 1993, Egypt*—A bomb exploding underneath an overpass as a tour bus traveled to the Giza pyramids kills two Egyptians and injures six British tourists, as well as Egyptians and Syrians.
- *October 1994, Peru*—The SL explodes a large bomb under a minibus in the parking lot near the departure terminal at Lima's international airport. The driver of a hotel shuttle bus is killed and about 20 others are injured.
- *August 1995, Oklahoma City*—A truck bomb at a federal building injures or kills hundreds, including children in a day care center. A member of a militia group is charged with the crime.
- *January 1996, Israel*—Suicide bombers continue to cause civilian deaths in Jerusalem and the West Bank. Hamas extremists take responsibility, in efforts to stop the peace process.

This list does not, of course, detail all of the bombings that have occurred in the past two decades. It is intended only to demonstrate the wide range of bombs used, the variety of targets chosen, and the worldwide nature of the patterns of use.

## Arson

Arson accounts for approximately 14 percent of all terrorist incidents. The use of this tactic often involves the employment of an incendiary explosive device.

Again, a brief look at some of the terrorist events in which this method has been employed may offer insights into its usefulness. It is, for example, used more frequently to destroy property and to create a climate of fear than to destroy lives.

- *March 1982, South Korea*—A U.S. International Communications Office in Pusan is burned by a band of youths, killing one visitor.
- *October 1993, Paris*—Terrorists throw a firebomb into the Turkish-owned Bosporus Bank in central Paris. No serious damage is caused.
- *November 1993, Europe*—The PKK stages a round of coordinated attacks against Turkish diplomatic and commercial facilities in six Western European countries. The assaults consist mainly of firebombings and vandalism, but 1 person is killed and about 20 others injured.

## Hostage Taking and Kidnapping

This tactic allows terrorists to maximize the publicity surrounding the event. By employing such a tactic, terrorists are able to control both the length of the event and media coverage of the event, at least in terms of interviews with the hostages. Because audience is important to terrorist events, this tactic is particularly enticing to terrorists. The feelings of power, of being in control, of playing before a worldwide audience are indeed heady sensations for terrorists.

The headlines have been full, in recent years, of spectacular, and not so spectacular, hostage takings. Indeed, as shock has succeeded shock, the taking of yet another individual by extremists in Lebanon or Turkey is no longer even newsworthy in some parts of the world. A brief glimpse at the endless list of hostage takings indicates why this should be so. Note also that virtually all such reports refer to the incident as "kidnapping."

- *October 1986, Lebanon*—Edward Austin Tracy, an American and longtime resident of Moslem-controlled West Beirut, is kidnapped. A group calling itself the Revolutionary Justice Organization claims responsibility.
- *June 1991, India*—A Kashmiri separatist group kidnaps one Dutch and seven Israeli tourists in Srinagar. One Israeli is killed in an escape attempt.
- *August 1991, Turkey*—The Kurdish Worker's Party (PKK) kidnaps 10 German tourists near Lake Van. The tourists are later released. Later this same month, PKK kidnaps three Americans, a Briton, and an Australian near Bingol, who are released a month later.
- *February 1993, Colombia*—Eight ELN terrorists kidnap U.S. citizen Lewis Manning, an employee of the Colombian gold-mining company Oresom, in the Choco area.
- *March 1993, Costa Rica*—Four terrorists kidnap 25 persons in the Nicaraguan Embassy in San Jose, including the Nicaraguan ambassador. The hostages are held for several days while negotiations are conducted.
- *October 1993, Algeria*—Terrorists kidnapped a Peruvian, a Filipino, and a Colombian, technicians employed by the firm, from the cafeteria of an Italian construction firm in Tiaret. Two days later, the three are found dead with their throats cut. The extremist Armed Islamic Group claims responsibility for this and other attacks against foreigners.
- *December 1996, Peru*—Tupac Amaru takes more than 500 people hostage at the Japanese Embassy in Lima, Peru. Most are freed early in the negotiation process, and the remaining 72 are rescued after being held for 126 days by Peruvian troops.

Unlike hostage taking, kidnapping is a covert act. Because it requires secrecy, kidnapping is usually preceded by considerable planning and rehearsal. Terrorists tend to kill the victims, even if their demands are met, possibly because a dead body is infinitely more dramatic than a quietly released hostage. Terrorism, to be effective, requires an element of drama.

In the news items cited here, the events could in some cases be termed "kidnapping," planned and executed in secrecy. The victims, however, were in a very real sense hostages to political and/or monetary demands made by their kidnappers. Some were killed, others remained in captivity as hostages to demands that could not be met.

## Assassinations and Ambushes

Targets for such attacks have been selected for both their publicity and their symbolic value. In Lebanon, victims have included officers involved in peacekeeping efforts, priests, and college personnel. This tactic, because it requires an element of surprise, usually involves careful planning and execution.

Assassins and their victims come in all shapes and sizes. While government officials make attractive targets, a variety of others have come under the assassin's gun. Note in the following brief list below the diversity of targets:

- *1984*—Malcolm Kerr, president of American University in Beirut, is shot and killed as he steps off the elevator to his office on the West Beirut campus. Islamic Jihad claims responsibility.

   Leamon R. Hunt, the American director of the Multinational Force and Observers peacekeeping force in the Sinai peninsula, is shot and killed as he drives to his home in southwestern Rome. A radical offshoot of the Red Brigades claims responsibility.

- *1985*—Terrorists shoot and kill 13 people as they sit in a sidewalk café in San Salvador. Two days later the Urban Guerrilla–Mardoqueo Cruz, associated with the FLMN, takes responsibility.

   A coalition of Palestinian and JRA terrorists attack airports at Rome and Vienna with grenades and machine guns, killing 18 and wounding 116. Abu Nidal's Revolutionary Fatah group is responsible.

- *1991*—The RAF claims responsibility for firing approximately 250 rounds of small-arms fire at the U.S. Embassy in Bonn—the first RAF attack against a U.S. target since 1985.

   An Iranian dissident leader is stabbed and killed in the lobby of his apartment building in Paris.

   Sendero Luminosa kills the Canadian director of the humanitarian organization World Mission in a Lima suburb.

   Former prime minister Rajiv Gandhi is assassinated by a suspected LTTE suicide bomber while campaigning in southern India.

- *1993*—An Italian businessman is shot and wounded by a terrorist as he leaves his residence in a suburb of Algeria.

   A police officer is killed and six others wounded when a group of terrorists open fire on two movie houses showing foreign films. Al-Gama's al-Islamiyya claims responsibility, stating that the attack retaliated for the screening of "immoral" films.

- *1995*—Yitzhak Rabin, prime minister of Israel, is assassinated by a Jewish student, claiming that Rabin had given away too much of Israel in the peace process.

## Aerial Hijacking

Skyjacking, as such events have been called, has been used by terrorists to maximize spectacular situations. This type of event allows the terrorist to maximize shock value and grab world attention. Moreover, it once provided the terrorist with an escape vehicle, until international law closed this loophole.

These "spectaculars" have provided extensive media coverage, at fairly minimal cost to the hijackers. Although the psychological costs for victims are high, the loss of lives has tended to be less than in other types of terrorist events—except when things go wrong.

- *1985*—Shiite gunmen hijack TWA Flight 847 from Athens, Greece. The hijackers shoot and kill U.S. Navy diver Robert Stetham in Beirut and disperse the remaining hostages throughout the city.

    Four Palestinian gunmen hijack the Italian cruise ship *Achille Lauro* off Alexandria, Egypt, with 80 passengers and 320 crew aboard, and sail to Syria and Cyprus (where it is refused port entry) and back to Egypt. While off the Syrian port of Tartus, the terrorists kill American Leon Klinghoffer.

    Arab gunmen hijack an Egypt Air flight and land at Malta after an in-flight gun battle with Egyptian security guards. Five passengers are shot at close range and dumped on the runway.

- *1986*—Pan Am Flight 73 is hijacked in Pakistan. At 5:55 P.M. (Eastern Standard Time), four Arab-speaking gunmen seize a Pan Am 747 at Karachi International Airport as the plane is loading passengers for a flight to Frankfurt, Germany. The hijackers hold 374 passengers and 15 crew members hostage for 16 hours while sporadic negotiations are attempted. Suddenly, at 9:45 P.M. the following night when the ground power units run out of gas and the lights are dimmed on the plane, the gunmen panic and begin firing indiscriminately at the huddled passengers. Before Pakistani commandos can storm the plane, 21 hostages are dead and more than 60 seriously wounded.

- *1991*—Four Pakistanis claiming to be members of the Pakistani People's Party hijack a Singapore Airlines flight en route from Kualu Lumpur to Singapore, demanding the release of several people reportedly imprisoned in Pakistan.

## Sabotage

Highly industrialized Western nations are particularly vulnerable to this type of terrorist tactic. It is possible, for example, to disrupt utility services or shut down industrial complexes. Japan in 1987 suffered a disruption of its commuter rail services by terrorists armed with nothing more than a few sharp blades. Such an incident can clearly have tremendous symbolic value, demonstrating to the watching governments the power that even a relatively obscure group may wield. Although such actions serve terrorist goals of disrupting and perhaps destabilizing governments, they are not necessarily terrorist acts, because no innocent victims are injured or killed in the action (disturbed, imposed upon, perhaps, but not casualties).

# Threat/Hoax

This is another low-cost tactic, with varying potential for disruption, without making innocent victims out of anyone. It forces governments to assess the vulnerability of the targets and the history of the group claiming responsibility. The cost of reacting to such a hoax may well be crippling to the authority involved, while the consequences of not responding could be equally dreadful.

# Chemical-Biological Attacks

Agents for this type of tactic are, as noted earlier, available commercially or can be developed without undue difficulty by some groups. The possibility of a successful poisoning of the water supply of a city has concerned some governments in recent years. Individuals in the United States have already demonstrated that it is possible to poison medicines on drugstore shelves and food supplies. The toxic agent attack on Tokyo subways in 1995 proved the effectiveness of this tactic and demonstrated that groups can no longer be assumed to be unwilling or unable to use them. Use of toxic agents against the Kurds by the government of Iraq during its conflict with Iran had already made it clear that states are increasingly willing to use these weapons.

# Nuclear Threat

As noted earlier, the technology and the materials are available to terrorists today. While the devices may be difficult to manufacture, it is not impossible to do so, and they could be stolen, purchased, or supplied by a supporting state. Sabotage or takeover of a nuclear facility is also feasible and far less expensive.

Information regarding these last four forms of terrorism is less readily available. Sabotage, as noted earlier, is not a terrorist act, in the strict definition of the term. Threat holders are not, according to most terror-specific statutes, legally punishable crimes of terrorism, either. Thus, the reporting for such crimes is less complete. The use of chemical and biological weapons by terrorists has thus far remained quite limited—no longer a "science fiction" tactic but not yet widely used. But the increased use of such weapons by nation-states at war makes the likelihood of terrorist acquisition and use of such methods much more probable.

In the Iran-Iraq war, as noted earlier, Iraq spread poison gas against its enemies. For a time such measures were reserved for "desperate" military situations, when confronted with overwhelming Iranian forces. But there was gruesome evidence of an increase in the use of this lethal weapon against villages and cities. The city of Halabja, near the Iran-Iraq border, was covered with a poison cloud, which one survivor described as "a dense choking pancake that settled over many square blocks."[11] Very few of those left in the center of town survived. Medical evidence suggests that Iraq dropped mustard gas, a relatively common poison; hydrogen cyanide, a chemical combination used for executions in U.S. prisons; and possibly sarin, a nerve gas that is one of the deadliest chemical weapons ever developed.

When nation-states themselves use such weapons, even on civilian populations, how can the civilized world prevent or even proscribe the use of such weapons by terrorists? Certainly the use of such weapons by nations engaged in conflict both lessens the strength of the laws designed to control or prohibit their usage and makes more difficult the means by which the production of such weapons is controlled. If production of such chemical weapons cannot be effectively limited, then their dissemination becomes even more difficult to control

Today, intelligence sources say that some 37 countries are full or potential members of the "chemical weapons club."[12] While all but six of these—North and South Korea, Laos, Angola, Albania, and Nicaragua—have signed the 1925 Geneva Convention banning chemical warfare, several signatory nations are flagrant violators of the pact. Iran is one whose violations are well documented. Evidence exists that others, including Ethiopia, Mozambique, Libya, Vietnam, and even the former Soviet Union violated the agreement.

## Evaluation

Terrorists today have a wide variety of tactics from which to choose and sufficient training and support systems to make the most of the tactics within their grasp, should they choose to use them. Although most terrorist groups continue to rely on the tactics proven successful in earlier years, such as bombing and hostage taking, recent developments make it possible that different choices may be made in the near future.

Two potentially conflicting forces seem to be influencing the choice of tactics. Consider these factors carefully, and decide what you think will be the trends in future terrorist attacks.

1. Some terrorist groups have become financially stable, with well-established ties to many governments. These governments supply training, arms, personnel, intelligence, and travel assistance. These same governments are, at the same time, somewhat more vulnerable than the group itself to retaliation in the event of a terrorist attack. The U.S. air strike against Libya in 1985 gives credence to this point. Moreover, the demise of the Soviet Union has made the political risks for supporting such groups much higher and the risks of military retaliation much less calculable.

2. The technology for developing more sophisticated weapons is now more readily accessible to terrorists. At the same time, restraints against the use of widespread violence in terrorist attacks appear to be diminishing. In other words, it is now possible to construct instruments of vast destructive power at a time when inhibitions against the committing of such atrocities seems to be vanishing. If terrorists groups (or states) are willing to be responsible for hundreds of deaths in an airline bombing, will they continue to be reluctant to use weapons capable of even greater destruction, such as toxins, if they can obtain them?

3. Terrorists today can inflict more harm with more sophisticated weapons, and with larger
quantities of weapons, than ever before in part because of the eagerness of the rest of the
world to sell arms to anyone who has the money to buy them. How much responsibility
rests with the arms merchants of the so-called civilized world for making weapons so
easy to obtain?

## Suggested Readings

Dobson, Christopher, and Ronald Payne. *The Carlos Complex: A Study in Terror.* New York:
Putnam, 1977.
Grossman, Lawrence K. "The Face of Terrorism." *The Quill,* June 1986, 24–41.
Hickey, Neil. "Gaining the Media's Attention." In *The Struggle against Terrorism.* New York:
Wilson, 1977.
Jenkins, Brian. "International Terrorism: The Other World War." A Project AIR FORCE
Report prepared for the United States Air Force, November 1985.
———. *Terrorism: Trends and Potentialities.* Santa Monica, CA: Rand, 1977.
———. "Will Terrorists Go Nuclear?" P-5541. Santa Monica, CA: Rand, November 1975.
Kupperman, Robert H., and Darrell M. Trent. *Terrorism: Threat, Reality and Response.*
Stanford, CA: Hoover Institution Press, 1979.
"New Horrors in a Long-Running Horror Show." *U.S. News & World Report,* April 4, 1988.
Russell, Charles A., and Bowman H. Miller. "Profile of a Terrorist." *Terrorism: An Inter-
national Journal,* 1 (1977): 24–48.

## Endnotes

1. Christopher Dobson and Ronald Payne, *The Carlos Complex: A Study in Terror* (New York:
Putnam, 1977), 34.

2. Quoted in ibid., 104.

3. Robert H. Kupperman and Darrell M. Trent, *Terrorism: Threat, Reality and Response*
(Stanford, CA: Hoover Institution Press, 1979), 80.

4. Ibid., 54.

5. In that year, evidence indicates that a Rhodesian airliner was shot down with an SA-7.

6. Brian Jenkins, *Terrorism: Trends and Potentialities* (Santa Monica, CA: Rand, 1977), 80.

7. Kupperman and Trent, *Terrorism,* 83.

8. Ibid., 57. This agent comparison was derived by Conrad V. Chester of the Oak Ridge National
Laboratory, transmitted in a June 20, 1975, letter entitled "Perspectives on the CB Terrorist Threat."

9. Brian Jenkins, "Will Terrorists Go Nuclear?" P-5541 (Santa Monica, CA: Rand, November
1975).

10. Charles A. Russell and Bowman H. Miller, "Profile of a Terrorist," *Terrorism: An International
Journal* 1, no. 1: 27–28.

11. "New Horrors in a Long-Running Horror Show," *U.S. News & World Report,* April 4, 1988, 11.

12. "A Plague of 'Hellish Poison,'" *U.S. News & World Report,* October 26, 1987, 32.

# The Media: A Weapon for Both Sides?

*For the press to ignore terrorist acts is clearly impossible in a democratic society, but coverage of terrorism almost surely invites the strong possibility of intensification or copycatism and more terrorism.*
—Martin Slann and Bernard Schechterman

## Key Concepts

amplification effect
right of access
prior restraint
censorship
prisoners of war
complicity
arousal hypothesis
disinhibition hypothesis
social learning theory
interactive relationship
built-in escalation imperative
publicity
tactical and strategic gains

favorable understanding
legitimacy and identity
destabilizing the enemy
criminality of the act
denial of a platform
information and cooperation
copycat operation
disinformation
getting a scoop
dramatic presentation
protection of rights
personal security

Terrorism has been called "propaganda by the deed." This particularly violent form of propaganda has captured the attention of millions of people. To what extent have the media today become a weapon of the terrorists about whom they report? Who is exploiting whom in this vicious scramble for worldwide audience?

Many of today's terrorists have learned an important lesson about this technological age: that television news organizations can be forced into becoming the link between terrorists and their audience. What is needed to forge this link is a crime sufficiently newsworthy, which has come to mean outrageous, dramatic, even barbaric enough. According to Brian Jenkins, a Rand Corporation expert on terrorism, "terrorists want a lot of people watching and a lot of people listening, not a lot of people dead. . . . I see terrorism as violence for effect. Terrorists choreograph dramatic incidents to achieve maximum publicity, and in that sense, terrorism is theater."[1]

Terrorists benefit from what has been called an **amplification effect,** when their activities are broadcast through the media to a much larger audience than would be available on the spot where the action occurs. For instance, insurgents carried on rural guerrilla warfare in several countries, including Angola and Mozambique, for more than a decade, without receiving much attention from the rest of the world. But when a similar number of Palestinians carried their warfare into the urban centers of Europe and the Middle East, their actions and their causes became dinner table conversation for TV audiences around the world, because in the urban centers of Europe and the Middle East, the terrorists were within reach of TV news reporters and their cameras.

This confluence of interest between the media—who thrive on sensational news—and terrorists—who are only too happy to provide the sensational events—has raised questions about the possible complicity of the media in today's terrorism. Students of terrorism have suggested that the media today *are* in fact a contributing factor, a weapon, in the hands of modern terrorists. A quick survey of the opinions of a few of these experts is illuminating.

Frederick Hacker, a California psychiatrist who has served as negotiator in terrorist incidents, notes that "if the mass media did not exist, terrorists would have to invent them. In turn, the mass media hanker after terrorist acts because they fit into their programming needs: namely, sudden acts of great excitement that are susceptible, presumably, of quick solution. So there's a mutual dependency."

Walter Laquer, chair of the International Research Council of the Center for the Strategic and International Studies, states: "The media are a terrorist's best friend. . . . [T]errorists are the super-entertainers of our time."

Raymond Tanter, political science professor at the University of Michigan, makes the relationship dilemma a bit clearer: "Since the terror is aimed at the media and not at the victim, success is defined in terms of media coverage. And there is no way in the West that you could *not* have media coverage because you're dealing in a free society."[2]

In Tanter's comments lie a key to the dilemma regarding the role of the media in terrorism. Censorship in any form is anathema to most free societies. Instead, it has been assumed that the media could be expected to exercise voluntary self-restraints where necessary in reporting such events. But the media is not wholly convinced that restraint is either necessary or desirable. There is still considerable conflict over the extent of the public's "right to know" in the coverage of terrorist events. Executives of most of the major news companies have stated that television's "right to report" is absolute, that, in any case, it is better to report than not report. ABC's William Sheehan has said, "I don't think it's our job to decide what people should not know. The news media are not the reason for terrorism even though they may sometimes become part of the story."[3]

Which is the more accurate picture of the role of the media with respect to terrorism today? Are they the responsible means by which the public is kept informed on events and individuals who are interacting in the international arena? Or are they, as one hijacker said, "whores" whose "favors" are available to anyone with a pistol?[4] If it is indeed true that the media are responsible for amplifying the effects of guerrilla warfare, to what extent are they responsible for the effects of that amplification? If terrorists have to move to increasingly more spectacular crimes to satisfy the increasingly jaded palette of TV audiences sated with violence, to what extent are the media responsible for whetting that appetite?

Some experts have suggested that the media are acting increasingly like a "loose gun," a weapon that terrorists are learning to use with rapidly improving sophistication. It is, moreover, a gun that democratic governments have provided, and continue to provide, essentially without controls, against itself. It would indeed be ironic if one of the fundamental freedoms of the free world—free press—were to be instrumental in its destruction, as the Libyan incident noted in the previous chapter suggests.

## LEGAL ISSUES OF THE RIGHT OF ACCESS

The issue of the relationship among terrorism, the media, and the law has received attention from scholars for more than a decade. Legal experts from law enforcement agencies and media services have benefited from the scrutiny of this complex web of relationships. A brief review of a few significant issues raised by experts on this subject may be of value at this point.

Both law and the media experts have frequently differed on the nature of the relationships that should exist among law enforcement, the media, and terrorists. Members of the media often claim to have an unlimited right to have access to, and the right to report, all news, including that relating to terrorist events. Those responsible for hostage rescue contend that such rights should not be regarded as unlimited and should never be exercised in ways that might endanger lives. The legal issues inherent in these contrasting viewpoints were explored extensively during the late 1970s and early 1980s. As one researcher has succinctly noted, "The media must not be the dupes of the radical scriptwriters, nor should they be the mouthpiece of government. There is a mean. Law enforcement and the media cannot be locked in combat."[5]

The U.S. Supreme Court during Warren Burger's tenure as chief justice did not regard the media's right to access as superior to that of the general public. Abraham Miller has created a significant review of case law decisions involving the issue of the press's **right of access** to terrorist events—that is, the press's right to get close to the events as they occur. He notes that, in the *Pell* decision, the Court stated that when the public is excluded from the scene of a crime of disaster, then the media may also be excluded, without violating the First Amendment to the U.S. Constitution.

Miller's study suggests that the Court, under Burger, viewed access by the media to a site where news is being made (as in a terrorist incident) not as a First Amendment right but as a privilege to be granted or revoked at the discretion of the law enforcement agency entrusted with ending the breach in the law. Even access to the perimeter between the tactical squad and the public (frequently established by law enforcement units in hostage-taking and siege situations for the purpose of permitting access for the media) is not a right guaranteed to the media by the Constitution but rather a privilege accorded at the discretion of the government law enforcement agency in charge of the situation. Miller concludes with the following observation:

> Access to the site where news is being made cannot be claimed by the press if the general public is also being excluded. Press access, largely a privilege under the most sanguine of circumstances, can be revoked, and where the situation is fraught with imminent danger of people being injured or killed, the media's claim to special access rings especially hollow.[6]

An earlier study by Miller and Juanita Jones reached similar conclusions about the legality of excluding the press from certain areas during hostage situations, particularly those in which law enforcement procedures require secrecy to save lives. However, this study also noted that the Supreme Court did not allow blanket denial of access through a set of preconditions. Case law, according to this study, did not support a total or standard ban on news access to terrorist events; only the circumstances surrounding each event could legally justify limitation of access.

**Prior restraint,** establishing specific legal limits on the press before the action occurs, has been a tool used successfully only during times of great national stress, when the security of the state could reasonably be said to be at risk. During the Civil War and both of the world wars, the United States imposed restraints on the press regarding the right of access to events. Fear that an unfettered press might irresponsibly jeopardize the lives of American soldiers or civilians by injudiciously printing too much information about an event led to restrictions on access of the press during wartime.

Even in such extreme circumstances, however, the right of the government to impose such restraints was vociferously challenged, not only by the press itself but by constitutional scholars who feared the precedent that such rules might set. In the more recent conflict with Iraq (1990–1991), the press in the United States were permitted to have briefings near the front lines, show flight recordings and raw data from the advancing armies often before it had been fully analyzed by the military intelligence staff, and allowed to film much of the fighting. Still, the press chafed at the restrictions that were imposed, sought to get even closer to the fields of battle (to the extent where some media personnel were captured by Iraqi soldiers), and demanded unlimited access to all military information available, to be broadcast live to a world-wide audience.

If the world can watch a war being fought, from start to finish, by 24-hour coverage via Cable News Network (CNN), if the press is allowed to broadcast live footage of Special Forces troops conducting a "stealthy" night landing in Somalia, then it is difficult to imagine the circumstances surrounding a terrorism event that would engender the need to limit press access. If national security was not jeopardized by the filming of the war with Iraq or by the broadcast depicting the landing in Somalia, then it is surely not endangered by filming a hostage rescue effort or televising the aftermath of a bomb attack.

It could be more effectively argued that self-restraint instead of prior restraint would be in both the press's and the nation's best interest. Few legal scholars have challenged court findings that restrictions on the media comparable to those imposed on the general public do not necessarily contravene the First Amendment's protection of a free press. Differences have arisen over the type of restrictions and the body empowered to impose them. Most recent research has focused on three alternatives: government-directed censorship, self-censorship by the media themselves, and restraints imposed by a special commission. All three options have difficulties, and the first two have been seriously discussed for more than a decade.

## CENSORSHIP: THE UGLY WORD

No one wants to use the term **censorship,** referring to efforts by a government to limit and edit what is said by the press about an incident, in conjunction with the press in its coverage of terrorist events. Yet many democratic states are hard-pressed not to desire to filter what reporters say to a general (and possibly credulous) public about the motives, lives, intentions, as well as the actions and individuals involved in perpetrating terrorist events. The power of the press to create heroes is sometimes frightening, and democratic governments are not blind to this danger. But few are willing to sacrifice cherished liberal values to keep the press from depicting a person who bombs a supermarket as a heroic "freedom fighter."

To impose censorship on the press in a democratic society would, as several scholars have pointed out, give to the perpetrators of the terrorist events a significant and unearned victory. When a democratic society, in panic and anger, abandons one of the cherished principles of law that make it democratic, the society has inflicted on itself a greater wound than the terrorists could achieve, were they to bomb a hundred buildings.

Yet anger, frustration, and unrelenting problems have led some democratic systems into just that deplorable situation. The problems in Northern Ireland have taxed the patience and the ingenuity of the British security forces past bearing, time after time. The fabric of democracy has sometimes worn thin in this troubled area, as restrictions have been placed on the press as a kind of "damage control." The damage done by censorship in such situations is difficult to calculate.

This issue has been of serious interest to many Western democracies because most have been challenged to resolve the tension between a need to guarantee as unfettered a media as possible while maintaining control over terrorist events. While most of the studies conducted have focused on the ability of the British government to cope with the continuous flow of terrorist events that, until recently, emanated from Northern Ireland, several studies of other Western democracies have also yielded significant insights into this problem.

Miller, a Bradley Resident Scholar at the Heritage Foundation, who conducted the study of the U.S. Supreme Court case law on this issue, expanded his study of this topic in 1990 with research into the struggles of the British government to balance the media's desire to be unfettered against special security needs generated by the struggle in Northern Ireland. As in the study of the Court decisions, Miller concluded that media access to information was not guaranteed by British law.[7] However, he found no evidence to support claims by the government of a need for censorship that extended beyond the limiting of access.

One of the most comprehensive research studies on terrorism and the media was conducted during the 1980s, examining the relationship among terrorist violence, the Western news media, and the political actors.[8] This study is an excellent empirical exercise, including careful scrutiny of terrorist violence, beginning with nineteenth-century anarchists. The study evaluates interaction among terrorists, the media, and political actors in many regions of the world, concluding that much of the blame for the increase in terrorism can be attributed to the media.

Schmid and de Graff summarize the arguments for and against censorship of terrorist news reporting. At the bottom of their list of 11 arguments against censorship is the only one even marginally relevant to the legality of such censorship. This argument is simply that "the assertion of insurgent terrorists that democratic states are not really free would gain credibility if the freedom of the press were suspended."[9] This does not suggest that censorship in such events would be unconstitutional but that it might be counterproductive in constitutional democracies.

Government-directed censorship has been most often studied in the context of Great Britain's efforts to restrain the media on the subject of the conflict in Northern Ireland. Of particular interest in this situation is the legislation banning television and radio broadcasts of interviews or direct statements by members of the outlawed IRA, along with nine other organizations. Two of the organizations are legitimate (or at least not proscribed) groups: Sinn Fein and the Protestant Ulster Defense Association (UDA).

This broadcasting ban was intended, in the words of then prime minister Margaret Thatcher, to deprive terrorists of "the oxygen of publicity" on which they thrive.[10] Ian Stewart, minister of state for Northern Ireland when the ban was enacted, stated that it was designed to "put an end to the practice of providing an easy platform for people who represent groups such as Sinn Fein and the UDA in Northern Ireland, who support political action by means of violence."[11]

Although the British legal system does not have a formal written constitution, it does possess a strong legal tradition of protection of civil liberties. There is considerable difference of opinion as to whether such measures are attacks on that legal tradition or simply reasonable precautions taken by a government faced with an extraordinarily difficult situation. As one British commentator has noted, "nobody calls it censorship when Mafia spokesmen are not allowed to explain, over the airwaves, why it is advisable to pay protection money."[12]

British governmental restraint of media reporting on terrorism has not been limited to the 1988 ban. Occasionally pressure rather than legislation has enabled the government to limit media coverage of terrorism. In his analysis, *Terrorism and the Liberal State,* Paul Wilkinson notes that the home secretary was able to pressure the British Broadcasting Company into banning the documentary "Real Lives: At the Edge of the Union," which was a portrayal of Northern Ireland extremism.[13]

The controversy in Northern Ireland highlights one dilemma faced by law enforcement officials assigned the task of coping with terrorism. Terrorism is, by definition, a political crime in that it involved political motives. Yet most of the laws created by democracies to deal with it have been crafted with a desire to prevent its classification as a political crime, to prevent the use of the "political crime exception" included in most extradition agreements, as discussed in an earlier chapter. Democracies, in general, allow a wide range of political dissent, with political parties and interest groups representing extremes on both the right and the left of the ideological spectrum operating legally within the system. Thus, it is generally not the political motive that is "illegal" but the action taken by the individual or group.

Most formal agreements and legislation concerning terrorism today focus on the illegality of the action taken, not on the group or its motive. Prevention of terrorist acts, not designation of terrorist groups, is the stated focus of law enforcement today. The motives of the group may be legal, even laudable; its actions may properly be subject to censure.

It is easier to censure such actions than to censor them. If the motive is not illegal, then it is not reasonable to expect the press not to investigate, evaluate, and report on the motive as it relates to a specific act of terrorist violence. In a system in which the press is allowed to interview perpetrators of violent crime (e.g., murder, rape, torture, etc.) and to interview their family, friends, coworkers, and any other relevant individuals, it seems unlikely that a clear standard could be established for the need to censor stories about individuals and groups involved in terrorist acts.

If terrorist acts are not political crimes, then the press cannot reasonably be censored from reporting information on the individuals and their motivations in such cases, as long as they are permitted to publish similar insights relating to other violent crimes. Such reporting may be in poor taste or reflect bad judgment, but it is scarcely worthy of the serious punishment of censorship.

Broadcasters in the United Kingdom, confronted with the censorship system created by the government to control media coverage of the situation in Northern Ireland, were quick to note this policy's ambiguity. Certainly it was inconsistent to prohibit Sinn Fein from having access to the broadcast media and to censor news stories about this political group, when it was by law allowed to function openly as a political party. If it is legal to report on the activities and the causes espoused by other legal political parties, it is not rational for it to be illegal to report on those same items with regard to Sinn Fein.

Neither the United States nor the United Kingdom has been willing, moreover, to recognize violent acts carried out by radical political groups as acts of war. Had they done so, it would have been a fairly simple matter to justify censoring media reporting that might give "aid or comfort to the enemy during time of war." But if the governments should declare that a state of war exists, then they would also be bound by international law to treat the individuals captured during the commission of those violent acts of terrorism as **prisoners of war,** combatants actively involved in a war who have been captured by the opposing side. This would make such prisoners subject to the appropriate Geneva Convention provisions and eligible for exchange. Governments are certainly aware that such a step would encourage the endless taking of hostages by groups committing acts of terror, to exchange them for the prisoners of war held by the government. This could create an intolerable situation, one certainly not worth the comparatively small advantage that the legitimization of censorship would give.

While the Northern Ireland situation has received the majority of research attention, other Western democracies also offer interesting viewpoints on the utility and effect of governmental restriction on the media's dissemination of information regarding terrorism. A study by Christopher Kehler, Greg Harvey, and Richard Hall offers interesting perspectives on the delicate balance that democracies are expected to maintain between the need for some form of media regulation and the need for a free press.

Kehler and his associates argue that some form of media regulation is essential simply because media coverage of terrorist events can endanger lives. They cite cases in which the press negotiated with terrorists, in which press corps members entered lines of fire and secured zones, and in which hostage rescue efforts were endangered by live broadcasts of the rescue forces moving in for assault. While such cases led these researchers to agree that it would be legally permissible for governments to regulate the media in their access to the scenes of these violent acts, it is interesting to note that these authors concluded that responsible standards created and enforced by the broadcast industry itself would be a preferable solution.

These conclusions are consistent with those of most other researchers on this subject. While almost all deplore the reckless endangering of lives that sometimes takes place when unrestricted media abuse their privileges of access, few scholars advocate government censorship as a solution. Most appear to agree with Wilkinson's assessment: "[A]ny suggestion that any external body is bringing pressure to bear and altering editorial judgement as a result of political considerations undermines not only the credibility of the media, but the credibility of democratic government."[14]

Moreover, the government cannot expect to hold the media to a higher standard than that to which the government itself is able to attain, with regard to the so-called bias in the media toward certain individuals and groups. When the U.S. government refers to one group as "freedom fighters" and to another, engaged in similar tactics with similar motives, as "terrorists," the lack of clarity is both debilitating and deliberate. Although government claims that the press evidences at times too much "sympathy" toward a particular individual, group, or cause may have merit, the standard for clear, precise, and consistent reporting of information about such individuals, groups, and causes must be set first by the government.

Governments must decide the legal status of a terrorist crime before the option of censorship can ever be explored. If it is a political crime or even a crime of war, then certain restrictions by the government might be applicable. If, however, it is treated by the government as simply a particularly vicious but essentially "common" crime, then the press should not be prevented from exploring every facet of it in the same fashion as it is permitted to explore other violent criminal activity.

## COMPLICITY: A VERY SERIOUS CHARGE

The relationship between terrorism and the media does not flow in a single direction; rather, terrorism reacts to and utilizes the media in a fashion similar to that in which the media react to and use (to sell papers and increase viewership) the terrorist events. This interactive relationship has allowed serious charges of **complicity,** a legal charge indicating active participation of a primary or secondary nature, in terrorist events to be leveled at the media by law enforcement and government counterterrorism officials.

Terrorism is a crime of theater. For it to be effective, the terrorists need to be able to communicate their actions and threats to their audience as quickly and dramatically as possible.[15] Statistically, terrorist incidents worldwide are insignificant, in terms of both the number of dead and injured and the number of incidents reported annually. But massive media coverage of individual terrorist attacks reach a vast audience, creating an impact far beyond that which the incident, in the absence of this media, could be expected to effect. Without intensive media coverage, it could be argued that few would know of terrorist actions, motivations, and actors. As Jenkins has noted:

> Terrorism is violence for effect—not primarily, and sometimes not at all for the physical effect on the actual target, but rather for its dramatic impact on an audience. Developments in world communications, particularly the news media, have expanded the potential audience to national and, more recently, to international proportions.[16]

The interaction of the media with terrorists in the Hanafi Muslim siege in Washington, D.C., in March 1977 gives evidence of interference by the media in law enforcement efforts and of the proactive role of some media in terrorist events. Live broadcasts from the scene continued throughout the siege, and overzealous journalists tied up the telephone lines interviewing the terrorists. This constitutes nuisance, perhaps, but not necessarily interference.

However, at least two incidents occurred that highlight the interactive nature of the media and terrorists in this event. One of the reporters, observing law enforcement officers bringing food to the terrorists, broadcast that the police were preparing for an assault. Eventually, the police were able to convince the Hanafi that the reporter was incorrect, but valuable negotiating time and trust-building efforts were lost. Another reporter called the leaders of the hostage takers, Hamas Abdul Khaalis, and suggested that the police were trying to trick him. Khaalis selected ten of the older hostages for execution, and police again had to try to defuse the situation by removing some of their sharpshooters from the area.[17]

These actions certainly constituted interference in the hostage negotiation process and generated much legitimate criticism of the press. A reporter who was one of the hostages in this siege observed:

> As hostages, many of us felt that the Hanafi takeover was a happening, a guerrilla theater, a high impact propaganda exercise programmed for the TV screen, and . . . for the front pages of newspapers around the world. . . . Beneath the resentment and the anger of my fellow hostages toward the press is a conviction gained . . . that the news media and terrorism feed on each other, that the news media and particularly TV, create a thirst for fame and recognition. Reporters do not simply report the news. They help create it. They are not objective observers, but subjective participants.[18]

This charge suggests that the media play an active role in terrorist events, sometimes even impacting the course of the event. Such a claim goes well beyond that commonly made by many who research this issue: that terrorists use the media for their own purposes. Few would argue that terrorists do indeed use the media to reach the large audience and to carry a specific message to that audience as quickly as possible. The hijacking of TWA Flight 847 in 1985 was, as Grant Wardlaw notes, "cleverly choreographed to ensure maximum media coverage and maximum exposure of [their] propaganda."[19] It remains a disturbing example of the manipulation of the free world's news media by groups involved in terrorist acts.

To propose an interactive relationship suggests that it is possible that the media's impact on terrorism goes beyond that of a reluctant tool, tending instead toward that of a generator of action. This does not mean that anyone truly believes that the media plan, or deliberately suggest, terrorist attacks to groups or individuals. But the action of the media has been scrutinized intensely in recent years to determine whether media coverage of terrorist events caused, for instance, terrorists to choose one particular choice of action over another (e.g., bombings over hijackings).

Schmid offers three hypotheses that attempt to explain the media's effect on terrorism. The first, called the **arousal hypothesis,** suggests that unusual or unique media content can increase a person's desire to act aggressively; that, in fact, any news story detailing some form of aggressive behavior can increase the potential for more aggressive behavior from members of the media's audience. The second is termed the **disinhibition hypothesis,** which suggests that violence portrayed in the media weakens the inhibition of the viewer to engage in similar behavior, which in turn increases the person's readiness to engage in aggressive behavior.

These are hardly as radical a set of concepts today as they were in 1982 when Schmid suggested them. Indeed, a great deal of time and attention has been devoted to determining whether the media encourage violent behavior in viewers, particularly young people. Results of research into these hypotheses have been mixed but have generated sufficient concern for the attorney general of the United States to issue a not too veiled warning to the television networks, strongly suggesting that they initiate self-regulation systems for limiting televised violence before the government decides that it must regulate the industry on this issue.

The third hypothesis suggested by Schmid involves **social learning theory,** which is premised on the belief that all behavior is learned by observation. Thus, if television depicts successful terrorist acts, then viewers will learn all about them; this will in turn increase the likelihood of terrorism. The media would thus be engaged in training individuals in terrorist behavior each time they report such acts.

Surely this is an extreme assessment of the situation. Although live media coverage has, perhaps, given greater importance to events in remote parts of the world, it seems unlikely that an individual would decide, on the basis of a news report of a terrorist incident, to begin engaging in terrorist activities. Although TV newscasts are more visually exciting than printed news articles, it has been possible to test this hypothesis by tracking the articles generated by terrorist events over a decade to determine whether increased coverage of terrorist events actually resulted in an increase in the number of such events.

All that could be determined by such an analysis was that an **interactive relationship** appears to exist—that is, that one of the variables acts on or influences the other. It was not possible, with this type of data, to determine much more than a rough estimate of the strength of the relationship and its apparent direction. Because other variables could also be acting on the ones being studied, without controlling for all other potential influences on terrorist behavior, it would be difficult to generalize about the results of this research. It did, however, become possible to comment more on the utility of the third hypothesis posited by Schmid, using this limited study.

According to the list generated by the U.S. State Department of terrorist incidents that took place from 1981 to 1989 (a time of fairly intense terrorist activity), a total of 119 incidents were recorded involving an American citizen in some respect. Because all of these incidents involved at least one U.S. citizen, it seems logical to assume that they would be reported in national newspapers, such as the *Washington Post* and the *New York Times*. Using these two papers, most of whose stories on these incidents were supplied by the Associated Press (thus eliminating most of the anomalies in the reporting of the data), and categorizing the incidents by type (to discover whether any type of event served better as a "learning tool"), it was possible to note several interesting phenomena:

1. Cumulative regression analysis of the data resulted in a multiple *r* of .843 and a square multiple of *r* of .710. This generally indicates a strong relationship, in this case between the type of event and the amount of coverage.

2. During 1981–1989, inclusive, the number of terrorist incidents increased overall, whereas the number of articles generated in response to these incidents actually decreased.

   a. There were exceptions to this trend. The number of bombings resulting in deaths remained relatively constant, actually decreasing toward the end of the period. This occurred in spite of the enormous increase in the number of articles generated by these attacks.

   b. The incidence of assassination (defined, in State Department terms, as "any time an American is shot and killed) peaked in 1984, with four incidents that generated a record 14 articles. In spite of the spate of press coverage, however, the number of incidents fell the following year to the 1981 level (one incident), producing only four articles. The following year there were three incidents, clearly not impacted by the previous year's limited press coverage of these types of events. In other words, many articles in one year did not generate many attacks in the following year; nor did a year when the number articles dropped to only four was there a decrease in the subsequent number of incidents.

   c. Hijackings (involving the willful seizure of a means of transportation for a political purpose) occurred in only three years during the decade studied. After three incidents generated a phenomenal 16 articles, there was only one further incident for the remainder of the decade.

   d. Kidnappings of Americans actually generated fewer articles than incidents, meaning that some incidents were not even reported in the national news. Nor was there a directional relationship between the number of articles and the number of incidents. Four incidents in 1985 generated only one article, whereas fewer incidents (three) in 1986 evoked seven articles. The same number of incidents (three) in 1987 produced only one article.

These data suggest that, although a relationship appears to exist between the number of terrorist incidents in a given year and the number of articles that they generate, this relationship varies with the type of incident. Moreover, even in the same category of incident, there is considerable variation in the number of articles evoked by the same number of incidents. This suggests, again, that other factors are at work in this process that are not accounted for in so simplistic an assumption as the "learned behavior" hypothesis. If all that was necessary for a terrorist to repeat his or her action, or for another terrorist to attempt a similar action, were news coverage of the event, then all of the types of events should have produced parallel growth lines between incident and article numbers. This was clearly not the case.

Instead, it is obvious that other factors influence the decision of an individual or group to engage in terrorist activities. The media may have some impact, but it is erroneous to assume that the action of the media causes terrorist events to happen, by the coverage of previous events. Hijacking incidents did not become less frequent because of limited press coverage; instead, press coverage was extensive. However, the enactment of several aerial hijacking conventions, and the subsequent closing of most safe havens for hijackers by the "extradite or prosecute" provisions in international agreements (discussed in the following chapter), may as easily be given credit for reducing the number of hijack incidents.

This limited study of news media in a role of "motivation" for terrorism suggests that, although terrorism and the media show a strong relationship, this does not mean that media coverage results in terrorist acts. Certainly, the mass media do serve to extend experience, present models, stimulate aspirations, and indicate goals for terrorists. But the media are clearly not responsible for terrorist acts occurring.

It is possible to infer from a variety of studies on this issue that the media can impact terrorists by what Schmid terms a **"built-in escalation imperative"** that requires that terrorists must commit more and more bizarre and cruel acts to gain media attention. Because kidnapping failed to generate continued media attention, even though most articles suggested that many times the ransom demands were met, terrorists turned increasingly to the use of assassination. When the shooting of a single American stopped generating many articles (as it did between 1985 and 1989), then bombings, resulting in multiple deaths, became the weapon of choice.

Although a relationship certainly exists between terrorists and the media, it is probably not a suitable target for intervention by the government. Intervention could skew the relationship in an undesirable direction. As Schmid notes, "the assertion of insurgent terrorists that democratic states are not really democratic would gain credibility if the freedom of the press were suspended."[20] Perhaps it would be more accurate to say that terrorism and the media may share some goals, which impacts the nature of their relationship. An examination of the goals of terrorists, the goals of the media, and the goals of democratic governments reveals some insights into the complex relationship that exists among these three actors.

## TERRORIST GOALS REGARDING MEDIA

In the view of several of the experts just cited, terrorists have goals that the media can help them to achieve. Let us briefly examine a few of these to determine more clearly the stakes in this very dangerous game.

### Publicity

Because terrorism is an act of theater and requires an audience, most terrorist groups welcome the opportunity to acquire free **publicity.** Getting information out to a large, even a global audience about the cause for which the acts are being committed is a vital part of the act itself. Press coverage that makes the world aware of the "problem" that the individual or group is seeking to resolve is clearly advantageous. This publicity can offer both **tactical** (short-term) and **strategic** (long-term) **gains** for the operation itself, and in some cases to the cause for which the terrorist act is being committed.

Tactical gains in publicity are usually measured in terms of getting information concerning demands that must be met within a time frame to more than just the law enforcement officers at the scene. If the general public can be made aware of the demands and the consequences threatened for lack of fulfillment, then pressure may be put on the legal officers to comply by a concerned public. Strategic goals can be met by increasing that large audience's awareness of the "justice" of the cause for which the act is being committed and the seriousness of the "problem" that the terrorists are trying to rectify.

## Favorable Understanding of Their Cause

This is a vitally important goal of most terrorists today. Everyone wants to be understood, and an individual or group that is clearly breaking important laws and norms of behavior has an intense desire for **favorable understanding,** for their audience to understand why they are carrying out these acts. Sympathy for their suffering and, more important, their cause can be generated by a press willing to convey their message. If, as discussed in a previous chapter, terrorists live with images of their world as unlike those of most of this audience, then it is critically important to them that they convey to that audience the justice for which they struggle and the reasons that have driven them to carry out acts of terrorism.

As one expert has noted, "good relationships with the press are important here, and they are often cultivated and nurtured over a period of years."[21] While not all terrorists have access or longevity sufficient to build such friendly relations with the press, most individuals and groups carrying out terrorist acts do want the press to share with the public a positive understanding of why the incident is occurring. This leaves the media in an invidious position, trying to decide what is news to be reported and what is rhetoric from the terrorist's pulpit. As Rushworth Kidder suggests, "the decision whether or not to broadcast or publish interviews with admitted terrorists brings journalists to the fine line between news and a forum for propaganda."[22]

## Legitimacy and Identity

To recruit effectively, groups must convey **legitimacy and identity,** a clear sense of purpose to those who might be seeking similar political goals. Proving to be both committed and effective in kidnapping, bombing, assassination, and other dramatic terrorist events can be a very useful tool in the recruitment of new members to a group's cause. Moreover, if the group needs funding for their operations, as most do, good publicity of a successful operation can be the key to drawing such support from nations and individuals who share a concern for the cause motivating the group.

When numerous groups exist that share a similar general "problem" focus, then a group may carry out bombings or assassinations simply to establish a separate and credible identity. Certainly in areas such as Northern Ireland and Israel this has been the case, as splinter groups commit acts of terrorism whose tactical goal seems to be establishing a separate identity.

## Destabilizing the Enemy

A goal often cited by terrorist groups has been to cause damage by **destabilizing the enemy**—that is, generating a sense of unrest, enhancing a fear that the government is unable to offer security and stability to its people. Because terrorism is an act designed to create a mood of fear, the press can be seen by terrorists as a valuable tool in achieving this goal. If the media can be used to amplify fear, to spread panic, and to make the population feel insecure, then the terrorists will have won an important goal.

# GOVERNMENT GOALS WITH RESPECT TO MEDIA

In democratic systems, journalists usually have substantial freedom to report news, including that of terrorist events. But unlimited freedom of the press has led, as noted earlier, to an escalation of events and a loss of life—results that neither the press nor the government desire. In many ways, the goals of the government in terrorist incidents are quite similar to those of the group carrying out the act.

## Publicity

Most governments know that the event will be publicized and therefore want the press to offer publicity designed to help the government to achieve its goal of ending the situation without loss of innocent lives. This means that publicity, from the government's perspective, should be carefully disseminated in a manner that will not endanger lives and that will help the public to understand the positive actions undertaken by the government to resolve the situation. This clearly is not compatible with the terrorists' goals, since from the terrorists' perspective publicity should be used to spread fear, not reassurance, about the government's handling of the action. The media are thus left with difficult choices about what news to release and how it should be worded.

## Criminality of the Act

Certainly, law enforcement would prefer that the media paint the terrorists as the "bad guys," and the simplest method for achieving that goal is often to stress the **criminality of the act**—its illegal nature. Whereas the terrorists will seek to have the press convey the "justice" of the cause for which they fight, law enforcement will want to focus on the serious breach of law being perpetrated. Because terrorism is, by definition, carried out against innocent victims, legal authorities will seek to have the media focus on the injustice of the actions being taken by the group, and the criminal nature of the offense will be highlighted by noting the innocence of the victims. If the public can be made to view the terrorists as common criminals of a particularly nasty sort, then the government will clearly be viewed as the "good guys" rescuing the victims and ending the violence. To achieve this goal, the government clearly needs the media's cooperation.

## Denial of a Platform

It is certainly in the government's best interest not to allow terrorists to use the free press as a "bully pulpit" for their propaganda, or to enforce **denial of a platform.** Not only can a platform be used to generate understanding and perhaps sympathy for the terrorist's cause, but it can also be used to generate tangible support. The 1986 hijacking of TWA Flight 847 in Beirut gave explicit indication of the dangers of publicizing a platform. The skyjackers reportedly offered the press tours of the plane for $1,000 and a session with the hostages for $12,500! Although few situations ever become quite so chaotic, it is in most government's agenda to separate the terrorist from the media as far as possible, so that neither propaganda nor funds can be generated from the event.

## Information and Cooperation

While for most law enforcement agencies the optimum solution would be exclusion of the media and other observers from the area in which a terrorist event occurs, this is seldom an option in democratic systems. Instead, governments may encourage **information and cooperation.** They may want the media to share information that they might have about the individuals involved and to be careful not to share information with the hostage takers about data that might be of use to them. Thus, the media will be asked by governments to be discrete, careful not to reveal how successful operations were performed, and cautious about revealing information about an event that might provoke or enable a **copycat operation,** one in which a terrorist act is copied by an observer in a subsequent act. Cooperation may even, in some cases, be interpreted by the government by a willingness on the media's part to share **disinformation**—that is, inaccurate information designed to confuse—when such cooperation will help in resolving the threat in the terrorist action.

# MEDIA GOALS IN TERRORIST EVENTS

Few of these goals by police and terrorists for working with the media are compatible. Indeed, most are absolutely incompatible, since both sides seek "good" publicity, legitimacy, and cooperation. Before considering methods for resolving this problem in conflicting goals, let us briefly consider the goals of the media in reporting such events.

## Getting a Scoop

In a world with fast-breaking news, 24 hours a day, being the first to report the news—or **getting a scoop**—is a crucial goal. High-tech communications make it possible, and increase the pressure, to transmit news stories in "real time"—that is, as the event actually happen. This leaves little option for editing or carefully evaluating the impact of such a news release on the situation. In such situations, this may mean that stopping to discuss the impact of their reporting with public safety officers, noted as part of several goals of the law enforcement community, may be costly to the journalists, who stand to lose that scoop to a less scrupulous reporter.

## Dramatic Presentation of News

The media, in this fierce competition for public attention, clearly need to create a **dramatic presentation** of the event as well as a timely one. During the hijacking of TWA Flight 847 in June 1985, ABC broadcast extensive interviews with the hijackers and the hostages. Indeed, in one dramatic reel, a pistol was aimed at the pilot's head in a staged photo opportunity for the interviewers.[23] The media argue that the intense scrutiny they give to each aspect of the event actually protects the hostages. This view assumes that the primary goal of the act is to communicate a cause, drawing support from this explication. If drama is needed to demonstrate the seriousness of the cause, however, then the lives of hostages could be jeopardized by a media demand for drama. If killing a hostage, or a plane load of hostages, becomes the price of "drama," then media may be held responsible raising the stakes in the hostage game.

## Protection of Rights

The media has a strong commitment to the **protection of rights,** specifically the public's right to know about events as they occur. Usually, this does not mean that the media see their role as being in opposition to law enforcement. Most media seek to be professional and accurate, careful not to give out disinformation, and playing as constructive role as possible in the event. Freedom of speech is not an absolute and inviolable value; most democracies have experienced times when civil liberties, including free speech, have had to be curtailed in the interests of national security. As one scholar notes, the conflict discussed here between the media and law enforcement "is between our commitment to unhindered public discourse and the need for public security."[24] The concept of censorship of the press in most democracies is unacceptable; the idea of voluntary restraints by the press on itself is advocated, but it is difficult to evoke in a form flexible yet effective enough to satisfy all concerned. If democracies give up free speech to stop terrorism, then regardless of the "success" of this effort, the terrorists win, because the government and its citizens lose a fundamental part of their system. But an absolutely free press can cost lives. In the hijacking of TWA Flight 847 mentioned earlier, radio broadcasts alerted the hijackers aboard the Lufthansa jet that the captain of the plane was transmitting information to authorities on the ground. The hijackers then killed the captain. The press was free, and the cost was the pilot's life.

## Personal Security

The Committee to Protect Journalists, based in New York, notes that more than 300 journalists have been murdered since 1986 as a result of their work. In 1995 alone, according to this group's records, 45 were assassinated.[25] Thus, one of the goals of media is increasingly **personal security,** to be able to protect themselves both during and after terrorist operations. Journalists who interview terrorists are at risk, and those who fail to satisfy terrorists' goals of favorable understanding and publicity may be vulnerable to attack by the terrorists and their sympathizers.

## CONCLUSION

Technological progress in communications systems has made the media a potentially significant weapon in the terrorist arsenal. Whether the media are "the terrorist's best friend," as Lacquer has suggested, or an unwitting ally, as described by Schmid and de Graff's study, it seems clear that the media play a significant role in the "propaganda by the deed" that is modern terrorism.[26] The line between reporter of terrorist events and participant in these events, between impartial journalist and partisan advocate, if often quite thin and easily, if unintentionally, crossed.

Studies suggest that violent behavior can be learned and that copycat behavior among individuals and groups is common. Therefore, it is not unreasonable to assume that portrayal of terrorist events in the news may actually motivate terrorist behavior. This observation does not suggest that journalists are intentionally involved in the increase in terrorist incidents. Although journalists have sometimes interfered in situations to a degree that may have altered the course of the event, this effect is the exception rather than the rule.

A strong case can be made for the need for media to work with the government to devise workable guidelines in matters of media coverage of terrorism. These should include recommendations for working with law enforcement in setting reasonable limits on access to events, where appropriate, as well as self-regulating rules on the use, nonuse, or delayed use of information, technology, and opportunity, in ways that will best protect the lives endangered by the situation and the needs of citizens for a full account of events.

The goals discussed of terrorists, law enforcement, and the media are clearly intensely related and fundamentally incompatible in many respects. There is no greater challenge for democracies in the struggle to deal with terrorism today than that posed by the need to find a policy that is compatible with the tradition of a free and vigorous press. Democratic governments are confronted with the demand that they be able to reconcile the goals of the media with those of law enforcement in ways that do not satisfy the goals of terrorists. Prior restraints placed on access and censorship of press coverage of terrorist events are too high a price to pay for the dubious value of decreasing press reports of terrorist acts. Terrorists win significant victories against democracies when they force such measures.

This is a formidable, but not necessarily an impossible, task. The Report of the Task Force on Disorders and Terrorism (1976) made constructive suggestions regarding the synthesizing of the protection of First Amendment rights with the need for public security:

1. Limiting interviews during hostage situations
2. Delaying the release of inflammatory or sensitive information
3. Minimizing the intrusiveness of the media in the course of the terrorist events
4. Striving for balanced and noninflammatory coverage of such incidents

The standards suggested by the media during the 1990s often coincide with these recommendations. Most call for balanced coverage, which avoid the use of provocative catchwords and phrases. There is also agreement on the need not to offer to terrorists a platform for propaganda. But the media have strongly resisted the concept of government regulation, regarding this as censorship, with the government restricting freedom of speech/press in ways not compatible with constitutional protections. While most governments have constitutionally sanctioned powers of emergency that may be invoked, with a consequent limiting of freedom of speech, most democracies are unwilling to concede to terrorists their goal of destabilization by having to invoke such emergency provisions. Deciding which goals must be met, and what the acceptable cost will be for meeting them, will be a challenge that governments in the twenty-first century *must* meet.

One scholar of this thorny issue has succinctly stated the essence of this dilemma:

> The potential power of these [terrorist] groups seems to lie not in their threat to overthrow society by force of arms *per se,* but in their ability to symbolize the fragility and vulnerability of the social order and to force that order to subvert itself by eroding the liberal and democratic values upon which its own legitimacy is based.[27]

## *Evaluation*

1. Ralph Perl suggests several voluntary press coverage guidelines that offer insights on the pattern of self-restriction that may emerge. Consider each of these briefly, and decide which goals are placed at risk by each.

    a. Limiting information on hostages that could harm them (e.g., number, nationality, official positions, personal wealth, etc.)

    b. Limiting information of military movements during rescue operations

    c. Limiting or agreeing not to air live interviews with terrorists

    d. Toning down information that may cause widespread panic

    e. Checking sources of information carefully

2. Ted Koppel, anchor of ABC television's *Nightline,* suggests that American media operate at the outer boundaries of what its European allies would view as acceptable. He notes that "[American television is] particularly vulnerable to misuse. We are vulnerable to misuse by our own leaders. . . . The fact that terrorism by definition tends to be dramatic [and] the fact that by definition it tends to involve acts which are pictorial, makes us even more vulnerable."[28] How can this "vulnerability" be diminished without allowing terrorists to use media as a weapon—eliminating the former two vulnerabilities by making it subject to a third?

3. David Hubbard, a psychiatrist who has interviewed scores of imprisoned hijackers, contends that TV news broadcasts of ongoing terrorist events is "social pornography" because it "caters to the sick, unmet needs of the public."[29] He is convinced that world terrorism would decrease if television brought its coverage under control. How accurate do you think this assessment is? What kind of controls can a democratic society afford to impose on its media? What are the dangers of such controls? How effective do you think voluntary or involuntary controls on media coverage of terrorism would be in reducing either the number or the violence of terrorist events?

## *Suggested Readings*

Alali, A. Odasno, and Kenoye K Eke. "Terrorism, the News Media, and Democratic Political Order." *Current World Leaders* 39, no. 4 (August 1996), 64–72.

Alexander, Yonah, and Robert Patter. *Terrorism and the Media: Dilemma for Government, Journalism, and the Public.* Washington, D.C.: Brassey's, 1990.

Bar-Illan, D. "Israel, the Hostages, and the Networks." In *Terrorism*, ed. S. Anzovin. New York: Wilson, 1986, 108–120.

Bassiouni, M. C. "Media Coverage of Terrorism." *Journal of Communication* 32: 128–143.

———. *Terrorism, Law Enforcement, and the Mass Media.* Rockville, MD: NCJRS.

———. "Terrorism and the Media." *Journal of Criminal Law and Criminology* 72: 1–55.

Bell, J. B. *A Time of Terror: How Democratic Societies Respond to Revolutionary Violence.* New York: Basic Books, 1978.

Bering-Jensen, H. "The Silent Treatment for Terrorists." *Insight,* November 21, 1988, 27–41.

Dobson, Christopher, and Ronald Payne. *The Carlos Complex: A Study in Terror.* New York: Putnam, 1977.

Finn, John E. "Media Coverage of Political Terrorism and the First Amendment: Reconciling the Public's Right to Know with Public Order." In *Violence and Terrorism: 98/99* (New York: Dushkin/McGraw-Hill), 1998.

Fitzpatrick, T. E. "The Semantics of Terror." *Security Register* 1, no. 14 (November 4, 1974), 17–35.

Grossman, Lawrence K. "The Face of Terrorism." *The Quill* (June 1986), 12–19.

Hickey, Neil. "Gaining the Media's Attention." In *The Struggle against Terrorism.* New York: Wilson, 1977, 45–62.

Jenkins, Brian. "International Terrorism: The Other World War." A Project AIR FORCE Report prepared for the United States Air Force, November 1985.

———. *Terrorism: Trends and Potentialities.* Santa Monica, CA: Rand, 1977.

———. "Will Terrorists Go Nuclear?" P-5541. Santa Monica, CA: Rand, November 1975.

Kehler, C., G. Harvey, and R. Hall. "Perspectives on Media Control in Terrorist-Related Incidents." *Canadian Police Journal* 6: 225–243.

Kidder, Rushworth M. "Manipulation of the Media." In *Violence and Terrorism 98/99.* New York: Dushkin/McGraw-Hill, 1998.

Kupperman, Robert H., and Darrell M. Trent. *Terrorism: Threat, Reality and Response.* Stanford, CA: Hoover Institution Press, 1979.

Livingstone, W. D. "Terrorism and the Media Revolution." In *Fighting Back: Winning the War against Terrorism,* ed. N. C. Livingstone and T. E. Arnold. Lexington, MA: Heath, 1986, 213–227.

Miller, A. H. "Terrorism, the Media, and the Law: A Discussion of the Issues." In *Terrorism, the Media, and the Law,* ed. A. H. Miller. Dobbs Ferry, NY: Transnational Publishers, 1982, 13–50.

———. "Terrorism and the Media: Lessons from the British Experience." In *The Heritage Foundation Lectures.* Washington, D.C.: Heritage, 1990.

"New Horrors in a Long-Running Horror Show." *U.S. News & World Report,* April 4, 1988, 35–41.

Perl, Ralph F. *Terrorism, the Media, and the 21st Century.* Washington, D.C.: Congressional Research Service, 1998.

Russell, Charles A., and Bowman H. Miller. "Profile of a Terrorist." *Terrorism: An International Journal* 1 (1977): 24–48.

Schmid, A. P., and J. de Graff. *Violence as Communication: Insurgent Terrorism and the Western News Media.* Beverly Hills, CA: Sage, 1982.

Wardlaw, Grant. "State Response to International Terrorism: Some Cautionary Comments." Paper presented to the Symposium on International Terrorism, Defense Intelligence Agency, Washington, D.C., 1988.

Wilkinson, Paul. *Terrorism and the Liberal State.* New York: New York University Press, 1986.

## Endnotes

1. "Terrorism Found Rising, Now Almost Accepted," *Washington Post,* December 3, 1985, A4.
2. These quotes were gathered by Neil Hickey in "Gaining the Media's Attention," in *The Struggle against Terrorism* (New York: Wilson, 1977), 113–114.
3. Ibid., 117.
4. Ibid., 112.
5. T. K. Fitzpatrick, "The Semantics of Terror," *Security Register* 1, no. 14 (November 4, 1974), 23.

6. A. H. Miller, "Terrorism, the Media, and the Law: A Discussion of the Issues." In *Terrorism, the Media, and the Law,* ed. A. H. Miller (Dobbs Ferry, NY: Transnational Publishers, 1980), 43.

7. Abraham J. Miller, "Terrorism and the Media: Lessons from the British Experience." In the *Heritage Lectures.* (Washington, D.C.: Heritage, 1990), 1–9.

8. Alex P. Schmid and Janny F. A. de Graff. *Violence as Communication.* (Newbury Park, CA: Sage, 1982).

9. Ibid., 172.

10. Rushworth M. Kidder, "Manipulation of the Media." In *Violence and Terrorism 91/92* (New York: Dushkin, 1991), 118.

11. Henrik Bering-Jensen, "The Silent Treatment for Terrorists," *Insight* (November 21, 1988), 34.

12. Ibid., 35.

13. Paul Wilkinson, *Terrorism and the Liberal State* (New York: New York University Press, 1986).

14. Wilkinson, 8.

15. Billy M. Turner, "America: Bull's Eye for Terrorists?" *Security Management,* June 1987, 45.

16. Brian M. Jenkins, "High Technology Terrorism and Surrogate War: The Impact of New Technology on Low-Level Violence." In *Contemporary Terrorism: Selected Readings,* ed. J. D. Elliott and L. K. Gibson (Gaithersburg, MD: International Association of Chiefs of Police, 1978), 101.

17. Schmid and de Graff, *Violence as Communication,* 77.

18. Ibid., 42.

19. Grant Wardlaw, "State Response to International Terrorism: Some Cautionary Comments," paper presented to the Symposium on International Terrorism, Defense Intelligence Agency, Washington, D.C., 1985, 8.

20. Schmid and de Graff, *Violence as Communication,* 172.

21. Rushworth Kidder, "Manipulation of the Media," *Violence and Terrorism 98/99* (New York: Dushkin/McGraw Hill, 1988), 151.

22. Ibid., 152.

23. On June 13, 1985, two Hizballah gunmen hijacked this flight en route from Athens to Rome, and murdered U.S. Navy diver Robert Stethem after the plane landed in Beirut for a second time. The U.S. State Department was highly critical of the impact of the media on this event.

24. John E. Finn, "Media Coverage of Political Terrorism and the First Amendment: Reconciling the Public's Right to Know with Public Order." In *Terrorism and the Media: Dilemma for Government, Journalism and the Public,* ed. Yonah Alexander and Robert Latter (Washington, D.C.: Brassey's, 1990).

25. See Web site http://w.w.w.cpj.org/.

26. Schmid and de Graff, *Violence as Communication,* 172.

27. Ralph Perl, "Terrorism, the Media, and the 21st Century" (Washington, D.C.: Congressional Research Service, 1998) 2.

28. Kidder, "Manipulation of the Media," 53.

29. David Hubbard, *Skyjacker: His Flights of Fancy* (New York: Wilson, 1997), 124.

# Legal Perspectives on Terrorism

*International and transnational terrorism are nothing more nor less than the wanton and willful taking of human lives, the purposeful commission of bodily harm, and the intentional infliction of severe mental distress by force or threat of force.*

—Robert Friedlander

## Key Concepts

innocent persons
innocence
civilians
special provisions in the Geneva
   Convention
protected persons
rule of proportionality
*hostis humanis generis*
skyjacking

novation
provisions for jurisdiction
extradite
"gentleman's agreements"
attentat clause
"political" crime
political offenders
loophole in the law

If Friedlander's assessment of the nature of terrorism is correct, then one would assume that such acts would already be designated as common crimes in the legal codes of most countries. One could also be forgiven for assuming that international law, if it truly reflects the laws and mores of the international community, would reflect a similar tendency to declare such acts illegal.

The fact that this is not the case is perhaps due less to a lack of consensus about the desirability of such a law or even the criminality of "a willful and wanton taking of human life" than to the nature of the international system itself. In the international community, although there may well be general agreement on the undesirability of such things as war, racial discrimination, genocide, and other violations of basic human rights, there has been a significant reluctance to translate that agreement into workable treaties with enforcement powers.

Why, if nations generally agree with the idea of reducing the incidence of such evils, cannot workable methods of getting rid of them be constructed? The answer to this question must be the same as that given by municipal leaders when confronted with a question as to why a society's problems (e.g., poverty, unemployment, discrimination) are not being effectively eliminated. Unfortunately, consensus about the undesirability at any level is often difficult to translate into acceptable, enforceable rules and regulations that might remedy the situation. General policy directions are always easier to formulate than specific legislation.

Moreover, the constraints that make progress in creating such legislation difficult at the local and national level are magnified many times at the international level. An examination of at least a few of these constraints may help us to understand the dearth of international law on terrorism.

The first problem involves a lack of legislative authority. However inept one may consider state and national legislators to be, at least lawmaking bodies can be said to exist at such levels. But on the international level, no body is invested with such authority. The United Nations was certainly never designed to "rule" the nations of the world or to create rules for its governance.[1] The UN offers a forum for discussion, for cooperation and consensus building on issues. It does not make laws in the sense that governing bodies make laws for subordinate individuals and groups in the national arena.

There is, too, a distinct lack of central authority in the international community. To describe it even as a confederation is to invest it with properties that it does not really possess. A confederal system has mechanisms for governing at the top level, whereas no such system exists in any real sense at the international level. Not only is there no legislative body empowered to make laws, there is also neither an autocratic nor a democratic chief executive who is able to speak with authority for, and issue commands to, the community of nations.

Moreover, there is no judicial system to which all have recourse and whose decisions are binding at the international level. The International Court of Justice's decision-making authority depends for the most part on states' willingness to resolve a difficulty amicably and on their willingness to submit their disputes to the court for adjudication.[2]

So the most serious infractions of international law often go untouched by the court, because many states are not willing to submit their disputes for adjudication. A voluntary judicial system that can neither hail an offender to the bar of justice nor enforce compliance with its judgments, and that has no provisions by which entities other than states (e.g., individuals, groups, or corporations) can seek recourse for injustice, seems to be sadly lacking in judicial accouterments.

The international system, then, has no central authority figure or figures, provides only a forum for debate rather than lawmaking, and possesses only a voluntary (and frequently ineffective) judiciary. It is thus even less able than municipal governments to deal with the difficulties inherent in enacting and enforcing laws designed to eliminate societal problems. The political and enforcement problems that hamper the making of effective laws within nations are even more capable of preventing the successful completion of treaties designed for dealing with sensitive issues in the international community.

This incapacity is made worse by the absence of law enforcement officers. With the possible exception of INTERPOL (which, until the 1990s, was strictly charged to stay out of political problems), there does not appear to be, at the international level, anyone with the authority to act in this capacity. Just as there are few procedures for bringing a miscreant to justice, there is no one authorized to physically do so.

Lacking these instruments of governance most commonly found at the national level, the construction of rules at the international level has become an extremely delicate and difficult task. Political considerations of the nations in the international community are usually accommodated as fully as possible, because compliance with any rules is largely voluntary.

The more highly politicized the issue and the greater the perception of "national interests" involved, the more difficult it becomes to construct an effective treaty—that is, one that is both strong and acceptable. This may, as one scholar suggests, derive from the nature and scope of national interests' inevitable tension with political reality. When diverse national interests appear to oppose perceived common goals, as they often do in discussions on terrorism, then this "tension" becomes heightened to unworkable levels, according to this scholar.[3]

Recent history provides lots of examples of the hazards that abound when international law extends itself further than the limits of assured compliance within the community of nations. The most striking instance of such overextension may be the attempts to outlaw war, notably through the Kellogg-Briand pact.[4] In spite of the majority consensus that may be presumed to exist on the undesirability of war, it is not within the power of international law to enforce a prohibition of war.

More successful, perhaps, have been efforts within the international community to restrict certain highly undesirable practices during times of war. This was partially accomplished by putting together "rules of conduct" for times of war. Conventions about the treatment of prisoners of war and innocent civilian personnel, as well as some involving prohibitions of certain methods of warfare and weapons of war, have been more effective, in terms of compliance, that the ill-judged and altruistic Kellogg-Briand pact.

This success in creating laws to deal with specific aspects of generally undesirable behavior has important implications in terms of understanding the attempts by the international community to deal with the sensitive issue of terrorism. Attempts by the international community to construct general treaties dealing with terrorism have been largely unsuccessful. But on treaties or conventions that deal instead with specific aspects of terrorism, greater progress has been made. A quick review of the provisions and "success" record in preventing or punishing terrorism could make it easier to decide on the most effective ways for handling the problem of current and future terrorism.

First, let us examine portions of international law that do not deal specifically with terrorism but from which laws and regulations on terrorism have evolved. Three areas of international law come immediately to mind in this regard: laws of war, laws on piracy, and laws concerning the protection of diplomatic personnel and heads of state.

## LAWS OF WAR

International law has been divided by some scholars into laws of war and laws of peace. This can be somewhat confusing dichotomy, since some peacetime laws continue to apply even during times of war. However, it is true that the rules of behavior change in many respects during wartime. This change is usually in the direction of allowing greater latitude for suppressing or eliminating ordinary protections and courtesies. It is fair to say that, during times of war, more types of violence may be employed against a wider range of targets with far fewer safeguards for human rights than are permissible during times of peace.

This is not a tautological statement. It is instead an important point when one considers that it is the laws of war that are most often invoked by terrorists in justification of their acts. If, even under the rules that permit a broader range of acceptable actions, there are certain significant prohibited actions, then those actions could be said to be always prohibited, regardless of the provocation. If the laxity of safeguards that exists during times of war still does not allow certain actions the semblance of legality, then those actions could be regarded as unacceptable to the international community, both in times of war and in times of peace.

While the mass of rules and laws that govern warfare today has grown to immense proportions, a number of fundamental rules meet the criteria described earlier, in that they involve the establishment of minimum standards of behavior, even for parties engaged in hostilities. Of these rules of war, perhaps the most significant for this study are those affecting the treatment of **innocent persons.**

This category of persons is an extremely important one for students of terrorism. It is crucial to establish a clear understanding of what is meant by the term *innocent.* Terrorists have claimed that "there is no such thing as an innocent person,"[5] yet the Geneva Conventions extend special protections to "persons taking no active part in the hostilities."[6]

Innocence, as it is used by the laws of war, has much the same meaning as that found in any expanded international dictionary definition of the term. In both cases, *innocence* signifies freedom from guilt for a particular act, even when the total character may be evil. It is in one sense a negative term, implying as it does something less than righteous, upright, or virtuous. Legally, it is used to specify a lack of guilt for a particular act/crime, denoting a nonculpability.[7]

Innocence is thus imputed to a thief found innocent of the crime of murder. By this logic, even a government official guilty only of indifference can still be said to be "innocent" of any crime committed by his government. That official, in other words, has been guilty of nothing that would justify his summary execution or injury by terrorists with a grievance with his government.

This concept of a lack of guilt for a specific act is particularly appropriate in examining the random selection of "any Englishman, any Israeli" by terrorists as acceptable targets.[8] If "innocent person" status can only be removed by guilt for a specific act or crime committed by the person (not by others of the same age group, nationality, race, religion, or other similar categories), then there can be no legal justification for such a random selection of targets.

International law, like that of most civilized nations, neither recognizes nor punishes guilt by association. Records of the Nuremberg trials give credence to this point, in terms of the efforts made to establish personal guilt for specific criminal acts (e.g., murder or torture), instead of prosecuting simply on the basis of membership in the Nazi Party or Hitler's SS troops.[9] In refusing to punish all Germans or even all Nazi Party members for crimes against humanity and crimes of war, the precedent was established for differentiating between a person guilty of committing a crime during times of war and those who were innocent of actual wrongdoing.

The importance of this legal concept of innocence as an absence of guilt for a particular act cannot be overstated. The reason for its significance lies in the justification set forth by modern terrorists for their selection of victims. Many organizations that commit terrorist acts today do so on the premise that they are legitimately engaged in seeking to overthrow an existing government or to radically change existing conditions and are thus engaged in warfare.

Accepting, for the moment, this claim to revolutionary action, it is logical to assume that the actions of these groups should still conform to the rules of warfare. Terrorists have rejected the laws of peace as too restrictive to their revolutionary efforts. Let us instead test the legality of their actions according to the laws of war.

The Geneva Convention on the treatment of **civilians** demands special protections for "persons taking no active part in the hostilities." Nonactive status, like innocence, does not imply that the person is good, virtuous, or even disinterested in the outcome of the conflict. A person need only be innocent of participation in the hostilities to be protected by the convention. This means that membership in the civilian population of a nation against which a group is waging war is insufficient reason for according "guilty" status to a person, thereby removing those special protections. Thus, the waging of war against "any Israeli" or "any Englishman" is not acceptable behavior under the laws of war.

What are, then, the **special provisions in the Geneva Convention** relating to the treatment of civilians? First, this convention states that such persons "shall in all circumstances be treated humanely." Article III lists various actions that are prohibited "at any time and in any place whatsoever with respect to such persons." These prohibited acts include "violence to life and person, in particular murder of all kinds, mutilations, cruel treatment and torture; taking of hostages; and outrages upon the personal dignity, in particular humiliating and degrading treatment."[10]

Furthermore, in Article 27, the Geneva Convention on Civilians emphasizes the degree of legal protection afforded to these noncombatants, stating that "they are entitled, in all circumstances, to respect for their persons, their honor, their family rights, their religious convictions and practices, and their manners and customs . . . and shall at all times be treated humanely, and shall be protected especially against all acts of violence or threats thereof."[11]

Article 33 of the Geneva Convention for the Protection of Civilian Persons (1949) provides that

> [n]o protected person may be punished for an offense he or she has not personally committed. Collective penalties and likewise all measures of intimidation or terrorism are prohibited.
> Pillage is prohibited.
> Reprisals against protected persons and their property are prohibited.

**"Protected persons"** in this convention are civilians who have the misfortune to be living in a combat zone or occupied territory. Not only does this convention specifically prohibit the use of terrorism against this civilian population, but it also, in Article 34, prohibits the taking of hostages of any sort. Such rules make it clear that the kidnapping or murder of any civilian, even during times of war, to exact punishment for an injustice real or imagined is not legal unless the victim was directly responsible for the injustice.

This prohibition against collective punishment applies to states as well as to revolutionary organizations. Control Council Law No. 10, used in the Nuremburg trials of war criminals, makes this point clear.[12] Neither side in an armed conflict, whether involved in the "liberation" of a country or in the efforts of the state to maintain itself while under attack, may engage in warfare against the civilian population.

Terrorist acts against innocent persons by the state, as well as acts of terrorism by nonstate groups, are as illegal in times of war as they are in times of peace. The laws of war offer neither justification nor protection for the willful and wanton taking of innocent life. If terrorism by its very nature involves victimizing an innocent third party to achieve a political goal and to evoke a particular emotional response in an audience, then it seems reasonable to say that terrorism is illegal under the laws of war.

While this convention was drafted with the protection of civilians in occupied territories in mind, Protocols I and II, drafted in 1976, extend these protections to civilians in nonoccupied territories. Article 46 of Protocol I codifies the customary international law doctrine that the civilian population as such, as well as individual citizens, may not be made the object of direct military attack. One significant provision in this article states, "Acts or threats of violence which have the primary object of spreading terror among the civilian population are prohibited." This article goes on to prohibit indiscriminate attacks that are "of a nature to strike military objectives and civilians or civilian objectives without distinction." It further states that "a bombardment that treats as a single military objective a number of clearly separated and distinct military objectives located within a city, town or village, or other area which has a concentration of civilians is considered to be indiscriminate and is therefore prohibited."

What does this mean, in terms of legal restraints on terrorism? It means, for one thing, that a state may not commit an attack on a city or town as a whole, just on the basis of information that insurgents or combatants may be making a base in that area. To do so would be to commit an act of terrorism under international law. These conventions, in other words, make it clear that states as well as groups are prohibited from punishing the innocent in efforts to stop the insurgents in guerrilla warfare. To do so would be to commit acts of terrorism.

Article 50 of Protocol I attempts to make clear the precautions that a state and a revolutionary army must make in conducting an attack. This article also codifies customary international law concerning what is called the **rule of proportionality.** Generally speaking, this refers to the need for the loss of civilian life to be minimal compared with the military advantage gained. It states specifically that those who plan or decide upon an attack must "refrain from deciding to launch any attack which may be expected to cause incidental loss of civilian life . . . which would be excessive in relation to the concrete and direct military advantage anticipated."

In simple terms, this provision, along with other provisions in the article, means that those launching or planning to launch an attack are legally responsible for making sure that the military objectives that they expect to gain justify the minimal loss of civilian life that may occur. This provision is extremely practical. It recognizes a basic fact of life during war: there are inevitably civilians on and around military targets who will no doubt be injured or killed during an attack on those targets.

There are two important points here. One is that the objective is assumed to be a military, never a civilian, target. The law makes it clear that, whereas legitimate attacks may be expected against military targets, there is no legal expectation or right to launch attacks against civilian targets. On the contrary, the civilians within the target zone are to be protected against the effects of that attack, as far as it is militarily possible.

The other point is that, although military reality makes note of the fact that some civilian injury may occur during an attack, the injury or deaths of civilians should be incidental to the operations, on a scale proportionate to the military objective sought. If civilian casualties are expected to be high, then the attack cannot be justified under international law.

Two thoughts come to mind with respect to these provisions. One is that guerrilla or revolutionary groups that select predominantly civilian targets are in violation of international law, even if there is a military target that may also be hit. Thus, the fact that a café is frequented by members of an enemy military does not make it a legitimate target, because there would be a great likelihood of many civilian casualties in such an attack. If the target area is populated predominantly with civilians, then it cannot be a justifiable military target.

The other thought that this provision evokes is that states may not strike civilian settlements, even if guerrilla soldiers are taking refuge or making their headquarters in such settlements. To attack such places would mean inflicting unacceptably high levels of civilian casualties in proportion to the military objective sought. Thus, those who seek to destroy Palestinian revolutionaries, for example, may not, under international law, drop bombs on Palestinian refugee camps, because such camps have large civilian populations, including women and children, the sick and the infirm.

It is true that those revolutionaries who make their headquarters in the midst of civilian encampments are deliberately placing those civilians at risk in the ensuing war. But this point does not justify the attacking of such settlements by the enemy. The civilians have, for the most part, no choice but to be there, in their own homes or shelters. The state seeking to destroy the revolutionaries cannot take advantage of their vulnerable state to make war on the insurgents at a cost of countless civilian lives. Even when seeking to destroy an enemy who takes refuge among protected persons, a state may not deliberately wage war on those protected persons.

## PIRACY OF AIR AND SEA

If, during times of war, terrorist acts against innocent persons are illegal, then it seems logical to assume that such acts are also illegal during peacetimes. Indeed, the term *crimes against humanity* used to describe war crimes at Nuremberg did not originate with laws of war but with laws of peace. The term was used in international legal writings to describe acts of piracy. The famous English jurist, Sir Edward Coke, in the time of James I, described pirates as ***hostis humanis generis,*** meaning "common enemies of mankind."[13]

National case law confirms this view of piracy as an international crime. The U.S. Supreme Court, in the case of *U.S. v. Smith* (1820), went on record through Justice Joseph Story as declaring piracy to be "an offense against the law of nations" and a pirate to be "an enemy of the human race."[14] Judge John Bassett Moore of the World Court reaffirmed this assessment in his opinion in the famous *Lotus* case (1927).[15]

In fact, from the Paris Declaration of 1856 to the Geneva Convention of 1958, the proliferation of treaties dealing with aspects of terror-violence on the high seas has helped to codify international law with regard to piracy.[16] Piracy—of the sea, at least—is one of the first and most universally recognized "international crimes."

Nations have not been so willing to deal, through international law, with modern **skyjacking,** which some legal experts have termed *air piracy.* One legal expert has suggested the "the legal status of aerial hijackers could become the same as sea pirates through the process of novation wherein the former would be presumed to stand in the shoes of the latter."[17] Theoretically, this would provide a way to bring perpetrators of skyjacking under the existing legal restrictions and penalties imposed on crimes of a similar nature (i.e., sea piracy), that were more common in an earlier era.

**Novation** is not a complicated process. Legally, it refers to the substitution of a new indebtedness or obligation, creditor or debtor, for an existing one. In other words, aerial hijackers would assume the legal "indebtedness" of sea pirates under international law. Thus, it would not be necessary to create new international law to deal with what is, in many respects, a very old form of criminal activity.

But modern nations have not seen such a process as an adequate or acceptable solution. Instead, three major agreements on aircraft hijacking have evolved in recent years, as well as a number of smaller agreements between nations concerned with this crime. A short review of these agreements sheds some light on the state of the law with regard to this modern form of piracy.

One of the more successful antihijacking agreements in recent years has been the Memorandum of Understanding on Hijacking of Aircraft and Vessels and Other Offenses signed by the United States and Cuba on February 15, 1973.[18] In spite of a denunciation of the agreement by Cuba in October 1976, there has been a rather impressive record of interstate cooperation in combating aerial hijacking between the two countries. Many of the hijacking attempts that have occurred between the United States and Cuba since 1978 have resulted in the prompt return of the hijacked aircraft and the somewhat less prompt seizure for prosecution of the hijackers.

But treaties of a broader nature have met with less success. Three issues that need to be addressed in any successful hijacking convention have not been adequately resolved: determining who has jurisdiction, establishing a prosecutable offense, and providing for prompt processing of extradition requests.

The Convention on Offenses and Certain Other Acts Committed on Board Aircraft, signed in Tokyo on September 14, 1963, provided a general basis for the establishment of jurisdiction—that is, legal authority to exercise control. The hijacking of an aircraft is an act that often takes place in flight en route between countries. Such planes are often registered to yet another country and carry citizens of many countries. So a decision as to who has the right to bring a hijacker to justice is often a difficult one.

Article 3 of the Tokyo Convention provides that the state of registration is the one that has the first and primary right to exercise jurisdiction.[19] But this convention does not place on any signatory nation the responsibility to ensure that all alleged offenders will be prosecuted. Thus, a nation may accept jurisdiction and then refuse or neglect to bring the offenders to justice.

The subsequent Convention for the Suppression of Unlawful Seizure of Aircraft, signed in The Hague on December 16, 1970, deals more specifically with the issues of extradition and prosecution. This convention obliges contracting states to make the offense of unlawful seizure of aircraft punishable by severe penalties.

This convention offers a definition for the actions that may constitute the offense of skyjacking, in Article 1, which states that any person commits an offense who on board an aircraft in flight

1. Unlawfully, by force or threat thereof, or by any other means of intimidation, seizes, or exercises control of, that aircraft, or attempts to perform any such act; or,

2. Is an accomplice of a person who performs or attempts to perform any such act.

Although not as explicit as the later convention drawn up in Montreal, this convention does provide an important legal framework for prosecution of an offense, reasonably and clearly defined in legal terms that are directly applicable in the legal systems of many states (meaning that the states are thus not given the sticky political task of creating laws to make such acts a legal offense).

Under this convention, too, **provisions for jurisdiction** were extended. Three states were legally given the responsibility for jurisdiction, in the following order of precedence: "(1) the State of registration; (2) the State of first landing; and, (3) the State in which the lessee has its principal place of business or permanent residence." Moreover, this convention requires each contracting state to take measures to establish jurisdiction, if the offender is within its territory and is not to be extradited.

This convention also addresses the issue of prosecution, obligating each contracting state to either **extradite** (i.e., to send the person to another state seeking to prosecute) an alleged offender or to submit the case "without exception whatsoever to its competent authorities for the purpose of prosecution." While it does not create an absolute obligation to extradite, the convention states that the offense referred to is deemed to be included as an extraditable offense in any existing extradition treaties between contracting states and in every future extradition treaty concluded between such states.

The Convention for the Suppression of Unlawful Acts against the Safety of Civil Aviation signed in Montreal on September 23, 1971, adds more detail to the description of the offenses affecting aircraft and air navigation. It includes

1. Acts of violence against a person on board an aircraft in flight if that act is likely to endanger the safety of that aircraft; or

2. Destruction of an aircraft in service or damage to such an aircraft which renders it incapable of flight or which is likely to endanger its safety in flight; or,

3. Placing or causing to be placed on an aircraft in service, by any means whatsoever, a device or substance which is likely to destroy that aircraft, or to cause damage to it which is likely to endanger its safety in flight; or,

4. Destruction or damage of air navigation facilities or interference with their operation, if any such act is likely to endanger the safety of the aircraft in flight; or,

5. Communication of information which is known to be false, thereby endangering the safety of the aircraft in flight.[20]

In spite of these efforts to specify the crime and to establish procedures for deciding who has jurisdiction over the crime, large gaps remain in international legal efforts to deal with skyjacking today. There is little to compel a contracting state to honor its paper commitment to extradite or punish a terrorist who has hijacked a plane. This matter has become painfully evident in recent years, as the pressure and threats from powerful terrorist organizations have forced several Western nations to evade their responsibilities under these conventions. There are no sanctions or enforcement procedures in any of these conventions; they are, in effect, **"gentlemen's agreements,"** dependent for their enforcement on the integrity of the contracting states.

Efforts to achieve an independent enforcement convention during the ICAO Extraordinary Assembly in September 1973 ended in failure. Several proposals were made at that assembly with the aim of broadening the effectiveness of international control over interference with aircraft. A new multilateral convention was proposed, establishing an international commission with the power to investigate alleged violations of the enforcement provisions of the Tokyo, Hague, and Montreal conventions. It provided for sanctions against states that refused to comply with the commission's recommendations. (One of the contemplated sanctions was the collective suspension of flights to and from such a state.) None of the proposals were passed by the assembly.

## PROTECTION OF DIPLOMATIC PERSONNEL AND HEADS OF STATE

Similar difficulties have hindered efforts to create effective protections against attacks on diplomatic personnel and heads of state. In light of the seizure of American diplomatic personnel in Iran, which was never formally "punished" as a crime under international law, it could be argued that there still exists no effective international law concerning such acts. However, laws do exist (in spite of the fact that they are broken without punishment) on this politically sensitive subject. Because these laws concern terrorism of a specific sort, they deserve consideration here.

Perhaps the unwillingness to punish, or even to condemn, those guilty of attacks on these "protected persons" has its roots in the venerable Western tradition of granting political asylum to offenders who have committed political crimes. Although concern for the preserving of societal order influenced some Western European governments to modify their positions on granting asylum for political crimes, political asylum remains the primary focus in extradition questions in many modern states.

In 1833, Belgium enacted a law providing for nonextradition of political offenders, a principle incorporated into a Franco-Belgium treaty in 1834.[21] Following attempts, both successful and unsuccessful, on the lives of heads of state in subsequent years, however, an **attentat clause** began to be incorporated into successive treaties. This clause made the murder or attempted murder of any head of state or his or her immediate family a common (not political) crime. These clauses stated essentially that such attempts "shall not be considered a political offense or an act connected with such an offense."[22]

In 1957, the European Convention on Extradition invoked the principle of the attentat clause by making assaults on heads of state and their immediate families non-political offenses.[23] The Vienna Convention on Diplomatic Relations gave evidence of a broadening concern for diplomats as well as heads of state. Under this convention, it is made "the responsibility of the States to prevent attacks on a diplomatic agent's person, freedom, or dignity."[24] This broadly stated concern and general delegation of authority, however, has failed to secure significant enforceable protections for diplomats. As one expert expressed it, "what was needed, beyond the incidental tightening of police measures, is a constant vigilance on the part of states, acting individually and collectively in an organized way, to prevent the occurrence of incidents."[25]

But while subsequent treaties on this subject have attempted to make clear the specific acts that are prohibited and the states that have a right to claim jurisdiction over the crime, serious flaws remain in the protection afforded to diplomatic agents today. No collective, organized approach to the problem has evolved.

Furthermore, the delegation of responsibility for protecting and punishing in the event of attacks on diplomats creates serious problems, when the government of a state is itself a party to, or a tacit accessory to, the taking of diplomatic hostages. It is clearly useless to expect a government that actively or tacitly approves of such a crime to prosecute its perpetrators. Such a requirement could mean that the government must at some point prosecute itself for committing what it obviously did not regard as an illegal act—a most unlikely scenario!

One further development in the law regarding the protection of diplomatic personnel should be noted. The Venice Statement on Taking of Diplomatic Hostages, issued by the Heads of State and Government of the Seven Summit Countries during their meeting in Venice in 1980, not only expressed grave concern about the Iranian hostage situation but also called on nations to ratify the recently completed Convention against the Taking of Hostages, adopted by the UN General Assembly on December 17, 1979. Completed shortly after the seizure of the American Embassy in Teheran, this convention effectively makes it a crime to take *any* person as a hostage. The protection of international law is extended to every individual, regardless of his or her position (or lack of one), with the exception of those in armed forces engaged in armed conflict.

This broadening of the law in this respect suggests that nations consider certain actions unacceptable to the community of nations. Just as in laws of war, we have noted that certain actions were prohibited at all times, whether at war or at peace, so we note that there are some actions that the international community has come to believe are unacceptable, regardless of the cause.

## SUMMARY: PROTECTION OF THE INNOCENT AGAINST SPECIFIC CRIMES

Although limitations persist on the extent of the protection provided by the conventions reviewed thus far, several significant points illustrate the strengths—and weaknesses—of international law on terrorism contained in these examples. Certainly, two international crimes already reviewed, air piracy and hostage taking, offer several interesting points that may be briefly recapitulated and summarized to good effect at this point.

Innocence, as noted earlier, connotes not virtue but an absence of guilt for a particular act. The international laws governing piracy protect those considered innocent in the most common meaning of the word, those whose only "crime" was to be in the wrong place at the wrong time. Similarly, the expanded law on hostage taking propounded by the 1979 convention offers legal protection to a similarly innocent person.

However, the laws on the protection of diplomatic personnel, including the 1979 convention, offer a broader concept of the innocent person and his or her right to the protection of the law. Diplomats, consular agents, and similar governmental agents are precisely that: agents who carry out the policies of a government. As the Nuremberg trials demonstrated, it is possible to hold such persons legally responsible if their actions transgress the laws of nations.

That is the crucial point, though: it must be their *own* actions, not merely any of a variety of actions of the government that they represent, that transgress the law. It is not enough that their government adheres to unacceptable or illegal policies. If the agent is to be punished for those policies, then personal guilt (in terms perhaps of the carrying out of illegal policies, such as genocide) must be established before the agent can be punished. Thus, although such persons are perhaps less innocent than, for example, the tourist who boards an airplane that is subsequently hijacked, government agents cannot legally be "punished" (taken hostage or executed) unless they can be proven guilty of a specific illegal action.

By the same token, the representative of a multinational corporation must be considered legally innocent unless proven guilty of a specific crime. Thus, the kidnapping of a multinational corporation employee for ransom, to redress perceived exploitation by the company of a nation's resources, would be without legal justification.

International law, it appears, extends its protection to those truly innocent of any crime as well as those who could only be considered guilty of association with a government or corporation whose actions may be unjust. The law regards both types of persons as being sufficiently innocent to merit protection. Indeed, as the Nuremberg tribunals demonstrated, even individual governmental agents thought to be guilty of heinous "crimes against humanity" were nevertheless given a trial by law rather than a summary execution.

This presumption of innocence, which precludes summary judgment, is a major stumbling block to the justification of terrorism. The taking of any innocent life, however meritorious the cause to which the act is designed to call attention, cannot be justified under international law. No wrong can justify, or require, the commission of another wrong to rectify it. To accept such a premise would be to agree that the end for which one strives can serve to justify the means that one employs to attain it.

This does not leave revolutionary groups with no legitimate targets. While the range of innocent persons protected by international law is fairly broad, it is not absolutely inclusive. Military and police officials, for example, are far less clearly "innocent," in any sense of the term, particularly in regimes that practice forms of state terrorism. International law prohibits the summary taking of innocent life. The extent to which terrorism violates this prohibition is a measure of its transgression of the law.

## TERRORISM: A POLITICAL CRIME?

The definition of what constitutes a "political" crime has become a crucial part of the modern legal debate concerning terrorism. The crux of the problem appears to be in deciding how one determines what is and what is not a political crime. It is a problem that is far from solved and one whose political ramifications may well make it, for the present, insoluble.

For centuries, the nature of a **political crime** rested largely on the intended victim of the crime. That is, the assassination of a head of state or of a diplomat was regarded as being political in nature, and therefore to be handled differently—more leniently or more severely, depending upon the state's system of laws—than an ordinary, nonpolitical offense, such as the murder of an ordinary citizen.

If such a criteria were applied to many terrorist acts today, such as the hijacking of an airplane or the bombing of a café, then such acts would not, on the surface, qualify as being political. The argument could be (and indeed has been) made that the real intended "victims" of such crimes are the governments who are forced to watch helplessly and perhaps ultimately capitulate as the events unfold.

But to make the assumption that a victim is involved beyond the obvious captives or casualties, one is forced to rely on knowledge or inference about the motives of the perpetrators. In other words, the action would be described as a political crime not specifically by its intended victim but by the motives that prompted its commission.

This reasoning poses at least two problems. First, to make such a determination concerning a motive for an action, the person rendering the judgment would have to have a knowledge of why the terrorists committed the crime. How is such knowledge to be obtained? Does it come from propaganda put out by the terrorists, which is designed to persuade but is not necessarily truthful? Does it come from interviews with the perpetrators or their allies, assuming such interviews could be arranged? Is there any way, indeed, to discover the facts concerning the motive for a crime? To search for a factual basis is not useless by any means, but the attribution of a motive for any crime, political or common, is essentially a judgment call. In the courts of most civilized nations, assessment of motivation may affect the degree of severity with regard to the prosecution or sentencing, but it has little effect on the decision as to whether or not a crime has been committed.

Yet if one allows motivation to be the determinant for delineating political from common crimes, there is reason to suspect that, for crimes judged to be political in motivation, there will in fact be neither prosecution nor sentencing. This is the second problem in allowing motivation to be the guiding factor in determining what constitutes a political crime. For under the laws of many nations, **political offenders** are accorded special status. Those believed guilty of political offenses are eligible for the granting of political asylum by friendly states. States granting such asylum are under no legal obligation to prosecute the perpetrator for the crime.

Even those who are prosecuted are afforded special treatment. Seldom are political criminals jailed with those who have committed common crimes. To be a political prisoner confers, in many nations, a unique status on the offender. There is nothing wrong with this: political crimes are not the same as common crimes. Their perpetrators are often regarded as being motivated by high ideals for political change for which they are willing to pay a high personal price, often imprisonment or even death.

That is another important point, however. Just like the perpetrator of any other crime, the political offender does so with the knowledge of, even the acceptance of, the penalty that must be paid for the crime. Perpetrators of political crimes in earlier centuries committed their offenses in the full expectation of being required to pay the legal penalty for their crimes. Those who would classify terrorism as a political crime today do so to enable its perpetrators to evade the payment of those penalties. The concept of "political offense" has become a loophole through which terrorists try to avoid having to pay the just penalty for their crimes.

This **loophole in the law,** which allows political offenders to escape extradition or even punishment, has worried international legal experts for years. Attempts have been made to advocate the creation of an international criminal code and an international criminal court. Under these innovations, terrorism could be specified as an international crime, punishable in international court. But although the efforts to create an international criminal court progressed dramatically in 1998, even lacking endorsement by the United States, the leaders working in Italy to construct the code for this court were unable to resolve both practical legal and political problems relating to international terrorism. Indeed, it is interesting and discouraging to note that the issue of terrorism was removed early in the conference as a crime for which this international criminal court would be expected to adjudicate. So the loophole of political offender still allows terrorists to commit heinous crimes for "political" purposes and escape the hand of justice.

## *Evaluation*

International law is perhaps most useful as a measure of international concern and opinion on an issue such as terrorism. Lacking methods and mechanisms for enforcement, it cannot be said to be an effective deterrent to terrorism, either on the national or the international level. Because its formulation is so ad hoc, relying on loose associations of states rather than any legislative body to draft conventions, it is somewhat less than coherent and often indecisive. Political considerations often weaken the resolve of nations to deal with politically sensitive subjects.

Lacking a judiciary empowered to adjudicate without the consent of all parties, and lacking an executive or police force to enforce the laws, international law on terrorism has evolved as a patchwork of treaties. Among the most successful have been those relating to specific types of terrorism. Even these treaties, however, have been seriously hampered by political concerns relating to issues of jurisdiction, prosecution, extradition, and political asylum. Nor will the new international criminal court, as it comes into fruition, be of significant help in filling this absence of international legal authority.

As a means for combating terrorism, then, international law appears to be a somewhat dubious tool. When agreements are entered into that have enforcement capabilities, then such laws can be used to curb terrorism. But to date, few such agreements are in force within the international community.

Two other types of international legal agreements on terrorism have been attempted, however. Consider each of the following descriptions of international legal efforts to deal with terrorism. Decide which, if any, have a reasonable chance of success, given what you now know about the problems of enforcement and adjudication.

1. From July 16 to August 11, 1973, three ad hoc UN committees met to define international terrorism, its underlying causes, and measures for its prevention. Virtually every participant in the general debate in the plenary session of the General Assembly before the issue was sent to the Legal Committee had found it necessary to issue a detailed separate position statement on the issue. The Legal Committee found the issue too politically hot to handle. Will it be possible for a body, such as the UN, to create general international law on an issue such as terrorism?

2. A Convention on the Suppression of Terrorism was adopted November 10, 1976, by the Committee of Foreign Ministers of the Council of Europe. Modeled after Europe's fairly successful Convention on Human Rights, which has both an active administrative and judicial arm, this convention seeks to outlaw certain types of terrorist acts. The problems regarding jurisdiction and prosecution appear to be somewhat resolved, but the issue of extradition was too politically sensitive to handle effectively. Can a general treaty on terrorism, undertaken by states with a common legal and political heritage, succeed where similar ones by the entire community of nations have failed?

3. The creation of an international criminal court (ICC) could have offered a solution to the "politicization" of the crime of terrorism. If the new ICC could have included in its code laws on terrorism, its impact might have been dramatic. Some who have advocated such a system suggest that it include such things as an international prison, to allow states to rid themselves of terrorist prisoners whom the states may be under pressure by other terrorists to release. On whose territory should this international prison be located? Who would supply the maintenance of such a prison? Who would have the right to release a prisoner from that prison on parole? Would anyone have the right to grant clemency to a prisoner? Would, in fact, placing such powers in the hands of the ICC create as many problems as it would solve, even with respect to terrorism?

## Suggested Readings

Bremer, L. Paul, III. "Terrorism and the Rule of Law." U.S. State Department, Bureau of Public Affairs, Current Policy No. 847, April 23, 1987.

Clough, Patricia. "Proposed West German Law to Tackle Terrorism Sparks Dissent." *Christian Science Monitor*, November 10, 1986, 2–3.

Friedlander, Robert A. *Terrorism: Documents of International and Local Control.* Dobbs Ferry, NJ: Oceana, 1979.

Howe, Irving. "The Ultimate Price of Random Terror." *Skeptic: The Forum for Contemporary History,* January–February 1986, 12–17.

Joyner, Nancy D. *Aerial Hijacking as an International Crime.* Dobbs Ferry, NJ: Oceana, 1974.

Levi, Werner. *Contemporary International Law: A Concise Introduction.* Boulder, CO: Westview, 1989.

Rozakis, Christos L. "Terrorism and the Internationally Protected Person in Light of the ILC's Draft Articles." *International and Comparative Law Quarterly* 23 (January 1974), 33–41.

Sofaer, Abraham D. *The Political Offense Exception and Terrorism.* U.S. Department of State, Bureau of Public Affairs, Current Policy No. 762, August 1, 1985.

Tokyo Convention on Offenses and Certain Other Acts Committed on Board Aircraft.

## *Endnotes*

1. As Werner Levi points out in his text *Contemporary International Law: A Concise Introduction* (Boulder, CO: Westview, 1979), a degree of political cooperation is only implied, not stated, in the UN Charter (P. 265–268). Considerable difference of opinion as to a legal obligation for political cooperation by member states continues to exist today.

2. See the Statute of the International Court of Justice, 6 U.S.T. 3517, T.I.A.S. No. 3043, 74 U.N.T.S. 244 (1944).

3. Stanley Hoffman, in his article "International Law and the Control of Force" (*International and Comparative Law Quarterly,* 32 [June 1995] 22), suggests, for example, that "peace" as a common goal is a weak tool. He asserts that many states embrace doctrines that have stated goals of protracted confrontation and ultimate conquest—goals that are incompatible with this "common" goal of peace.

4. See the Treaty for the Renunciation of War (Paris: August 27, 1928), 46 Stat. 2343, 94 L.N.T.S., 57.

5. Statement credited to Emile Henry, a nineteenth-century French anarchist who bombed a crowded Paris café, killing 1 customer and wounding 20 others. At his trial Henry is reported to have said that his only regret was that more people had not been killed. His reply to the judge's exclamations that "those were innocent victims that you struck" has formed the dogma of "collective guilt" that is often invoked to justify indiscriminate acts of terror.

6. Convention Relative to the Protection of Civilian Persons in Time of War, U.S.T. 3516, T.I.A.S. No. 3365, 75, U.N.T.S. 287 (1949).

7. See Funk and Wagnall's *Standard Comprehensive International Dictionary* (Chicago: Ferguson, 1987) vol. 1, 653.

8. Irving Howe, "The Ultimate Price of Random Terror," *Skeptic: Forum for Contemporary History* 11, no. 58 (January–February 1976).

9. See the Judgment of the International Military Tribunal, Nuremberg, September 30, 1946. vol. 22 Trial of the Major War Criminals before the International Military Tribunal Proceedings, 411, 427, 459, 461, and 463 (1948).

10. Marjorie M. Whiteman, *Digest of International Law* (Washington, D.C.: Department of State, 1968), vol. 11, chap. 35, Article 2, 3518–3520.

11. Whiteman, *Digest of International Law,* Article 32, 3528.

12. This law defines as criminal "atrocities and offenses, including but not limited to murder, extermination, enslavement, deportation, imprisonment, torture, rape or other inhuman acts committed against any civilian population . . . whether or not in violation of the domestic laws of the country where perpetrated."

13. Quoted by Robert Friedlander, *Terrorism: Documents of International and Local Control* (Dobbs Ferry, NJ: Oceana, 1979), 18.

14. *U.S. v. Smith,* 18 U.S. (5 Wheat.) P. 71, 73–75 (1820).

15. The case of the *S.S. Lotus,* P.C.I.J., Series A, No. 10 (1927), 2 Hudson, World Court Rep., 20.

16. See "Harvard Research in International Law: Piracy," *American Journal of International Law* 26 (1932): 739, 754, 759–60. See also the text of Geneva Convention on the High Seas, 13 U.S.T., 2312, T.I.A.S. No. 5200, 450 U.N.T.S. 82, and Article 100 of the Third United Nations Conference on the Law of the Sea, A/Conf. 62/WP. 10/Rev. 1 (April 28, 1979).

17. Friedlander, *Terrorism,* 13. For further insights on this subject, see Nancy Joyner, *Aerial Hijacking as an International Crime* (Dobbs Ferry, N.J.: Oceana, 1974).

18. 24 U.S.T. 737, T.I.A.S. No. 7579 (1973); *International Legal Materials* (1973), vol. 12, 370.

19. Tokyo Convention on Offenses and Certain Other Acts Committed on Board Aircraft, signed September 14, 1963.

20. Convention for the Suppression of Unlawful Acts against the Safety of Civil Aviation, signed in Montreal on September 23, 1971.

21. Extradition Treaty, November 22, 1834, France-Belgium, Articles 5 and 6, *Recueil des Traites* (France), 278, 84 Perry's T.S., 456.

22. See, for example, the Treaty of Extradition between the United States and Venezuela, January 19, 1922, Article 3, 43 Stat. 1698, T.S. 675, 49 L.N.T.S. 435.

23. Convention of Extradition, December 13, 1957, 24 Europe T.S., 173–175.

24. Signed April 18, 1961, 500 U.N.T.S. 95.

25. See comments by Christos L. Rozakis in "Terrorism and the Internationally Protected Person in Light of the ILC's Draft Articles," *International and Comparative Law Quarterly,* 23 (January 1974), 72.

# Counterterrorism:
# The Use of Special Forces

*As soon as men decide that all means are permitted to fight an evil, then their good becomes indistinguishable from the evil that they set out to destroy.*

—Christopher Dawson

## Key Concepts

| | |
|---|---|
| Munich massacre | secrecy and surprise |
| strike forces | killer course |
| Sarayat Matkal | GSG9 |
| Special Night Squads | Mogadishu |
| Irgun | Joint Operations Command |
| King David Hotel | Delta Force |
| Entebbe raid | Seal Team Six |
| SAS | Special Operations Wing |
| Operation Nimrod | Operation Eagle's Claw |

Although international laws of war and peace make it clear that terrorist acts have begun to be regarded as illegal, a cohesive framework capable of guiding the actions of nations confronted with, or perpetrating, terrorism does not yet exist. In the absence of such a framework, the burden of regulating the acts has fallen on individual nation-states.

Recent history abounds with examples of individual state efforts to combat the problem of international terrorism, revealing both the dangers and the degree of success they have achieved. The success and failure of the efforts, and an assessment of the price paid for both success and failure, provide interesting insights into the strengths and limitations of nations waging single-handed war on terrorism.

Moreover, if international law truly grows or evolves from international norms, then it may be that strategy for dealing with international terrorism internationally will strongly resemble those strategies found to be successful among nations individually. Thus, a review of the responses of nations to terrorism today may provide some clues as to the shape of international responses in the future.

## NATIONS WITHOUT DEFENSES

It has been said that the Munich massacre of Israeli athletes by Black September terrorists at the Olympic games in 1972 marked the turning point in the Western world's indifference toward terrorism.[1] Until then, few if any of the nations most frequently the victims of terrorist attacks had made any coherent policy for combating terrorism. Although CIA analysts have concluded that "terrorists continue to prefer operations in the industrialized democracies of Western Europe and North America,"[2] the very characteristics that cause nations to be included in this category also make it difficult for them to organize defenses against terrorist attacks.

In liberal democracies, dissent is part of the very fabric of the social and political milieu. This adherence to an almost absolute right to disagree sometimes creates conditions that allow radical dissent to become violent opposition before governments are able to prepare for this transformation. In West Germany, for example, before the publicized exploits of the Baader-Meinhof gang, any hint of the formation of an elite army or police unit to combat terrorism would have provoked a storm of protest inside (and outside) the country. Similarly, the United States, where both the army and the public bore scars from the traumas of Vietnam and Watergate, was in no condition to prepare for terrorist threats. This was due partly to the demoralizing effect of the Vienam War on the army's special units and partly to the perceived need to curtail (rather than expand) domestic surveillance operations.

Nor were these nations alone in their lack of preparedness. France (in the wake of their protracted Algerian war) shared Germany's abhorrence of secret or special armies, while the British, with their problems in Northern Ireland, were perhaps too confident in their assumption that their anti-IRA network would also deal effectively with any international terrorist. Italy, at this time, was oblivious to the growing potential for terrorism within its borders, misled by a belief that most contemporary terrorism was confined to participants in the Arab-Israeli conflict. In fact, virtually every Western nation, except Israel, lacked either the equipment or staff to combat the growing terrorist threat, and they also lacked a realization of the impending danger.

At Munich, this complacency and the inattention was effectively shattered. When a group of Black September terrorists, with logistical support from German and French sympathizers, captured the Israeli athlete's dormitory in the Olympic village in Munich in 1972, West Germany's response was firm, but it failed to prevent disaster. As the world watched transfixed in helpless terror, an ambush was set up by the Germans at Furstenfeldbruck Airport. Five sharpshooters succeeded in killing five of the terrorists, but not before the terrorists had killed all nine hostages.[3]

# STRIKE FORCES: A FIRST LINE OF DEFENSE?

This spectacular attack and the equally spectacular failure of the government troops to secure the hostages' safety prompted several Western governments to reevaluate the quality of their counterterrorism strike forces. Since 1972, the creation of effective **strike forces,** military or police units specially trained, equipped, and organized to combat terrorism, has become a fairly common practice—with varying degrees of success and divergent degrees of legality. A review of the strike forces created by a few nations, their methods of operation, and their patterns of success and failure may help us to understand the problems and pitfalls of their use.

## Israel's Sarayat Matkal

Israel has been engaged in antiterrorism warfare for perhaps longer than any other nation. It has, as a result, a more extensive history in the use of strike teams. As such, it serves as an interesting case to study to determine the strengths and weaknesses of this tactic for combating terrorism.

In Israel, the Talmudic injunction "If someone comes to kill you, rise and kill him first" has become the slogan of the **Sarayat Matkal.** This specialized Israeli antiterrorist strike force is so secretive that the Israelis rarely even mention it by name. This unit has been responsible for raids into Beirut to murder Palestinian leaders and for the Entebbe rescue operation in 1972. It has both successfully thwarted terrorist attacks and, in its zeal to "strike before being struck" and to punish terrorists, been guilty of the murder of innocent persons. When Prime Minister Golda Meir unleashed "hit teams" the day after the Munich massacre, with orders to roam the world seeking out and summarily executing those responsible for the attack, the results were neither entirely legal nor wholly desirable.

One of these hit teams assassinated the wrong man. At Lillihammer, Norway, in 1973, an innocent Moroccan waiter was gunned down by a hit team in front of his pregnant Norwegian wife. The team had mistaken the waiter for the architect of the Munich massacre, Ali Hassan Salameh. International indignation forced Israel to temporarily restrain its hit squads.

This was, however, only a brief setback in Israel's use of strike forces in its war on terrorism. In January 1979, one of Israel's hit teams succeeded in blowing up Salameh with a radio-controlled car bomb in Beirut. This bomb also killed his four bodyguards and five innocent people who happened to be passing by at the time. It may also have been responsible for the assassination of Khalil al-Wazir, the PLO's mastermind of terrorist strategy against Israel, in Tunis on April 16, 1988.

One of the ironies of Israel's response to this incident is that, as an excusatory footnote to their (unofficial) admission of regret at the loss of innocent lives, the Israelis suggested that these people were just "in the wrong place at the wrong time."[4] This statement has unfortunate echoes of the "justification" offered by terrorists of harm to innocent people caused by their bombs.

The innocent persons killed, including Susan Wareham, a British woman working as a secretary for a construction company in Beirut, committed only the mistake (crime?) of being too near Salameh's car when it exploded. Although counterterrorist attacks such as this one may not deliberately take innocent life, they are undoubtedly culpable of a wanton disregard for the safety of innocent persons. Callous uncaring or deliberate disregard for the safety of innocent persons—the difference may be in the degree of regard for the sanctity of human life. The net result for the innocent bystander is unhappily the same.

Not all of Israel's counterattacks on terrorism have been so counterproductive. Indeed, the Sarayat Matkal is one of the best-trained and best-equipped special forces unit in operation today, with an impressive record of successful missions as well.

This unit is not part of the regular army and reports only to the chief of intelligence. Its members do, however, wear uniforms. This unit does not rely on trained volunteers but instead draws on raw recruits from the Kelet (the recruit depot). Usually an officer of the Sarayat Matkal will go the the Kelet to select about 15 to 20 recruits to form a team.

This team does much of its training in enemy territory, where the bullets are as real as the enemy. Recruits who survive this basic training become permanent members of a squad. Such squads are trained in the use of the .22 Baretta pistol as well as the Uzzi, the Israeli-invented machine pistol, and the Kalishnikov, the Russian assault rifle.

The willingness of such teams to commit acts of terrorism to counter terrorism may perhaps lie in the very roots of Israel's history. The joint British-Jewish **Special Night Squads,** of which Moshe Dayan was a member, operated during the 1930s. These squads were trained by their leader, Orde Wingate, to kill rather than wait to be killed.

The **Irgun,** a successor to these squads in the increasing spiral of violence in the region of Palestine, boasted Menachem Begin as a member. This organization was responsible for the bombing of the **King David Hotel** on July 22, 1946, which took 91 lives—British, Jewish, and Arab. The terrorists of the Irgun who perpetrated this violence still meet annually to observe the anniversary of this bombing—at the King David Hotel. Thurston Clarke's account, *By Blood and Fire: The Attack on the King David Hotel* (1981), is a detailed and well-documented reading for those interested in a further review of this incident.

Given this concept that it is better to kill than to wait to be killed that seems to have pervaded Israel's brief and bloody history, it is perhaps easier to understand both the brilliant successes that reflect the intense training and dedication and the ruthless determination that has occassionally resulted in disaster of this special strike force.

This unit conducted a raid inside Lebanon in December 1968 that was described as an attempt to force the Lebanese to prevent Palestinian terrorists from mounting their attacks from Lebanon. Earlier that year, the Palestinians had carried out a successful hijacking, taking over an El Al airliner en route from Rome to Tel Aviv. They had also attacked another El Al plane at the Athens airport in Greece, damaging it with automatic fire and grenades. Israeli intelligence reports showed that both terrorist incidents origniated in Beirut.

So a commando raid, carried out by the Sarayat Matkal, was launched against Beirut International Airport. Thirteen Arab aircraft, including nine jetliners, were destroyed. There were no casualties, because all of the airplanes were cleared of passengers and crew first.

Although the raid was a tactical success, its long-term effects were less rewarding. President de Gaulle of France condemned the raid as a violation of the sovereignty of a nation-state and used it as a reason for cutting off all arms shipments to Israel. This cutoff came at a time when the Israeli Defense Forces were relying heavily on French equipment. The other major supplier of Israeli arms, the United States, expressed its displeasure over the raid but stopped short of cutting off arms shipments. Furthermore, the Palestinians acquired both publicity, and a certain amount of public sympathy, for its cause. Finally, the airline company that owned and operated the planes, Middle East Airlines, was able to purchase a whole new fleet of jetliners—with the insurance money from the destroyed planes!

Other assault operations were equally "successful" but had perhaps less negative impact. It was the Sarayat Matkal that in 1972 successfully ended the hijacking of a Sabena Boeing 707 jetliner, Flight 517 from Brussels to Tel Aviv. When four members of the Black September Palestinian group hijacked the plane and forced it to land at Lod airport, they announced that they intended to blow up the plane, with its 90 passengers and 10 crew members, unless the Israeli government met their demands for the release of over 300 Arab prisoners.

The Sarayat Matkal assault force succeeded in storming the plane and freeing the passengers and crew members. Although one passenger and two of the hijackers were killed, this minimal loss of life became the pattern for similar feats, such as that carried out by Germany's GSG9 at Mogadishu.

When the Palestinians struck again, it was at the Olympic Games in Munich, only months after the Lod Airport rescue. Israeli atheletes were the target, and the Sarayat Matkal was excluded from the attempts to free those hostages.

This unit was responsible, though, for the successful **Entebbe raid** in Uganda in June 1977. When an Air France Airbus, Flight 139 en route from Tel Aviv to Paris, was hijacked after a stop at Athens ariport, Israel responded by organizing a brilliant and successful military rescue operation. The plane, which landed at the Entebbe airport, carried 248 passengers and crew members. All but 106 of these hostages were released by the terrorists before the Israeli raid. Only the Israeli citizens and Jews of other nationalities were retained, to increase pressure on Israel to agree to the release of 53 "freedom fighters" imprisoned in Israeli prisons.

The military incursion mounted by Israel succeeded in freeing all of the hostages held at the airport, with the exception of three who either misunderstood or did not hear orders by the commandos to lie down as they opened fire on the terrorists. All seven of the terrorists (two of whom were German and five Palestinian members of the PFLP) were killed, along with a number of Ugandan soldiers, who tried to prevent the Israeli commandos from escaping with the hostages.[5]

International opinion, for the most part, supported Israel, in spite of the fact that Israel had militarily invaded Uganda. Part of this approbation derives, no doubt, from a common love for a "winner." But part is due to the perceived legal right of a nation to intervene for "humanitarian" purposes in another country. While this right of "humanitarian intervention" is limited, it seemed to most of the community of nations to be acceptable in this case.[6]

## The British SAS

On May 5, 1980, Britain's 22nd **SAS**, the Special Air Service Regiment, supported by special police units, carried out **Operation Nimrod,** an assault on the Iranian Embassy in the heart of downtown London. As thousands watched, black-clad SAS members swung down from ropes and burst into the building through windows. Wearing gas masks, the assault force moved from room to room throwing stun grenades mixed with CS gas. As they moved through the building, they identified the terrorists, shot them with their Heckler and Koch MP5s or Browning automatic pistols, and bundled the hostages out of the burning building.

This was not the only successful counterterrorist attack carried out by Britain's SAS, but it was unique in at least one way. Most nations do not have the opportunity to see their special strike forces in operation on their home soil. Most operations of such forces take place on foreign soil, far from home and citizen attention.

Even in Operation Nimrod, however, Britain worked very hard to preserve the speed and secrecy that have become the hallmark of SAS operations. The assault team wore hoods, which served to hide their identities as well as to frighten the terrorists. When the incident was over, the unit handed authority back to the police and quietly made their way to the St. John's Wood barracks for a small celebration, before returning to their permanent station at Bradbury Lines in Hereford.

**Secrecy and surprise** have been the watchwords of this regiment since it was formed over 40 years ago. Lieutenant David Stirling, of the Scots Guard, is credited with creating this special unit. Under his plan, the SAS was designed to operate in units of five (later reduced to four) men, which continues to be the standard SAS stick.

The units have tended to be made up of a high percentage of Scottish Roman Catholics, perhaps because its founder Stirling was himself a Scottish Catholic and perhaps because the Catholics of Scotland have had generations of history of guerrilla warfare and traditions of secrecy. All of its members are volunteers, mostly from the Parachute Regiment. It is not a "young" regiment; the average age is about 27.

Each recruit is required to give up his rank and pay (most have already reached the rank of corporal or sergeant before attempting to join) and go back to the rank of trooper. Training in the Welsh countryside is rigorous, literally a killer. Three men died on Brecon Beacons during solo treks in 1979 and 1980, in terrible weather through the Welsh mountains.

Recruits are trained in surviving combat, surviving in Arctic conditions, and swimming fully clothed. They also receive special parachute instruction, including night jumps from extraordinary heights. Emphasis is also placed on weapon training, using the SAS weapons, the aforementioned Heckler and Koch submachine gun, the Browning .45 automatic pistol, the pump action shotgun, and the Sterling submachine gun fitted with a silencer. In addition, they are given training in foreign weapons, so that they can both use captured weapons and be familiar with weapons that their enemies may use on them.

Of every 100 men who apply, only about 19 will meet the physical and mental requirements. The initial tests include a series of treks across the Welsh hills, carrying weighted packs. The final trek covers 37 miles, carrying a 55-pound pack, over some of the toughest country in the Brecon Beacons. It must be covered in 20 hours, and it is literally a **killer course.** As noted earlier, men have died trying to complete it.

Once they have passed these initial courses, they continue to receive specialized training in such subjects as explosives, battlefield medicine, and the operation of communication equipment of various sorts. They train in the use of various personal weapons, knives and crossbows for "silent" killing, and submachine guns fitted with silencers. They learn about desert and jungle warfare and wilderness survival.

After this, they continue to specialize. Their specialities may be in such fields as medicine, languages, skiing, mountaineering, or underwater warfare. Individual skill development is encouraged at all times.

The SAS finds itself operating more often than most other national strike forces, with the possible exception of the Sarayat Matkal, because of the continuing violence in Northern Ireland. Although the SAS rarely figures in press reports on antiterrorist activities in that region, many operations are carried out by this unit in cooperation with the British occupying forces. The SAS has also seen overseas service in Aden, Oman, and Borneo. Indeed, much of its training for the guerrilla warfare that it faces in Northern Ireland finds its origins in the SAS experience in Aden in the mid-1960s.

In Northern Ireland, the SAS has served as a backup for the regular army units and the Royal Ulster Constabulary. It has been a largely thankless and often a very dangerous job. As members have somewhat cynically noted, if the Sassmen (as the Irish have called them) are killed or injured in an ambush, little public mention is made of the incident. But if the SAS is responsible, even indirectly, for the injury or death of any civilians, then public indignation is quite vocal.

Britain, unlike Israel, has indeed been willing to criticize its own strike forces when their actions have resulted in needless injury or loss of life. One judge, in whose court two Sassmen were on trial for responsibility in the death of a civilian in a stakeout of an arms cache, stated that although terrorists might consider themselves outside the rule of law, the army could not.

Forty years of experience as a special forces regiment has made the SAS into one of the best counterterrorist strike forces in the world today. Many nations today benefit from training and assistance offered by this unit to their own strike forces. Relations between the SAS and Germany's GSG9 are quite cordial and have resulted in considerable mutual training and assistance efforts.

Relations between the SAS and Israel's Sarayat Matkal, however, are far less amiable. Both units can remember a time when the British, under the Palestine Mandate, formed Q Squads to hunt down Jewish terrorists, particularly those of the infamous Stern Gang. In one particularly nasty incident, Roy Farran, who was responsible for the formation of the Q Squads on SAS principles, was acquitted in a court-martial of the murder of a suspected member of the Stern Gang. Israeli terrorists, not satisfied with the verdict, sent a book bomb to Farran's home in England. Roy's brother, Rex, opened the package and was killed as the bomb exploded in his face. The memory of such tragedies, and the vindictiveness that caused them, make the relations between these two special forces units strained.

Moreover, the Sassmen are frequently called on by their government to protect the leaders of various Arab states. Because many of these states and their leaders are regarded by some as the natural enemies of Israel, the SAS and the Sarayat Matkal often find themselves on the opposite side of these security situations.

## Germany's GSG9

Grenzschutzgrupps 9 (called **GSG9**) makes no claim to be a "killer troop" or "hit squad." This group, formed when the Bavarian state police were unable to deal adequately with the Munich situation in 1972, has made a point of being less dependent on weapons than on the talents, discipline, and training of its men. The Federal Border Guard was the parent unit for this special unit, which works out well because it is the only force in Germany that is directly under the control of the central government. GSG9 became the ninth unit of the Border Guard, making its headquarters at St. Augustin just outside Bonn. It was formed along very much the same lines as the SAS, operating with five-man sticks.

Within GSG9 there is a headquarters unit, a communications and documentation unit, and three fighting units. Its three technical units deal with weapons, research, equipment, backup supply, and maintenance services. Each of its three strike forces has 30 men, comprising a Command Section and five Special Tactical Sections (composed of 4 men and an officer)—the five-man stick.[7]

This group differs from the Sarayat Matkal and the SAS in that it is a civilian police force. Although much of the training given to its members is similar to that of the SAS, it is unique in its training in knowledge of the law, particularly as that law applies to counterterrorism operations. Members of this regiment are more conscious of the law, and of their need to stay within its bounds as far as possible, than are other similar strike forces.

This does not mean that GSG9 does not train its personnel in active counterterrorism techniques. In fact, Germany's elite force has one of the most sophisticated arsenals in the world. Because the deplorable shooting at Furstenfeldbruck Airport demonstrated the need for marksmanship training, every man of GSG9 is taught to be an expert marksman, using the Mausser 66 sniper's rifle, equipped with infrared sights and light intensifiers for night shooting. Like the SAS, they favor the Heckler and Koch MP5s for their routine work, but they are also armed with .357 Magnum revolvers.

Because they are required to be able to reach any part of Germany within two hours, ready for action, units are supplied with Mercedes-Benz autos of special design and BO 105 helicopters. They are trained to descend from hovering helicopters, via special ropes.

These units spend a great deal of time studying the origins and tactics of known terrorists, to determine how best to defeat them. Every member of a team learns such useful tricks as how to pick locks and how to handle airport equipment, to facilitate efforts to mount successful attacks against terrorists who have hijacked an airplane.

GSG9 practices assaults on hijacked airliners, training on mock-ups of aircraft and sometimes on aircraft on loan from Lufthansa. Such training stood them in good stead in **Mogadishu** in 1977. In October of that year, Zohair Akache's terrorist team hijacked a Lufthansa Boeing 737 with 82 passengers, in support of the Baader-Meinhof gang. After touring the Middle East in search of an airport willing to let them land, they finally landed the plane at Mogadishu in Somalia.

Unlike the situation in Uganda faced by the Israelis, the Germans found Somalia more than willing to cooperate with them in their efforts to end the hostage situation. Twenty-eight hand-picked men stormed the airliner, rescuing all hostages without harm. It was, if not a perfect raid of its kind (the original assault ladders were too short), a very good example of careful planning and execution. No laws were broken, no unnecessary injuries to innocent persons allowed, and both hostages and plane recovered.

## Delta Force: One U.S. Option

American counterterrorist forces are based in the United States, far from the Middle East, where many terrorist attacks against Americans have occurred. The Joint Special Operations Agency, headed by a two-star general, is charged with preparing guidelines and plans to guide counterterrorist forces during their formation, training, and operations. But this agency has no command authority over the forces.

The **Joint Operations Command** is a secret unit stationed at Fort Bragg, North Carolina. It is reported to have control over units that might be used to repel terrorists or to rescue Americans held hostage. Such units include the Army's **Delta Force,** composed of specially selected soldiers stationed at Fort Bragg, and Task Force 100, which is composed of high-speed helicopter pilots at Fort Campbell, Kentucky.

The navy also has a counterterrorism force, **Seal Team Six,** made up of frogmen and stationed at Little Creek, near Norfolk, Virginia. Similarly, the air force boasts its own strike force as well, the **Special Operations Wing** at Eglin Air Force Base in Florida. This latter unit is trained to fly specially equipped C-130 transports in counterterrorist operations.

The problems with U.S. counterterrorism forces are obvious, brought on by the lack of cohesive command illustrated by the abortive attempt to send a strike team into Iran to free Americans held hostage in the U.S. Embassy in Teheran. **Operation Eagle's Claw,** as this mission was called, was characterized by a confusion of command, insufficient training, and critical equipment failure. Cloaked in so much secrecy that even some of the military officers involved were not told the aim of the mission for which they were preparing, this operation became a model for what can go wrong in a strike force manuever. In addition to too much secrecy, there were too many chiefs and not enough cooperation between military units. An army officer, Maj. Gen. James Vaught, was in overall command; Col. James Kyle of the Air Force had responsibility for fixed-wing aircraft. Col. Charles Pitman of the Marines also had command responsibility, and Col. Beckwith controlled Delta Force.

Delta Force lacked sufficient training and experience for such an operation. It had been created less than five years earlier by Col. Beckwith, and its training program was incomplete and not designed for the type of situation that evolved. It was underfunded and ill equipped to handle the hostage raid, having trained primarily in guerrilla warfare and low-intensity conflict.

Even today, the United States lacks the will to create a single unit in which to vest this specialized training and command. Within the armed services strong rivalries remain that make it difficult for one branch to create and recieve support for such a specialized unit. Although in the wake of Operation Eagle's Claw's disaster there was a call to establish a new special counterterrorism unit, with personnel drawn from all of the armed services, there has been little success in creating such a unit. Interservice rivalries make its creation very unlikely in the near future.

The Delta Force unit has, according to government reports, been deployed several times, other than the highly publicized Eagle's Claw fiasco and the *Achille Lauro* incident. It has, for instance, been sent to Venezuela to advise the armed forces there on the ways to retake a hijacked airplane. It was sent on a similar mission to Oman, to prepare to retake a hijacked plane in nearby Kuwait. At the time of the TWA hijacking, Delta Force was deployed to the Mediterranean. But in each of these cases, its activities stopped short of assault; it simply made preparations for, or advised in preparations for, the assault.

This has, some have argued, had a detrimental effect on the morale of the individuals in Delta Force. To be always preparing and never doing counterterrorist activities is infinitely frustrating, as the men in GSG9 and SAS could attest. But the United States has been singularly reluctant to field a strike force against the terrorists that have struck at it so often.

Delta Force remains among the best that the United States has to offer in terms of a strike force. It has, since the Iranian fiasco, proved itself to be capable of successful missions. The "skyjacking" of the *Achille Lauro* hijackers was an outstandingly successful operation, whose questionable legality has been overshadowed by its brilliant execution, giving a much-needed boost to Delta's morale.

Having, unlike Germany and Great Britain, few if any violent indigenous terrorists, the United States has focused its attentions on training its special forces to operate overseas. Emphasis seems to be placed less on secrecy of identity than on rapid-response capabilities and combat training. If coordination of command problems can be surmounted, these forces may develop into units as efficient and respected as the SAS and GSG9.

In the wake of the Operation Eagle's Claw debacle, the Pentagon began to establish the closest thing this nation has ever had to a secret army. Small, specially trained units were developed, which were designed to operate much more covertly than some of the older paramilitary units, such as the Navy Seals. In addition to being given rather exotic code names, such as Yellow Fruit and Seaspray, these units were armed with newer, more sophisticated types of equipment. These included such items as the small, high-tech helicopters with which Task Force 160, which operates out of Fort Campbell, train. These new units also received more sophisticated communications gear, including one-man satellite communications radios and dishes.

More important than these technological "toys," however, was the creation of the Intelligence Support Activity (ISA), a far-ranging intelligence organization that gave the army, for the first time, the ability to engage in full-fledged espionage, fielding its own agents. Through this organization, the strike forces were able for the first time to gather the information that they needed to plan their counterterrorist activities. They were no longer dependent upon the CIA or other intelligence services for vital data, which was too often not available or kept classified at a critical juncture in the planning process.

Even with these innovations, however, these units have been unable to rise above the bureaucratic infighting and bungling that has long plagued U.S. strike forces. While the units still exist, their morale, and even their preparedness, is in disarray. Seaspray, Yellow Fruit, and the ISA became involved in clandestine operations in Central America, which has seriously impaired their credibility with Congress and within U.S. military and intelligence units. The use or misuse of counterterrorism forces in this area has jeopardized the United States' efforts to develop a credible and respected strike force, respected by or capable of working with such units as the SAS and GSG9.

## CONCLUSION

The use of special forces to combat terrorism has both assets and liabilities. Too little commitment can result in an insufficiently trained and equipped force, as Operation Eagle's Claw demonstrated. Too zealous a desire to use such forces can result in the loss of innocent lives, as Israel has found.

Determination, unsupported by sufficient training or equipment, is also a recipe for disaster, as became evident in November 1985. An Egyptian airliner en route to Cairo from Athens was hijacked and diverted to Malta. Egyptian troops stormed the plane the next day, after the hijackers began to kill some of the hostages on board. As the troops rushed onto the plane, the hijackers tossed grenades at passengers. The death toll was put at 60, 57 of whom died in the rescue attempt.

It is not enough just to have such a force. Nations must train and equip them with adequate information and weaponry to meet an increasingly sophisticated terrorist threat. Nations need also to instill in its strike forces, as Germany has sought to do, a respect to the law and its restraints on strike force activities. So equipped and so trained, such forces can operate to significantly reduce not necessarily the number but the success of terrorist attacks worldwide.

## *Evaluation*

There are many conflicting views on whether strike forces are a legitimate and useful tool in combating terrorism. Some view such strike teams as potential threats to democracy, creating elite troops that could be used to quell demonstrations as well as to stop terrorist attacks. Others view them as essential to a nation's security, operating in ways not open to a large military unit to safeguard a nation's citizens, both at home and abroad.

Presented here are two quotations that reflect, in part, this divergence of view. Each viewpoint is a bit extreme, tending toward opposite ends of the spectrum of opinion. Read each, and decide which more accurately reflects the appropriate assessment of the need and use for such forces in today's world.

1. "The danger inherent in the war against terrorism is, of course, the prospect of desparate societies willing to substitute state terror for [nonstate] terrorism, to trade individual rights and freedoms for relief from chaos and violence, reconstituting what were once relatively benign governments into coldly efficient, centralized tyrannies, whose populations are held in close check by armies of secret police and informers, widespread electronic eavesdropping, and a constant deluge of propaganda."[8]

2. "The Israeli argue the case for pre-emptive strikes: it is better to kill their enemies in their own bases and so prevent them mounting their operations, rather than conduct elegant sieges inside Israel. While appreciating the excellence of other forces' pieces of electronic wizardry and the skill of the talk-out experts, their aim is to prevent the need for such expertise arising. Such a policy has its attractions, especially for a beleaguered, small nation like Israel under continual attack from enemies based round its borders. When national survival is at stake all manner of actions become permissable that would not be countenanced in more secure societies."[9]

## *Suggested Readings*

Dobson, Christopher, and Ronald Payne. *Counterattack: The West's Battle against the Terrorists.* New York: Facts on File, 1982.

"International Terrorism." Issue Brief No. 1874042. Washington, D.C.: Congressional Research Service, 1987.

Livingstone, N. C. "Taming Terrorism: In Search of a New U.S. Policy." *International Security Review: Terrorism Report 7*, no. 1 (Spring 1982), 12–17.

"Patterns of Global Terrorism: 1994." U.S. Department of State Publication 10136. Washington, D.C.: U.S. Government Printing Office, April 1995.

Rivers, Gayle. *The Specialists: Revelations of a Counterterrorist.* New York: Stein & Day, 1985.

Sederberg, Peter C. *Terrorist Myths: Illusion, Rhetoric and Reality.* Upper Saddle River, NJ: Prentice Hall, 1989.

## *Endnotes*

1. Christopher Dobson and Ronald Payne, *Counterattack: The West's Battle against the Terrorists* (New York: Facts on File, 1982), xvi.

2. *Patterns of International Terrorism in 1980: A Research Paper* (Washington, D.C.: National Foreign Assessment Center, 1980), iii, 1–6.

3. "International Terrorism," Issue Brief No. 1874042 (Washington, D.C.: Congressional Research Service, 1978), 41–42.

4. Dobson and Payne, *Counterattack,* 84.

5. Seventy-four-year-old Dora Bloch was not being held with the hostages at the airport. She had been transferred to a Ugandan hospital. After the raid, she disappeared, amid reports that she was dragged screaming from her hospital bed and murdered, on Ugandan president Idi Amin's orders. She has never been seen or heard from since that time.

6. See the editorial by Christopher Joyner in the *Washington Post, (*November 18, 1983), section A, 18. Joyner concludes that, except in certain carefully limited situations such as this, "armed intervention *per se* remains an act that contravenes sovereign rights of states that are legally inviolable."

7. Dobson and Payne, *Counterattack,* 96.

8. N. C. Livingstone, "Taming Terrorism: In Search of a New U.S. Policy," *International Security Review: Terrorism Report 7*, no. 1 (Spring 1982): 20.

9. Dobson and Payne, *Counterattack,* 83.

# 11

# Terrorism, Intelligence, and the Law

*The greatest threat posed by terrorists now lies in the atmosphere of alarm they create, which corrodes democracy and breeds repression. . . . If the government appears incompetent, public alarm will increase and so will the clamor for draconian measures.*

—Brian Jenkins

## Key Concepts

Red Brigade
FLQ
War Measures Act
Northern Ireland Act
Prevention of Terrorism Act
Irish Republican Army
ETA
Baader-Meinhof gang
Red Army Faction
"contact ban" law
"propagation of violence" law
Virginio Rognoni

Carlos Alberto Della Chiesa
"penititi"
INTERPOL
"the Kommisar"
PIOS
target searches
TREVI
Operation Chavin de Huantar
phases of modern terrorist
  incidents
Ottawa Ministerial Declaration
  on Countering Terrorism

## LEGAL INITIATIVES TO COUNTER TERRORISM

Politicians and scholars have expressed grave doubts about whether any government can remain strong, but not oppressive, in the face of severe emergencies. If a government is to make a measured but effective response to the great emergencies generated by terrorist acts today, then coping strategies other than sole reliance on the use of strike forces must be considered.

It is not feasible to evaluate all of the options available to nations in their efforts to deal with terrorism, as both an internal and external threat. Various nations have

**180**

devised different ways to address this recalcitrant problem. Some have tried to fashion a broad spectrum of legislative initiatives designed to make it clear that terrorists and groups resorting to terrorism operate outside the law of the land and can expect neither sanctuary nor quarter to be given them at the hands of the law.

These efforts have met with mixed success, depending in large measure on the determination of the government to enforce the laws that it creates and also on the degree of entrenchment that the terrorists enjoy within the society. Canada's efforts to curtail the activities of the FLQ, for example, have met with considerable success. Italy's offer or pardon to "penitent" terrorists, combined with its efforts to close all havens in which those engaged in terrorism might hide, also enjoyed some measure of success.

In both cases, legal initiatives were combined with efforts at social reform designed to reduce the grievances that terrorists voiced with the existing system. Italy's success in its efforts is less clear than Canada's, because of Italy's geographic location. Canada, with the help of a friendly nation on its only border, was able to keep terrorists from either escaping across its border or receiving help from other similar groups. Italy has had to contend with both indigenous and imported terrorism. Middle Eastern terrorists, as well as terrorists from several other European nations, have been able to offer support in the form of training, arms, personnel, and safe haven to Italy's indigenous terrorists. Thus, Italy's strongest indigenous terrorist group, the **Red Brigade,** has been able to survive several intensive police crackdowns. Its ability to revive after each such effort is perhaps due less to Italy's lack of diligence in its efforts to eradicate the group than to the inability of the Italian government to effectively shut its borders to other terrorist support groups.

The following case studies offer insights into the effectiveness — and the lack thereof—of legal initiatives in coping with terrorism. These cases were chosen to illustrate two crucial points:

1. Legal initiatives alone are insufficient to eliminate a terrorist problem.
2. The use of extraordinary legal measures is not without risk, particularly to democracies.

# CANADA'S LEGAL WAR WITH THE FLQ

Canada offers an instructive example of emergency legislation, enacted and applied on a limited scale, in terms of both scope and time. As the first North American nation to face a vigorous and violent native terrorist campaign, Canada from the late 1960s throughout the early 1970s was force to create its own answer to terrorism. Faced with a series of violent attacks by the Front du Liberation du Quebec **(FLQ)** in early 1970, culminating in the kidnapping of James Cross (British trade commissioner for Quebec) and Pierre Laporte (minister of labor in the Quebec provincial government), Prime Minister Elliott Trudeau decided to take firm, but extraordinary, measures.[1]

In 1970, Trudeau invoked the **War Measures Act,** which empowered him to call in the army to enforce his refusal to be coerced by terrorists. Although Trudeau agreed to deal with the kidnappers, allowing them to be flown to Cuba in return for Cross's release, he was determined to rid Canada of the terrorists in the FLQ.

He was willing to use any means at his disposal to accomplish this aim. He was willing to subordinate civil rights to the preservation of public order. As he noted:

> When terrorists and urban guerrillas were trying to provoke the secession of Quebec, I made it clear that I wouldn't hesitate to send in the army and I did, despite the anguished cries of civil libertarians.[2]

To a large extent Trudeau succeeded in ridding Canada of its indigenous terrorist organization. To do so, he saturated the Montreal area with troops, which acted to pin down terrorist cells, and used the Royal Canadian Mounted Police to concentrate on locating the cells that had organized the terrorist attacks. Using broad local powers of search and arrest, more than 300 suspects were apprehended.[3]

Excesses were no doubt committed during the course of this crisis. Nevertheless, the crisis had an end point, when civil liberties were restored, the army withdrawn, and local police once again constrained by strict laws on search and seizure operations. It may be true, as David Barrett, head of the opposition New Democratic Party once stated, that "the scar on Canada's record of civil liberties which occurred [at that time] is a classic illustration of how the state, in an attempt to combat terrorism, overstepped its boundaries and actually threatened its own citizens."[4]

But it is also true that after Trudeau's crackdown, Canada enjoyed a decade relatively free of terrorism, with civil rights and liberties fully restored. It is also worth noting that Trudeau was astute enough to accompany the repression of this period with political measures designed to end some of the grievances that may have contributed to the terrorism. These political initiatives included creating compulsory French courses for English-speaking persons in Quebec and heavy government investment in the French-speaking minority areas. Such measures helped to deprive those advocating terrorist actions of the support of the moderates among the French community.

The problems, ironically, that Canada faced in the 1990s over the efforts of Quebec to secede stem at least in part from the success of the government in "co-opting" the frustrated French-speaking population that had offered some support to the FLQ. By making the option of "working with the system" to achieve their objectives more attractive, Canada diminished its terrorism problems but may well have enhanced the probability of secession.

# THE "TEMPORARY" BRITISH PROBLEM IN NORTHERN IRELAND

At what point should the general welfare of a nation take precedence over the rights of its citizens, in a democratic society? How long and to what extent can those rights be reduced or taken away to secure that "general welfare" without doing irreparable damage to the fabric of democracy within that society?

Totalitarian and authoritarian states often justify the suspension or severe curtailment of civil and political liberties on the basis of a "need to secure the general welfare." But it is not only undemocratic states that have been guilty of repressing civil rights for this reason. This very issue has confronted the United Kingdom during the last three decades of the twentieth century, in its struggle with terrorism in Northern Ireland.

The periodic outbreaks of violence in Northern Ireland prompted the British Parliament to enact the **Northern Ireland** (Emergency Provisions) **Act,** in 1973. Parliament renewed this act each year for the next two decades, retaining in its title the term *emergency* even though it had been in effect for more than a decade. This draconian measure

- allows suspects to be detained by the executive authority,
- gives police powers of arrest without warrant for up to 72 hours,
- gives security forces broad authority for search and seizure, and
- makes it possible for those charged with terrorism to be tried by a judge, without benefit of a jury.

This extraordinary legislation was followed in 1974 by an act called the **Prevention of Terrorism** (Temporary Provisions) **Act.** Under this act, the home secretary was given special powers:

- to exclude from the United Kingdom, without court proceedings, persons "concerned with the commission, preparation, or instigation of acts of terrorism"
- to detain a suspect for up to seven days without bringing him or her to court (after his arrest by police officers without a warrant, as allowed under the Emergency Provisions Act)

The Temporary Provisions Act also allowed the prohibition in the United Kingdom of organizations considered to be connected with terrorism.[5]

Both of these acts were renewed annually by Parliament, though often with heated debates. So, although they carried the titles of "Temporary" and "Emergency," such terms are not really appropriate. *Emergency,* by definition, refers to a "sudden condition or state of affairs calling for immediate action."[6] Used in reference to a state of affairs that has persisted for more than a decade, it is meaningless.

These two legislative acts clearly demonstrate the extent to which a democratic state is willing to compromise on civil rights to combat terrorism within its borders. The prolonged curtailment of fundamental civil rights (e.g., the right to a trial by jury, the right to be charged with a crime when arrested, the right to be free to associate with organizations of one's choosing) and the granting of extraordinary powers to police (allowing them to violate certain rights in the process of search and seizure) surely diminish the democratic ideals of a state, even one that has been as committed to democracy as has the United Kingdom.

To create some measure of social order, Great Britain has given away some rights and freedoms of its Northern Ireland citizens. Unlike Canada, whose restriction of liberties was of relatively brief duration, the United Kingdom faced a restrictive situation that, because it showed only sporadic signs of improvement, seemed likely to assume an indefinite, if not a permanent, position in the governing of this nation. Only the agreement reached in 1998 has offered substantive commitment to a change in this governing position.

In Canada's case, the terrorists were not well organized or well armed, and they lacked substantive support from either other terrorist groups or supporters in other nations, particularly from the nation with which it shares a border. So a determined effort by the Canadian government succeeded fairly well in wiping out the terrorist threat. Given these conditions, the curtailment of rights and liberties was of short duration.

The situation that the United Kingdom faces is very different. The **Irish Republican Army** (IRA) has been a well-organized, heavily armed, and well-funded resistance group in this region. It received both training and weapons from supporters in many places. Other terrorist organizations contributed to the arms and training of IRA operatives, while supporters and sympathizers from several nations, particularly the United States and the Republic of Ireland, have given these terrorists money, arms, and logistical support.

There are many difficulties in fighting, on one's home soil, an entrenched and heavily supported organization committing terrorist acts. As Spain found in dealing with the Euskadi Ta Askatasuna **ETA,** Spain's militant Basque separatists, the presence of a friendly or neutral border over which terrorists can escape and find safe havens makes counterterror operations almost impossible for a nation to carry out on its own.[7] Cooperation between nations to thwart terrorists (as between Canada and the United States) can help to make counterterror legislation unnecessary or at least short term; the absence of such cooperation, particularly when linked with transnational support for the group engaged in terrorist acts, makes it very difficult for national "emergency" legislation to be effective in eliminating the terrorism.

## GERMANY'S "MODERATE" LEGISLATION

Several nations have tried to deal with the need for national legislation on terrorism by enacting more "moderate" legislation. West Germany in 1978 enacted a package of antiterrorist laws that, given the scope of the terrorist problem that the nation faced (remember the excesses of the **Baader-Meinhof gang,** the indigenous organization carrying out terrorist acts, and its successor, the anarchist **Red Army Faction**), were regarded as fairly moderate. Two of the most prominent of the antiterrorist laws enacted during the 1970s by West Germany were the **"contact ban"** and the **"propagation of violence" laws.** These laws illustrate the dangers in even such generally moderate legislation.

The curtailment of a prisoner's right of access to counsel provided for in the contact ban law was designed to restrict the flow of communication between imprisoned terrorists and their comrades still at large. German authorities believed that information was being passed between these two groups by sympathetic lawyers. But the only time that the law was invoked, information continued to flow. To many experts on German law, this made it appear that a fundamental principle of due process was being sacrificed without any appreciable benefit.[8]

The propagation of violence law was even more general, and possibly even more counterproductive. This law was used against student protestors, as well as persons engaged in acts of terrorism, with the unfortunate result that it helped to transform some nonviolent protestors into terrorists.[9]

Germany, like Canada, has been able through a combination of legislation and investigative intelligence to rid itself of many of its internal terrorist problems. The cost in Germany, though, has not been localized in one province, as it was in Canada, nor has it ended. In fact, in 1983 West Germany's minister of the interior, under whose jurisdiction much of the counterterrorism effort was made, steered through the cabinet several controversial amendments to the national demonstration law. These amendments were designed, for example, to make it easier for police to move into a crowd of peaceful demonstrators and arrest those who look as if they might be planning to riot or resist!

Germany has also enacted in recent years several legislative programs that have had, so far, no noticeable counterproductive effects and have in fact been helpful in reducing the internal terrorist threat. These legal efforts have been geared toward bringing terrorists "to a sense of reality."

## ITALY AND THE *"PENITITI"*

Italy has experimented with a similar legal strategy, with considerable success. In June 1983, Italians voted for the first time in more than a decade without an array of urban guerrilla groups holding the nation's political system at gunpoint. Long regarded as the Western European country most vulnerable during the general upsurge of terrorism in the 1970s, many of Italy's politicians and media experts hoped that their country was finally beginning to emerge from its terrorist nightmare.

The man credited with a large share in Italy's success in its war on internal terrorism was Interior Minister **Virginio Rognoni,** who assumed his office in the wake of the kidnap-murder of former prime minister Aldo Moro. At the time in which he took office, the Red Brigade terrorists appeared to be acting with impunity.

Statistics issued by the Interior Ministry indicated that, in 1978, there were 2,498 terrorist attacks within Italy. Between 1968 and 1982, 403 people were killed in terrorist incidents in Italy, and another 1,347 were injured. These people came from all walks of life. One out of every four was a police officer. Apart from politicians such as Moro, businessmen and journalists were favorite targets. But the bulk of the dead and injured were ordinary citizens unlucky enough to be on a train or in a piazza when it was blown up.

After 1980, a significant drop occurred in Italy's internal terrorist activity, apparently a result of a combination of legal initiatives and coordinated police efforts. Nearly 2,000 convicted urban guerrillas, including most of the leading members of the Red Brigade, were imprisoned. The Italians gave the task of hunting down these persons to a portly general of the Carabinieri named **Carlo Alberto Della Chiesa.** Armed with about 150 carefully chosen men, his antiterrorist cadre, he was responsible only to the minister of the interior, Rognoni, and to the prime minister.

With his support, the government enacted a number of decrees: strengthening sentences for convicted terrorists, widening police powers (allowing police to hold suspects longer for questioning and to search without a warrant), and making abetting terrorism a crime. Increased powers were also given to the police in matters of detention, interrogation, and wiretapping.

Rognoni, during this increased police activity, began to exploit what he saw as a growing disillusionment with the efficacy of terrorism as a problem-solving instrument. He helped to have enacted in 1982 a law that promised "repentant" terrorists lighter sentences if they confessed. Beset by gathering doubts, large numbers of the *brigandisti* began to confess. One of the most prominent of the *"penititi"* was Patrizio Peci, a former Red Brigade commander from Turin. He commented that, while he had been driven to become an urban guerrilla by police harassment for bomb outrages (which were later discovered to have been committed instead by neofascists), he no longer believed that the Red Brigades could create a better society in Italy using terrorism.

Terrorism was not, in any sense, eliminated in Italy. Both left- and right-wing terror continue to destroy individuals and property. Right-wing terrorists were responsible, in 1981, for an explosion in the Bologna train station that killed 85 people. But for a time, terrorism was significantly reduced. Consider the following facts:

- During 1980, deaths from terrorism occurred every three days on the average.
- In the first six months of 1983, in the wake of the government's police and legislative initiatives, only one terrorist-related death was reported.

The cost to Italy's democracy has been, arguably, substantial; due process was certainly impaired by the expanded police powers, for instance. But it is also possible that Italy's democracy could not have lasted much longer as a democracy under the barrage of terrorist attacks. Citizen's right to vote, to security of person, as well as to life and liberty were under constant, serious threat of attack by terrorists. To have stabilized the situation without a civil war and without transforming Italy into an authoritarian regime is quite an accomplishment, and continues to make Italy relatively free from terrorism as the twenty-first century begins.

Much could be learned from Italy's experience. The judicious blending of strong police investigative and arrest action, coupled with the offer of a government pardon for "penitent" transgressors, proved a potent and effective mixture. By closing most of the places to hide, while holding open a friendly government door to pardon, Italy has made serious efforts to resocialize a large number of its disaffected youth without unnecessary violence.

That Italy remains under occasional attack by terrorists is due, in large measure, to the fact that its ties in the Arab world, and its position in the Mediterranean, make it a natural staging ground or pathway for terrorism from the Middle East. Most of Italy's terrorist activities in the late 1980s were conducted by foreign terrorists, mostly Middle Eastern, who were easily able to enter and exit this democratic nation.

Thus, general legislative initiatives, as well as emergency legislation, can be effective in reducing the threat of terrorism within a nation, without undue damage to democratic institutions. As one U.S. government publication noted:

> There is an almost irresistible tendency to react to terrorism by enacting laws and practices that diminish the rights of the accused or increase the authority of the state. The adverse consequences of that reaction are magnified by the equally predictable tendency to apply these specialized laws and mechanisms to an ever-increasing class of investigations. While the facts may justify certain changes, we must guard against overboard, non-productive, or counter-productive changes.[10]

## INVESTIGATION: THE INTELLIGENCE INITIATIVE

There is at least one other coping strategy that nations have used with some degree of success that merits further attention: investigation. Since most nations, and many terrorist groups, are currently engaged in the use of this strategy, an examination of the promises and pitfalls that it offers provides some interesting insights into the way in which nations can, and cannot, cope with the rising threat of terrorism today.

Investigation is an initial and certainly the most universal technique used by governments in their efforts to combat terrorism. Its potential as an antiterrorism tool is enormous. It has been effectively used to both prevent and punish terrorism. At the same time, its potential for abuse has been all too evident in recent years. Indeed, investigation has shown itself to be a powerful, two-edged sword, capable, when improperly applied, of resulting in serious loss of civil rights, though seldom of human life.

The successful use of investigative techniques to counter terrorism is of relatively recent vintage. Although Israel has had, for decades, an intelligence operation that accumulates vast amounts of information about Arab terrorists, even Israel has been unable to keep pace with the internationalization of terrorism, particularly of the Palestinian movement.

However, until West Germany turned its attention in the 1970s toward intelligence gathering, Israel had the most active antiterrorist information system. In fact, it flooded Western European governments and police forces with information about terrorists, their movements, and planned actions. Indeed, the French complained at one point that the mass of information gathered by Israeli agents (who had infiltrated Arab groups in France) was just too much for them to manage.

There is, of course, an international body that has existed for some time that would seem to be useful to national governments trying to cope with the investigation of international terrorism. **INTERPOL,** the international police organization, with its data banks on criminal activity worldwide, would appear to have many of the resources necessary for such investigations. Under its charter, however, this organization was, until near the end of the twentieth century, restricted to investigations of ordinary crimes. Because not all of its charter members are as yet convinced that terrorism is indeed a crime, INTERPOL has been, until recently, unable to offer much substantive assistance in intelligence research. In October 1984, changes in the rules governing this organization have broadened its ability to assist nations in investigation of terrorism.

Germany, on the other hand, has developed and is sharing what is doubtless one of the most sophisticated antiterrorist intelligence operations in existence today. In Weisbaden, a computer nicknamed "**the Komissar**" plays a vital role in that country's battle against terrorism. It is controlled by the Federal Criminal Investigation Department (the BKA). During the 1980s and early 1990s, it has experienced an enormous growth in the federal resources put at its disposal.[11]

The heart of this computer system is an index of information called **PIOS** *(Personnen, Institutionen, Objekte, Sachen),* in which is stored every clue (such as addresses, contacts, movements) about known and suspected terrorists. Every address found in a suspect's possession, every telephone number and the name of every person who writes to him or her in prison is stored in this system. Information about every object found at the scene of a terrorist attack or in a place where terrorists have been becomes a part of this computer's data banks.

This information has been effectively used by another German intelligence investigative tool—a special unit of investigators operating in small teams on *Ziefahndung* (**target searches**). Target searches are instituted, according to German officials, for the apprehension of terrorists wanted under an arrest warrant, with priority given to a "hard core" of about 15 violent offenders. Every police officer in the Federal Republic carries at all times a set of cards bearing the photographs and identification data on all of these "targeted" persons. This is perhaps comparable to the U.S. Federal Bureau of Investigation's "Ten Most Wanted" list, except that this list, coming out of Weisbaden, focuses on terrorists.

Each target search team takes one terrorist and immerses itself in his or her life, using the computer at Weisbaden. All of the information about a suspect, however trivial it may seem, can be useful to the search team. If they know, for instance, that a suspect always telephones his or her mother on her birthday, the mother's phone can be wiretapped. Support for a certain soccer team indicated by the subject can lead investigators to attend that team's matches.

These intensive search methods have had documented success. Using such methods, 15 terrorists were tracked down in one six-week period in 1978. At that point, however, the success rate becomes somewhat less impressive. Having tracked the terrorists to other countries, the difficulty became one of securing their arrest and return for trial.

Four of the aforementioned 15 terrorists sought in 1978 were traced to Bulgaria. According to the lawyer for Till Meyer, Gabrielle Rollnick, Gudrun Sturmer, and Angelika Loder (the four suspects), four hired cars containing heavily armed German police drew up outside a café in Sonnenstrand, a Bulgarian resort. The four were over-powered, taken to a nearby bungalow, and tied up. At 2:00 A.M., they were taken to Bourgas Airport in a minibus with German customs license plates and put on a plane with 25 other armed German police. The cooperation of the Bulgarian authorities in this "kidnapping" of terrorists makes this a remarkable instance of cooperation between a communist and a noncommunist state in the apprehension of terrorists.[12]

Similar success was achieved in a cooperative effort with France in May 1980, when five women wanted on terrorism charges by Germany were arrested in an apart-ment in the Rue Flatters on the Left Bank in Paris. Again, no complicated extradition procedures hampered the operation. France simply sent the five to Germany.[13]

These stories do not mean that cooperation on all such intelligence ventures is guaranteed. Indeed, the French, in another famous case, refused to extradite Abu Daoud, one of Black September's commanders, to either Germany or Israel. Daoud had arrived in Paris (under an assumed name) for the funeral of the Palestine Liberation Organization's representative. The French, who had photographed the funeral party, circulated the pictures to friendly governments, asking for information in their efforts to solve the murder of the representative.

When British intelligence identified Daoud from a photograph, French police promptly arrested him, much to the French government's embarrassment. Israel and West Germany immediately requested his extradition, but the French government quietly set him free—outside their borders.

Daoud had, in fact, been formally introduced to senior government officials and entertained at the Quai d'Orsay. France's decision not to extradite or prose-cute was partly due to the embarrassment of having officially entertained Daoud, but more a result of the French government's ties to Arab states, whose sympathies lay with the PLO. Because these ties were attributable in part to France's dependency on Arab oil, the decision not to extradite was the result of both political and economic factors.[14]

Similarly, France arrested the German terrorist Wilfred Bose (whose connection with Carlos the Jackal was known to them) but released him. In this case, an extradition request was made, based on intelligence information on the crimes committed by this man. In spite of the fact that this intelligence information was made available to France, the French government decided to neither extradite nor punish this offender. Lacking a treaty or convention that could create a legal obligation to do one or the other, France was free to act, as it did, in what it perceived to be its best national interest.

Nor is France the only nation to refuse either to extradite or prosecute when given intelligence information about suspected terrorists. The former Yugoslavia, for example, refused to arrest Carlos when informed (in detail in an intelligence report) of his presence and his crimes, by a German target search team. Yugoslav officials did arrest four of West Germany's most wanted terrorists (Rolf-Clemens Wagner, Brigitte Mohnhaupt, Sieglinde Hofmann, and Peter Boock) on information given by a German target search team. Subsequently, however, these suspects were released without either a trial or extradition proceedings.[15]

The point is that intelligence gathering, as a weapon against terrorism, is often of erratic value in the absence of either a legal system with established guidelines for the treatment of terrorist suspects or an alternative method of compelling cooperation among nations in the prosecution or extradition of such persons. Today, if a government thinks that its national interests will be best served by letting a known terrorist go free, it can (and will) usually do so. Where no overriding national interests are involved, cross-national intelligence-gathering and arrest operations are feasible; where such interest are perceived to be at stake, they are far less likely to succeed.

Today, some international police cooperation structures do exist that facilitate sharing intelligence concerning terrorism. In Europe there is a permanent though comparatively secret structure, code-named **TREVI** for terrorism, radicalism, and violence international. This is a formalization of the "old boy" police network, which regularly brings together police chiefs from European Union countries. It also engages in day-to-day consultations through national bureaus. At a secret meeting in April 1978, the nine Common Market countries plus Austria and Switzerland agreed to pool resources to combat terrorism on the continent. The French have also been involved in this agreement since September of that year.

Furthermore, NATO has an antiterrorist network that allies Canadians and Americans with Europe. This system facilitates the exchange of information on terrorists, their organizations, techniques, and weapons.

# Case Studies: Government Use of Intelligence/Investigation

Two interesting cases of the use of intelligence and investigation as tools in counterterrorism offer helpful contrasts in these techniques in the late 1990s. Both involve the use of violent force, rather than legal initiatives, to resolve the situation, but both also are critically dependent for success on intelligence-gathering and investigation efforts by law enforcement agencies.

## Peru: A Rescue Mission "by the Book"

On December 17, 1996, rebels from the Tupac Amaru seized the Japanese embassy residence in Lima, Peru, during a festive cocktail reception. Demanding the release of 400 of their comrades who were in Peru's prisons at the time, the 14 Tupac Amaru guerrillas gradually released hundreds of the hostages, retaining only 72 for the entire siege. Alberto Fujimori, Peru's president, saw little chance of resolving the situation peacefully, since he was determined not to release the prisoners, but he gave the negotiators an opportunity to try. Attempting to alleviate the tension, he arranged the promise of safe passage to Cuba for the rebels if they wished (which they did not choose to accept, as most wanted to remain in Peru) and appointed Archbishop Juan Luis Cipriani to be the special negotiator.

The 72 hostages, who were held for 126 days, included senior Peruvian officials, Fujimori's brother Pedro, foreign diplomats, and the Japanese ambassador. Britain, Germany, Israel, and the United States all offered to help in the rescue attempt, but all were turned down. Fujimori was under intense pressure to resolve the issue as expeditiously as possible.

Yet he resisted the calls for a quick solution, opting instead to allow time for the creation and implementation of **Operation Chavin de Huantar** (named in honor of a pre-Inca archaeological site that was honeycombed with underground passages). What evolved was a masterpiece of months of planning, using 140 Peruvian special forces troops and professional miners. During the endless weeks of standoff and negotiations, professional miners were brought into the area near the residence to construct large, ventilated and lighted tunnels through which the troops could reach the inside of the compound.

The spectacular success of the rescue mission (only one of the 72 hostages was killed) can be attributed to split-second timing, well-planned diversions, and superb intelligence. During the months of the incident, listening devices of all sorts were smuggled into the residence. Some were hidden in a guitar and thermos bottle that the Red Cross workers were allowed to deliver, others were placed in buttons on clothing brought to the hostages as changes of clothing were needed. During the final four days, intelligence agents posed as doctors and were allowed to enter to check on the health of the hostages, implanting while they were there matchstick-sized two-way microphones that allowed intelligence officers on the outside to communicate with the military and police commanders being held inside.

With this intelligence access, those planning the operation were able to monitor the movements of the guerrillas and the hostages each day, noting patterns of behavior that made planning a carefully timed assault possible. The intelligence officers were able to learn that the 14 Tupac Amaru regularly had a makeshift game of soccer each afternoon at about 3 P.M. in the ground-floor living room and that prior to beginning this recreation, they stacked their rifles in a corner of the room. Audio and video sensors confirmed this pattern.

The government's special forces had plenty of time to train on mock-ups of the building. Construction of the tunnels, if detected by the rebels, could have precipitated a massacre. To prevent this, Peru's leaders used blaring martial music, played day and night outside the compound, to mask the noise (and to deny rest to the hostage takers, demoralizing or at least weakening their resistance and their stamina). Moreover, the tunnels were built to offer as many as six different accesses to the compound, which would increase the confusion of the rebels when the assault began.

At 3:10 P.M., the listening devices indicated that the afternoon soccer game had begun, with at least eight of the rebels participating. By 3:17, the hostages, who were being held upstairs, were alerted by a hidden receiver, smuggled into the hands of a high military official who was a hostage. The hostages moved a desk blocking the second-floor entrance and took cover. Three minutes later, nine pounds of explosives were set off in the tunnel directly under the reception room (where eight of the rebels were playing soccer), killing four of them and opening a hole through which troops began to pour.

The Peruvians' patience in waiting out the terrorists with protracted negotiations, while using the time to gather intelligence, to build tunnels, and to practice many times the assault, paid off, when the hostages were successfully rescued with the loss of only one hostage's life. Peru presented to the international community an excellent example of the value of careful intelligence and planning in such terrorist attacks. The rescue efforts broke no laws, wasted no civilian or innocent lives (except for the one who was shot by a rebel as the attack commenced), and were given all of the time necessary to plan the final act successfully. Patience and careful planning based on up-to-the-minute intelligence were rewarded.

This success, when compared to the botched U.S. 1993 assault on the Branch Davidian compound in Waco, Texas, offers dramatic evidence of the importance of accurate and current intelligence. At Waco, as one analyst noted, "the assault went disastrously wrong in part because agents relied on months-old intelligence that those in the compound were always separated from their weapons at 10 A.M."[16] The inaccuracy of this information contributed to the loss of four agents. Clearly, intelligence is a critical factor in counterterrorism exercises.

## U.S. Strikes in Afghanistan and Sudan: On the Edge of the Law

Bombings devastated U.S. Embassies in Kenya and Tanzania on August 7, 1998. More than 250 people, including 12 Americans, were killed. Intense investigation by federal officials from the United States, working with officials from Kenya and Tanzania, identified several suspects, including Khalid Salim (a Yemeni citizen) and Mohammed Saddiq Odeh. Salim was sent to the United States to stand trial less than three weeks after the bombing, while Odeh was arrested by Pakistani authorities on a flight from Nairobi the day of the bombing. He reportedly confessed under interrogation in Pakistan to a role in the bombings.

While continuing to seek evidence and to bring suspects in the bombing incident to trial in this country, the United States did not wait to complete the investigation. Instead, on August 20, it carried out a missile strike against two targets: camps in Afghanistan used by Osama bin Laden, the man believed to be responsible for orchestrating and funding the embassy attacks; and a pharmaceutical plant in Khartoum, linked by intelligence information to bin Laden.

Investigators at the time stated that gathering information admissible as evidence of bin Laden's connection to the embassy bombings would take at least weeks, perhaps months. The circumstantial evidence seemed clear but was insufficient to warrant an indictment in early August. Political pressure at home to take action, however, was intense and unlikely to accept the need to exercise patience while intelligence was accumulated. Hence, the bombings were ordered, although intelligence on the targets of the missile attacks was not clear, in that it lacked information about whether the camps in Afghanistan were in use by bin Laden or his leaders at the time.

The links of bin Laden to the embassy bombings were numerous and dated back at least two years. In 1996, the United States pressured Sudan to cut its ties to the multi-millionaire, indicating that the United States considered him to be masterminding and funding terrorism in the region. While bin Laden did subsequently leave Sudan, the resulting threats to the United States led to a removal of most U.S. Embassy personnel to Kenya and Egypt, without, it should be noted, increasing embassy security in Kenya, where it was fairly "soft." Thus, the ties of Salim and Odeh to bin Laden were not surprising to those tracking the actions of this leader of dissidents. But the gathering of sufficient admissible evidence to substantiate guilt is a very time-consuming operation.

The cruise missiles inflicted serious damage on the physical facilities at both targets, with minimal loss of life. This effort to prevent civilian casualties in Sudan was important because the United States gave Sudan no warning of the attack or of its concern with the facility itself. This unprovoked attack, as Sudan and many of its neighbors viewed the bombings, was both illegal and unjustified. Had the attack resulted in a high civilian casualty count, the anger of the international community might well have been formidable. Instead, the small amounts of evidence that the United States was willing to offer to public scrutiny concerning the alleged use of the facility frustrated many allies, who deplored the lack of firm intelligence prior to the attack and the lack of diplomatic interaction between Sudan and the United States that have prevented its necessity.

Although it provoked less concern in the international community in terms of the legality of the action (since most of the evidence clearly indicated it use as a training facility for rebellious groups), the attack on Afghanistan was less clearly effective because little evidence gathered before the attack indicated that bin Laden or any of his people were at the site when attacked. Destroying empty, relatively inexpensive shacks used for mercenary training may have satisfied domestic desire for "action" but did not eliminate the threat of bin Laden. Indeed, it may well have offered him further reason to hate the United States and to lead further actions of vengeance against its citizens.

The lack of intelligence concerning the presence of bin Laden at his headquarters, and the lack of admissible evidence against the Sudanese factory, diminished the value of the American actions in August 1998. While the productivity of both actions, in terms of counterterrorism, cannot yet be determined, both were impugned by the lack of up-to-date intelligence.

# INTELLIGENCE GATHERING
# AND COUNTERINTELLIGENCE BY TERRORISTS

The use of intelligence gathering and counterintelligence is not limited to those opposing terrorism. These have long been tools of terrorists as well. Indeed, the better organized and funded of the terrorist organizations could probably give lessons on the techniques of such operations to many governments today.

Study of the **phases of modern terrorist incidents** indicates that terrorists give considerable attention to intelligence gathering. Most terrorist acts entail both a preincident phase and a postincident phase. Essentially, this means that before and after the incident actually occurs, the terrorists are involved in gathering and evaluating intelligence information.

In the preincident phase, terrorists are concerned with planning, reconnaissance, and usually a rehearsal of the event. To effectively carry out the planning necessary to launch an event in a country perhaps hundreds of miles from the group's home territory, considerable intelligence gathering is clearly essential. Much of this is done not by members of the group itself but by members of an indigenous group sympathetic to the terrorists' cause. In incidents in which timing is crucial, intelligence information is also essential—information that will allow for a realistic rehearsal according to a carefully constructed plan.

This concept of planning for a well-orchestrated terrorist event is neither new nor radical. What many observers do not realize, however, is that today terrorists also have an extensive postincident phase to most events. In this phase, the terrorists (the ones who survive the event) usually regroup and critique the event. They learn from their mistakes, far more rapidly, it sometimes appears, than do the police forces charged with combating them. Those lessons are shared, becoming a part of the intelligence information available to terrorists in many areas of the world.

This pattern does not mean that there exists a network of terrorists who share intelligence information on a regular basis. But information and incidents have led many observers to conclude that such sharing does in fact occur, on a regular but not an organized basis, among many terrorists. This seems to be particularly true in Europe, where anti-American and anti-NATO feelings have served to unite several diverse groups in a common cause.

Like TREVI, however, the links in intelligence gathering and sharing between terrorists appears to be rather loosely organized and based more on informal "contacts" than on regular channels for the dissemination of information. As long as terrorists are no more organized than the law enforcement organizations that seek to combat them, then neither side can effectively win—a situation that neither side will be willing to tolerate indefinitely. The U.S. attack on the training camps in Afghanistan may have been most significant if it destroyed the base of such a network of intelligence sharing for terrorists. It is at least one more play in the endless intelligence-counterintelligence struggle between law enforcement and terrorists.

## CONCLUSION

> For a democratic society, the issue is not merely survival, but the way in which
> society chooses to survive.
>
> —Robert Friedlander

Just as terrorism is essentially a war against both the state and all of civilized society, so the struggle to eliminate, or at least to restrict, terrorism is also war of a sort. The cost of this "war" on terrorism, if carried by each state alone, can be quite high both politically and economically. Moreover, as noted earlier, when a state tries to pursue a strategy unilaterally, its effectiveness can be quite limited.

The heads of state and government of the seven most industrialized nations and Russia, meeting in December 1995 in Ottawa, discussed countering terrorism by collective effort. The **Ottawa Ministerial Declaration on Countering Terrorism** stated that these nations

> are determined as a group to continue to provide leadership on this issue to the international community, using bilateral and multilateral measures and agreements to counter terrorism. We will continue to develop specific, cooperative measures to deter, prevent, and investigate terrorist acts and to bring terrorists to justice.[17]

Collectively, these nations pledged to strengthen the sharing of intelligence and information on terrorism and to promote mutual legal assistance and extradition. This network of shared intelligence and cooperative effort could tip the balance in the struggle of law enforcement with terrorist groups. It is of very recent vintage and thus has too small a record to assess its impact, but in the coming decades, with such cooperative work states may well begin to win the war.

### *Evaluation*

Two areas of concern have been raised in recent years as governments grope for strategies with which to combat terrorism. Both involve the collection and dissemination of information—an issue of vital interest in most democratic countries today. One concerns the potential for abuse by governments using intelligence services to track potential terrorists. The other concerns the role of the media in reporting terrorist events. Consider each of these issues, as described here, and decide what potential for abuse, as well as legitimate security concerns, are involved in each.

1. The identification or "tagging" of people to keep track of potential terrorists might well be abused. If any person who participated in a peaceful demonstration or sit-in was tagged by intelligence services, that person's right to privacy could be violated without recourse to law. Indeed, would the investigative searches conducted out of Weisbaden be constitutional in the United States? Should they be?

2. Legal reforms that threaten the fabric of democracy are very dangerous weapons in the fight against terrorism. Are such initiatives justified by the reality of terrorism, or are they more of a danger to democratic society than the terrorism that they are designed to control? Which, if any, of the nations discussed would be a good role model for the fashioning of national antiterrorism legal initiatives?

## *Suggested Readings*

Beaton, Leonard. "Crisis in Quebec." *Round Table* 241 (1971), 8–14.

Dobson, Christopher, and Ronald Payne. *Counterattack: The West's Battle against the Terrorists.* New York: Facts on File, 1982.

Friedlander, Robert A. *Terrorism: Documents of International and Local Control.* Dobbs Ferry, NY: Oceana, 1979.

Jenkins, Roy. *England: Prevention of Terrorism (Temporary Provisions)—A Bill.* London: Her Majesty's Stationery Office, 1974.

Moore, Brian. *The Revolutionary Script.* New York: Holt, Rinehart, & Winston, 1971.

"Ottawa Ministerial Declaration on Countering Terrorism." Released at the Ottawa Ministerial on December 12, 1995.

"Report on Domestic and International Terrorism." Subcommittee on Civil and Constitutional Rights of the Committee on the Judiciary (First Session, April 1981) Washington, D.C.: Government Printing Office, 1981.

Weinberg, Leonard B., and Paul B. Davis. *Introduction to Political Terrorism.* New York: McGraw-Hill, 1989.

## *Endnotes*

1. See Brian Moore's *The Revolution Script* (New York: Holt, Rinehart, & Winston, 1971) for an account of these kidnappings; see also Leonard Beaton, "Crisis in Quebec," *Round Table* 241 (1971): 147–152.

2. Quoted by Robert Friedlander, *Terrorism: Documents of International and Local Control* (Dobbs Ferry, NY: Oceana, 1979), vol. 1, 113.

3. Christopher Dobson and Ronald Payne, *Counterattack: The West's Battle against the Terrorists* (New York: Facts on File, 1982), 113. For six months, Trudeau flooded the Montreal area with troops. It took nine weeks to track down those responsible for Laporte's murder.

4. Dobson and Payne, *Counterattack,* 113. It was Barrett's contention that "democratic governments cannot legitimately establish consent by the use of force."

5. For information on these two acts, see Great Britain, "Report to the Commission to Consider Legal Procedures to Deal with Terrorist Activities in Northern Ireland" (London: Her Majesty's Stationery Office, 1972). For analysis of the Temporary Provisions Act, see Roy Jenkins, *England: Prevention of Terrorism (Temporary Provisions)—A Bill* (London: Her Majesty's Stationery Office, 1974).

6. See Funk and Wagnall's *Standard Dictionary of the English Language,* international edition, (Chicago: J. G. Ferguson, 1977), vol. 1, 413.

7. French Basques are living north of the Pyrenees, and there is little doubt that they give help to people they consider to be compatriots in Spain. ETA men on the run frequently cross the border to find refuge in safe houses in France. In 1979, the French government finally removed the political refugee status of ETA members.

8. "Report on Domestic and International Terrorism," Subcommittee on Civil and Constitutional Rights of the Committee on the Judiciary (First Session, April 1981) (Washington, D.C.: Government Printing Office, 1981), 6–23. In spite of the concept of some lawyers as "fellow travelers of terrorism,"

little evidence was gathered to support this concept. In 1972, a lawyer in the Steinham trial was suspected of having transported a letter; however, after seven years of investigation and suspicion, no charges were brought.

9. Ibid., 22. For example, one person was sentenced to 18 months in prison for blocking the road in the anti-Springer demonstrations; he subsequently became a participant in acts of terrorism in Germany.

10. Ibid., 4.

11. Ibid., 18. This report includes an evaluation of German officials on the effectiveness of this intelligence system. The officials included Siegfried Froelich, state secretary; Gerhard Siegle, administrative head of the terrorism office; Dieter Osterle, deputy head of the Director's Office of the Police Superior Commission; and Capt. Ulrich Grieve, representative of GSG9.

12. Dobson and Payne, *Counterattack,* 101.

13. Bundeskriminalant (BKA) men stripped the apartment where the five women lived and carried back to Weisbaden railway timetables, cigarette stubs, fingerprints, even information on kitchen utensils that were "fed" into "the Komissar."

14. See the *New York Times*, January 12, 1977, sec.1, 1, for a concise recounting of this incident. This was not, of course, the only time that France refused to extradite known terrorists. However, recent French efforts to capture and prosecute Carlos indicate a significant change in French attitude toward the problem.

15. In this case, the reasons were both legal and political. The Yugoslavs demanded that the Germans give them in return a number of anti-Tito Croatian nationalists, some of whom were in German jails serving sentences for acts of terrorism against Yugoslav property and officials inside Germany. Germany could not, it decided, overcome the legal and moral complexities of meeting this demand.

16. "Peru Takes No Prisoners," *U.S. News & World Report,* May 5, 1997, 38.

17. "Ottawa Ministerial Declaration on Countering Terrorism," released at the Ottawa Ministerial on December 12, 1995.

# Security Measures:
# A Frail Defense

*Power, in its most primitive sense, can be defined as the capacity to disrupt or destroy. Terrorists through the use of selective, yet often indiscriminate, violence have been able to force governments to negotiate and often grant concessions to their demands. They have been able to attract worldwide attention to themselves and their goals. Terrorism has forced governments to expend vast amounts of time and resources on security.*

—M. K. Pilgrim

## Key Concepts

physical security
penetration teams
operational security
personnel security
hardening the target
training programs

taggants
trace detectors
general threat indicators
local threat indicators
specific threat indicators

Confronted with a growing tide of terrorist destruction, governments have indeed been forced to spend increasing amounts of time and money on the problems related to security. Modern society is both fragile and complex, with much interdependence within systems. As such, the possibilities for interference by terrorism are almost infinite.

Some aspects of security have, owing to their spectacular selection as targets of terrorism, received more attention than others. It is more than possible that this focus will shift, as new technologies make current security measures obsolete and as successful security systems harden certain targets against attack.

Technological developments during the past few decades have increased dramatically the potential targets and weapons available to persons committing terrorist acts. While the technology accessible to governments has also grown, governments are to some extent more hampered than helped by the technology boom. Governments are confronted with a rapidly growing number of targets that must be secured and simultaneously constrained by democratic principles from using many technological devices to secure those targets. Creating an effective security system that protects against a wide range of terrorist attacks while it continues to afford a maximum exercise of democratic freedoms and privileges is a formidable task indeed.

# THREE FACETS OF SECURITY

Security is not a one-dimensional issue. Instead, those confronting security problems are faced with at least three aspects to the situation that must be considered: physical security, operational security, and personnel security. Each of these facets of security is closely related to the others and cannot be easily differentiated in an analysis of counterterrorism security efforts. But certain features of each aspect can, if explained, offer a better understanding of the security measures that nations and businesses are taking, even now, against terrorist incidents and threats. Let us examine each of these aspects of security briefly.

**Physical security** has as its objective the hardening of the target against which an attack may be made. While no blueprint for successful physical security measures against terrorist attack has been in any sense adopted, certain considerations and countermeasures have begun to achieve acceptance in both the government and the business community.

Both these communities are slowly recognizing, for instance, that security measure against terrorism must go beyond the level of normal crime prevention. These are not "normal" criminals. Their goals, their willingness to sacrifice innocent lives, and their willingness to die in their attacks make them extraordinary criminals, against whom extraordinary measures must be taken if security is to be achieved and maintained.

To determine what, if any, extraordinary security measures are needed to protect against a terrorist attack, government and business have employed a number of relatively ordinary tactics. A physical security survey, by professionals who are aware of the dangers in a particular area or to a particular business or region, is standard procedure. This approach has, in recent years, begun to include the use of **penetration teams** whose job it is to discover holes in security systems through which other teams, such as terrorist attack teams, could presumably penetrate and sabotage or destroy the target.

The penetration team, or the organization conducting the physical security survey, may suggest in their report that the business use certain devices that have proven to be useful in guarding against attack or sabotage. For example, a fairly wide variety of intrusion detection devices are on the market today. Or an evaluation may emphasize the importance of such factors as lighting, access control, or physical security and access control codes. Organizations may be advised to inhibit surreptitious approaches by increasing lighting of entryways, fences, hallways, and other points of access. Greater access control is often recommended, usually in the form of limitations on the numbers of individuals cleared to work in the facility as a whole or in specific, sensitive parts of the operation. One of the more common recommendations for improved physical security is that security and access codes be changed fairly frequently, to make penetration of the operation more difficult.

Some operations that have experienced, until recently, relatively minor security problems are being urged to consider the use of personnel, such as guards, whose specific duty it is to ensure physical security. Others, who have already taken this step, have discovered from security surveys that they need additional guards or specially trained counterterrorist guards.

Physical security is clearly dependent on other types of security—operational security and personnel security. Fortress walls, barbed fences, and barred gates are not, in modern times, either reasonable or sufficient protection against determined terrorist fanatics. The operation of the facility itself must be secure, and its personnel well trained in security procedures, to circumvent modern terrorist attacks.

**Operational security** has as its objective the denial of opportunity for terrorists to collect such information on either the facility on its activities as might enable them to predict those activities. To be able to predict those activities would help terrorists to successfully penetrate the facility or activity and disrupt or destroy it. By denying that information to terrorists, organizations significantly decrease the risk of terrorists' carrying out an attack against the operation's activity or facility.

Prediction of operational activities usually relies on discerning patterns of behavior, so operational security analysis focuses on identifying those patterns and how they are communicated to personnel. Emphasis is placed on making such patterns less predictable, randomizing activities as far as possible without creating chaos within the organization. Too often, repeated activities create in the minds of the individuals responsible for security a numbness, a lack of alertness to small differences that may be crucial. The arrival of a particular car at the same time every morning, the use of a van of a specific color and model delivering goods at the same place and time—these routines can deaden the alertness of personnel to such factors as the driver's identity or the presence of an authorized person in the vehicle. Such a failure to notice, to carry out a thorough security check, can prove fatal to the organization or to some of its personnel.

The training of personnel in operational security measures is also important. Organizations are advised to train personnel in the recognition of intelligence-gathering activities, so that they can more readily spot individuals engaged in such activities. Screening of both employees and casual but regular contacts (e.g., vendors) is also a major focus of operational security efforts, as all such individuals can constitute a threat to the operation.

Moreover, the organization as a whole is often encouraged to improve its own operational security by a variety of fairly obvious but essential measures. These include the maintenance of a low profile, so that the organization does not become an attractive, publicity-provoking target; concentrating on the improving of communications security, so that it is less possible to penetrate the flow of commands or patterns of communications; and the development of counterintelligence capabilities within both management and security-related personnel, so that the organization need not always be on the defensive in this struggle against terrorism.

Neither operational nor physical security can function effectively without the third crucial type of security: personnel security. **Personnel security** focuses on training personnel to take responsibility on their own for security, by teaching them to know how to recognize and respond to a potential terrorist threat. For many years, this type of security was directed toward "high-threat individuals," those whom the organization regarded as being at a greater risk of attack than most of the rank-and-file personnel. Many organizations have developed individual crisis management files, which help management to decide which individuals need special security training and protection. Using those files, these at-risk individuals are often advised on how to randomize travel routes and maintain a low profile. Training is also given to certain individuals in special antiterrorism devices, such as bulletproof clothing.

But today, personnel security has taken on added dimensions. Organizations routinely schedule periodic training for all personnel in counterterrorism procedures. Such training is usually designed to heighten awareness among employees of the potential for terrorist attacks and the preincident activities—particularly intelligence gathering—that may alert personnel to a terrorist attack in progress. The proper use of security measures at all times is stressed, so that employees are less likely to be lulled by a sense of routine into a possibly fatal breach of security procedures.

Most of all, the need to tell someone about suspicious or threatening behavior, to alert the proper authorities to potential threats, has become a major focus in personnel training in many organizations. The alertness of personnel to security breaches may well mean the difference between the success and failure of a terrorist attack.

## CASE STUDY: AIRPORT SECURITY IN THE UNITED STATES

Nations such as the United States have, at present, managed to institute some security measures at one of terrorism's favorite targets: airports. Travelers of commercial airlines in this country are routinely subjected to electronic or manual luggage inspection and to electronic or physical body searches—a practice virtually unknown only a few years ago.[1] In several major U.S. airports, too, individuals without purchased airline tickets can no longer meet incoming plane guests at the arrival gates, nor can they take their friends or relatives to the departure gates.

These are potentially controversial measures, involving some invasion of privacy and some searches without a warrant of persons not accused of any crime. Yet few citizens today have serious objections to these measures. Even the presence of air marshals on randomly selected flights has been accepted with complacence by most citizens, in recognition perhaps of the fact that threat to their lives and property created by a terrorist wielding a bomb is greater than that incurred in airline security measures.

Such security measures, of course, only offer a measure of protection, in one country, against only one type of terrorism. If such measures are not universally applied by all nations, then the potential for skyjacking or bombing remains substantial, even for citizens of countries having such security systems.[2] Moreover, even U.S. measures recently have not been completely successful in thwarting the hijacking of airplanes, partly because the measures are incomplete and poorly enforced.

Consider the results of recent investigations of airport security in several major U.S. airports. Federal auditors, testing X-ray procedures for carry-on luggage, reported recently that major airports missed, on the average, about 20 percent of the auditors' dummy weapons. One airport missed 66 percent of these weapons! This is clearly a breakdown in both physical and operational security.

Other surveys suggest that the problem does not lie exclusively with laxity in X-ray procedures. One audit, for instance, found that Los Angeles International Airport could not account for 6,000 employee identification badges. Two thousand were missing at Dulles International Airport near Washington, D.C. Obviously, personnel security is also somewhat lax in this industry, contributing to a breach in operational security.

Consider the results of the informal "penetration team" of *U.S. News & World Report* reporters who checked several American airports:

1. At Reagan International, a reporter with a suitcase walked right past a security checkpoint on the side where arriving passengers walk out of the arrival gate. The reporter pretended to make a call at a row of pay phones near the checkpoint, then slipped by when the guards' backs were turned. What if his suitcase had contained a bomb?

2. At Chicago's O'Hare International Airport, a visitor found a baggage room security door open. He walked through with his briefcase into the baggage truck passageway, onto the tarmac where planes fuel and load, and up a jetway staircase. He then entered the terminal as if deplaning and caught another flight—without ever going through security. He could have sabotaged either luggage or a plane, without any contact with security.

3. A reporter watched in amazement as janitors at Midway airport in Chicago pushed large trash cans up to the passenger checkpoint. The janitors went through the metal detectors, but they pulled the cans through on the unscreened side. Guards neither inspected the trash cans—a serious security breach—nor did they check parcels brought into the same area by food vendors.

4. A reporter at Atlanta's Hartsfield Airport watched as an employee punched a code into a security door's lock. She then tried the same code on several other doors in the concourse. It opened them all. These doors led, among other things, to the planes on the tarmac.[3]

Such lapses in airport security must frighten and worry both those responsible for such security and the passengers and crew whom such security is designed to protect. The lapses are clearly in both personnel and operational security. The argument is made that security personnel operate under the disadvantage of a mandate by their employers to make air travel as pleasant as possible. In other words, we want airport employees to be both unfailingly courteous and unrelentingly suspicious—of everyone. They are trained to put the comfort and convenience of the passengers first but also to regard all individuals, including those same passengers, as potential threats to the airline's peace and security. It would appear, on the surface, to be an almost impossible task.

Moreover, physical security is still not completely effective. Weapons experts have testified before Congress on the possibility of smuggling guns through metal detectors, by carrying them on certain spots on the body. Nor are these metal detectors, on which much airline physical security relies, effective at all heights.

At this time, a system is not in place to X-ray checked baggage on domestic flights, according to the Federal Aviation Administration (FAA). The argument is made that the volume of such baggage is too high and that many weapons forbidden in carry-on baggage (for which the current detectors are designed) are still permitted in checked baggage. Because an explosive sniffer that would detect bombs is still years away, this means that it is still quite possible to send a suitcase bomb through checked luggage in domestic flights within the United States.

So what are airports to do to harden themselves as targets against terrorism? They could retrain their personnel to be more security-conscious, but it might well be at the cost of a loss of the friendly image with which airlines have sought to market their services. They could install more, and better-maintained, detection devices; but, again, unless the laws regarding the type of weapons that may be carried in checked luggage change, and unless the public becomes more reconciled to delays in flights due to essential security checks, then the cost of such measures to the airline industry may seem prohibitive.

## THE COSTS OF SECURITY

The costs of such antiterrorism measures are great, materially as well as politically. Unfortunately, a great deal more money is required to erect defenses against terrorist attacks than to commit such acts.

If the cost of defending just one type of industry against attack is so high, then the cost of erecting coordinated international defenses against a multitude of types of terrorist attacks may well be prohibitive. The protection of specific targets against terrorists, including air transport facilities, would be a mammoth task. It is also one that would not in itself be sufficient to secure entire nations and persons against terrorist attacks of all kinds.

The difficulty, as Kupperman has noted, is that potential targets for terrorist attacks are not limited to airports. Numerous vulnerable targets exist in our sophisticated society. Electrical power systems, for example, are very tempting as accessible targets. A well-placed bomb or shots from a high-powered rifle could conceivably cause a blackout in an entire city. The same is true about the potential for destructive attacks on telephone systems, gas pipelines, dams, and water systems.

Kupperman has also noted that, with the extensive reliance on computer information systems—for banking, credit cards, real estate, and so forth—that now characterizes industrial societies, the potential for economic disruption by terrorist attacks on those systems may also be substantial.[4] As any computer hacker knows, no matter how carefully a computer system's security may be designed, a blend of time, patience, knowledge, and a little bit of luck will usually suffice to break into it.

Concern has surfaced in recent years, too, over the protection of oil rigs in international waters. By the end of the next decade, there will no doubt be thousands of oil rigs in the Gulf of Mexico and a rapidly growing number in the North Sea. All of these are quite vulnerable to terrorist attacks. Recent movies and novels depicting attacks on such rigs serve to highlight the plausibility of this potential disaster.

This industry, so vital to modern economies, is particularly open to attack, according to some experts, not only at its drilling operations but at a variety of points. Although established petroleum and natural gas operations, their pipeline interties, and associated tankage and storage facilities have been the most attractive targets to date, there is "no part of the industry that is immune to being seriously damaged by someone who has little knowledge of it, or who makes an effort to learn its frailties."[5]

The point is that the list of potential targets that could require security measures is fairly extensive and growing with the development of modern technological interdependence. While it might be possible, although incredibly expensive, for a nation to undertake to protect its own citizens and structures, destructive attacks in another nation can have a substantial impact on the economy and lifestyle of the "protected" nation.

An attack on a North Sea oil rig, for example, not only would affect the cost of oil in Britain (and any nations that Britain supplies) but also could damage the North Sea countries' fishing industries. A successful attack on the computerized international banking system could have serious consequences for many national economies. The poisoning of a water supply in one nation could affect all of the other nations who share the use of that poisoned river or lake.

Just as no nation can entirely protect itself from terrorism by securing all potential terrorist targets, it is probably impossible for any nation, acting alone, to prevent or control the flow of weapons to terrorists. If targets cannot be fully protected, the next security step logically would appear to be an effort to curb the number and types of instruments of destruction available to terrorists. But again, the vast array of security measures required are staggering.

Some of the security measures in place or under consideration involve what is called **"hardening the target,"** which involves efforts to make targets less accessible. As noted earlier, these strategies include installing metal detectors and X-ray machines at points of entry, using sensor or closed-circuit television to monitor accessways, and employing other similar technical devices. Such measures also can include the erection of fences, vision barriers, and heavy barriers around the perimeters of the installation. Related security measures can involve increased use of such items as armored cars, security guard forces, and bulletproof vests. An increasing number of executives are enrolling employees in expensive **training programs** designed to teach skills in such things as high-speed car chases, surviving a kidnapping, and how not to look like a businessperson traveling abroad.

Indeed, companies offering to help to make a business or a businessperson more "secure" from terrorism have grown in number in recent years. One enterprising woman launched a business in 1987 that offered fake passports from nonexistent countries. Most of her clients have been military personnel and businesspeople traveling in the Middle East, South America, and Europe. Donna Walker, president of International Documents Service, points out that, "When you're up against a bunch of gun-waving crazies, you should have an option," such as a passport that does not label you as an American.[6]

Whether such exercises in protecting the target are useful or not, they continue to generate both interest and money for the companies providing them. What is not clear is the extent to which they offer real protection against a terrorist attack that is commensurate with the money expended on them. Nor is it clear whether such measures are either legal or acceptable in a democratic society. Fake passports could well be used by criminals to baffle legitimate customs officials. The erection of heavy barriers and guards around public buildings, while perhaps necessary to protect them from attack, are still unpopular with a democratic public, accustomed to easy access to, for example, their nation's capitol buildings. As the United States found in the wake of the Oklahoma City bombing, it is neither popular nor practical to harden all buildings that have federal offices against the public that they serve.

# CASE STUDY: PROTECTING PUBLIC TRANSPORTATION

Public transportation networks in large cities are enticing targets for terrorists because

- they typically carry large numbers of people;
- they move in concentrated, predictable geographic areas under routine time frames; and
- they are highly accessible, "public service" operations that cannot be hardened easily against their primary users—the general public.

Thus, in terms of physical, personnel, and operational security, public transportation is an attractive target for those seeking to reach a large audience and disrupt a system with little effort. The U.S. State Department, in its record of international terrorist attacks in 1996, noted that 92 of these—almost a third—were against transportation and transportation infrastructures. Although European, Middle Eastern, and Asian countries rely on their public transit systems much more heavily than the United States and have consequently developed more expertise in protecting these systems, their officials were unable to prevent the sarin gas attack on the Tokyo subway or the bombings of Paris trains.

Attempts to share learning experiences and technologies have evolved among some of the nations with a shared interest in this security threat. The advanced industrial nations (Canada, France, Germany, Great Britain, Italy, Japan, and the United States—the G-7) plus Russia have met several times in recent years to discuss the need for cooperation. On July 30, 1996, these nations met at the Lyons Summit in France, adopting a 25-point plan for international cooperation to combat terrorist acts. This plan included several significant points:

1. Tightened control on firearms and explosives
2. Improved bomb detection methods
3. Prevention of terrorist communications on the Internet
4. Faster exchange of information on terrorist activities, including those involving chemical, biological, and nuclear materials

Based on the progress made at this summit, two further meetings focusing on land transportation security were held in Washington, D.C., in 1996 and 1997. In April 1998, domestic and international presenters (primarily from the G-7 plus Russia) met in Atlanta, Georgia, to discuss current and emerging terrorist threats, results from case studies, lessons learned and techniques developed during to terrorist actions, and new technologies useful in protecting land transportation systems. Some of technologies under development discussed at this meeting, which may be of particular service in this target area, include weapons detection systems that can identify a weapon containing little or no metal at a distance of 30 feet, less than lethal incapacitation technologies that are both legal and socially acceptable (such as laser dazzlers, pyrotechnic devices, enhanced pepper spray delivery systems, and net devices), and sniper fire identification systems capable of detecting and locating a sniper within a 10- by 10-foot area of an urban environment.[7]

Cooperation with other states is indispensable in the effort to provide security for land transportation systems. The techniques and equipment developed by other nations, if shared, may make future attacks on these vulnerable targets more difficult. But, as the officials at these meetings noted more than once, security for such accessible targets is not possible without a loss of freedom unacceptable to democracies.

# PREVENTIVE SECURITY

Security has not been exclusively concerned with the hardening of targets that terrorists may select today. Some efforts are also being directed at what has been termed "preventive security," meaning the lessening of the likelihood of terrorist attacks themselves.

One such security technique in use today involves efforts to tag and trace various weapon components. **Taggants**—chemically identifiable agents—exist for many types of explosives. It is also possible, although not as easy, to use **trace detectors** for chemical agents, which would enable security agents to detect the presence of dangerous or hazardous chemicals in innocuous-looking containers.

The use of tagging devices and trace elements for person-portable rocket security, in addition to more complete inventory control measures, is also under advisement. The advantage in the use of taggants, in addition to an ability to detect certain substances, is an ability to determine the country, and sometimes even the company, of origin. Although this information would not necessarily be of immediate use in preventing terrorist attacks, it would be of considerable use in determining responsibility and perhaps thereby making future such attacks less likely.

However, companies and countries manufacturing such materials, from explosives to handguns, from nuclear to chemical and biological weapons, have resisted many attempts to institute a comprehensive tagging effort. Most have argued that laws requiring such security measures violate the rights of businesses engaged in lawful enterprises.

Political reality has made it clear that nations cherish their right to sell arms to whomever they please, under whatever conditions they deem advisable. Even nations that have made no secret of the fact that they sponsor terrorist groups with arms and war matériel have little difficulty securing those arms on the world arms market.

# CASE STUDY: WHO ARMS IRAN?

In spite of all that is known about the active support that Iran gives to terrorism worldwide, neither this nation nor Iraq, its adversary in its ongoing conflict, experienced any difficulty in securing a wide variety of lethal weapons. During the course of this war, at least 50 nations have sent arms to either Iran or Iraq, or both.

Iran, with its record of support for terrorism, is the focus of this case study. It got small arms from the East bloc nations and North Korea, SCUD-B surface-to-surface missiles from Syria, tank parts and radar systems from Britain, and speedboats (which it has used to attack shipping in the Persian Gulf) from Sweden. It concluded a deal with China to buy tanks, fighter planes, artillery, rockets, and Silkworm missiles. In the 1980s, Iran's biggest sources for arms were China and North Korea. China reportedly sold Iran more than $1.6 billion worth of military equipment, while North Koreans were engaged in filling a $250 million order for small arms, munitions, and mines.

Arms deals make strange political bedfellows. While the Soviet Union primarily supported Iraq in the conflict, 11 of its satellite states were busy providing Iran with artillery pieces, radar equipment, heavy machine guns, and mortars. South Africa became a key supplier of armored vehicles, aircraft, and explosives for Iran, because Iran was one of the few nations that did not embargo South African goods.

Stranger still was Israel's relationship with Iran during this decade. Israel sold at least $500 million worth of arms of various sorts to Iran in just one year, in an effort to help Teheran defeat Iraq, which Israel regarded as its enemy. Yet from Teheran have come terrorist teams that have struck against Israelis, both at home and abroad. In the arms market jungle, it is evidently difficult to decide who is friend and who is foe.

Part of the motivation for such sales is clearly monetary. Arms merchants must export to survive, so many governments have turned a blind eye to the illegal sale of arms to belligerents owing to an unspoken understanding of this need. The sale of arms, even on the legal market, is a multibillion-dollar annual industry that few governments, including the United States, can afford to ignore or cripple. But another part of the motivation is equally clearly political, as Israel's sales to Iran and the U.S. Iran-*contra* deals indicate. Some arms are sold simply to make a profit; others are bartered for political advantage.

Regardless of the motivation, however, it is obvious that arms are increasingly available to anyone with the money (or a moneyed sponsor) to pay for them. This makes the efforts to limit terrorist access to weapons, as a form of preventive terrorism, largely futile. What terrorists cannot purchase legally on the open arms market, they can surely procure illegally on the black market. Fake end-user certificates are readily available from several countries, such as Nigeria.

Moreover, it is difficult, in the shadow world of illegal arms sales, to use most preventive measures effectively. Shell companies, Swiss bank accounts, and the routing of weapons from country to country three or four times to hide the country of origin make the labyrinth of arms deals difficult to penetrate with regulation or preventive action.

Although using taggants might make the tracing of the country of origin feasible (even through this maze of sale and resale), it is also highly probable that nations that wink at such sales by their industries are going to be unwilling to force those industries to institute measures that might make it easier for a finger to be pointed accurately in accusing violators of arms agreements. For monetary reasons they may have tacitly agreed to the sales; for political reasons they do not want such arms sales easily traced home. Preventing terrorism becomes, in such cases, less crucial than being held accountable for violation of arms control laws and agreements.

# THREAT ASSESSMENT:
# HOW DO YOU KNOW WHEN YOU ARE AT RISK?

How do nations or businesses decide which of their operations or activities are likely to be victims of terrorist attacks? Nations and individuals use three types of indicators to assess the potential threat of terrorism: general threat indicators, local threat indicators, and specific threat indicators. Let us look briefly at each type.

**General threat indicators** are used to determine whether, within the nation or state, conditions exist that might stimulate or provoke terrorism. Such indicators are extremely general and consequently of little use in predicting the likelihood of a specific terrorist attack. Instead, they are used to assess the climate—political, ideological, religious, and so forth—that might influence the willingness of a portion of the population to resort to terrorism. Politically, for example, the presence of an unpopular, repressive, or corrupt government is considered a positive indicator of the probability of terrorism. Similarly, an economic climate that includes extreme poverty and/or high unemployment is regarded as conducive to terrorism.

These observations do not mean that any nation or region possessing these political or economic conditions will necessarily have a large degree of terrorism. They simply mean that the presence of such conditions makes the likelihood of terrorism greater in such places than it might be in areas without similar political or economic climates. These are indicators only, not predictors of terrorism. For instance, one geopolitical indicator has been the concentration of large foreign populations within a nation. Yet in the United States, many such concentrations exist in major cities without outbreaks of terrorism. But in occupied territories or nations involved in border disputes, such populations have indeed been useful indicators of the probability of terrorism.

**Local threat indicators** are used to assess more specific and localized possibilities for terrorism. Usually, they focus on the forms that dissent tends to take on the local level and the degree of violence involved in the expression of such dissent. The formation of radical groups; reports of stolen firearms, ammunition, and explosives; violence against local property, including looting and arson; violence against individuals, including murders, beatings, threats, and abductions; and the discovery of weapon, ammunition, and explosives caches are all considered to be local threat indicators. Again, this point does not mean that any radical group that forms must necessarily be a terrorist threat or that any demonstration against a government or a company must be the prelude to a terrorist attack. These are just some indicators of the possibility of terrorism in a particular location.

**Specific threat indicators** are used to evaluate the vulnerability of a particular target to terrorism, not the likelihood of terrorism in a nation or neighborhood. These indicators include such things as the history of attacks on similar targets, the publicity value of the target, the target's access to infiltration, its counterterror and its communications capabilities, the tactical attractiveness of the target, and the availability of the police or other security personnel. Some of these indicators are essentially judgment calls, such as the determination as to whether the industry involves a "sensitive" installation, which is generally used to refer to a nuclear, chemical, or other similar facility. Others are very easily quantified, such as the population density in the immediate area.

None of the three types of indicators can be said to predict the probability of a terrorist attack. Nevertheless, government and industry are beginning to rely increasingly on such indicators to help them to decide what, if any, terrorist threat exists and what direction such attacks may take. With the cost of installing, staffing, and maintaining security systems spiraling, no one is anxious to spend more than is warranted on protection against a threat that may never materialize. But few are willing, either, to risk remaining unsecured where strong indications exist that terrorist attacks may cripple or destroy costly facilities and irreplaceable lives.

## CONCLUSION

The question basically is how much a company, a government, or a people are willing to sacrifice to achieve greater security from terrorist attacks. For some, as long as the attack happens to "somebody else," the sacrifice of rights to prevent terrorism will always seem too high a price. To others, the prevention of terrorism will justify the loss of precious rights and freedoms. Governments, trying to strike a delicate balance between the need for its citizens to be secure and the need to protect its citizens' rights, have an increasingly difficult task.

Terrorism is fundamentally an attack on the state. Just as offshore maritime terrorism is a crime waiting to happen, terrorism with nuclear, biological, or chemical weapons is an international disaster waiting to occur. Neither national nor international security measures have proved adequate in terms of either protecting targets or preventing the dissemination of such agents of mass destruction.

As governments and industries come to grips with the rocketing costs of securing themselves against terrorism, serious questions continue to be raised concerning the priority that security should have in the allocation of resources. However real the terrorist threat may be, few are willing as yet to meet the exorbitant costs, both political and economic, of providing adequate security against that threat.

Unlike the issues raised with intelligence gathering and investigative counterterrorism measures, security measures costs are reckoned less in terms of political ideals such as civil liberties. Instead, the costs are felt to be more in terms of convenience and, more important, money. Until terrorism is felt to be enough of a threat to the economic well-being of both nations and industries to justify the expenditure of countless millions of dollars, security will remain a weak weapon in the arsenal of nations against terrorism. Until terrorism seriously pinches the pocketbook of nations and businesses, that pocketbook will be slow to open to defeat or prevent that "pinch."

## *Evaluation*

Making a decision to take on the cost—in economic, political, and public relations terms—of installing and enforcing security systems is seldom easy. Seldom is there a clear indicator that makes such a decision simple or obvious. Governments and industries continue to wrestle with the problems, and, while their solutions seldom satisfy everyone, it is often difficult to state, unequivocally, what they should do in a given situation.

Consider the following cases, and try to formulate an appropriate response. Remember to take into account both monetary and political costs of any decision. Could you justify your decision to a corporate board or an irate citizen in terms of cost-effectiveness? That is, does the security measure that you may recommend pay for itself in terms of the security gained, in a way that would recommend itself to a stockholder or taxpayer?

1. In spite of the gaps in airport security in the United States noted earlier, the FAA and air industry officials stress that U.S. aviation works pretty well. In 1987, airlines screened 1.2 billion passengers in this country and seized 3,000 weapons. Only four persons tried to hijack planes that year; none of them were successful and none carried a gun. In light of this record, should the FAA require increased security training for airline employees, as well as the installation of more and better screening devices for baggage? Do the airlines and airport personnel deserve an indictment, for the flaws noted earlier, or a commendation for the record of terrorism prevention that it has accumulated in recent years? In light of that record, could you justify spending large sums for increased security? As a citizen, passenger, and potential target of aircraft terrorism, do you want better security systems in place? Are you willing to pay for them, in higher-priced airline tickets, longer lines, and more flight delays?

2. Israel has resolved to pay the price, both monetary and political, involved in increasing airport security in Tel Aviv. Passengers boarding at this airport are warned to expect to spend several hours in security checks. Checked luggage, carry-on luggage, and handbags are scrupulously examined. Detailed scrutiny is also made of the passengers themselves, their contacts and personal histories. These searches are often what would, in the United States, be considered "unreasonable" in that there is no effort to establish a probable cause for believing that the individuals subjected to such searches and invasions of privacy are terrorists. The delays while these security measures are implemented are tedious and time-consuming. But Israel has so successfully hardened its airport as a target that terrorists seeking to focus on Israeli airlines or tourists have been forced to choose airports in other nations from which to launch their attacks. Are such measures justified, in terms of monetary costs, political costs, and inconvenience? Do they continue to be justified, even though Israel's airlines continue to be an accessible target through other airports in other nations? What more can Israel do to prevent its airlines from being vulnerable to terrorist attacks, if other nations do not institute similar security measures at their airports?

3. The development of plastic handguns is a security nightmare. This deadly technological breakthrough enables terrorists to carry handguns through most checkpoints and detection

devices without fear of discovery. The plastic gun only existed in 1988 as a concept and computer model patented by a five-person company called Red Eye Arms, Inc., in Winter Park, Florida. This gun employs state-of-the-art plastics and a design that allows gases to be vented when a shot is fired (which eliminates recoil). The basic design can be used for anything from handguns to howitzers. Furthermore, plastic weapons are lighter, less expensive, corrosion-proof, and almost completely maintenance-free. What a break-through this was, not only for military arsenals but for terrorists, who often have to hope that their weapons will last for many years! It is a terrorist's dream, and a security night-mare—this weapon that would slip undetected through the most sophisticated equipment now in place in most industries. Cost-efficient, undetectable, with a potentially long life-time, it would be an ideal weapon. What kind of security, if any, would be useful against such an innovation? If it cannot be discovered (because it has no metal) by metal detec-tors, would it be feasible to require that its makers build in a microchip that would set off a detection device? How could you be sure that a manufacturer would in fact build in such a chip or that it could not be readily removed by an unscrupulous owner? How can security measures best be developed to meet not only today's arsenal of weapons, which is quite formidable, but also weapons of the not very distant future? Is there a point at which secu-rity measures become increasingly futile, as the sophistication of the terrorist threat grows to match technological development? If so, to what do you as a nation, a business, an indi-vidual turn to protect yourself and your people from this growing threat?

## Suggested Readings

Aberlin, Mary Beth. "Trace Elements: Taggants Can Help Finger Terrorists and Counter-feiters." *The Sciences* 36, no. 6 (November/December 1996): 8–10.

Fenelo, Michael J. "Technical Prevention of Air Piracy." *International Conciliation*, 585 (1971), 117–124.

"Gaping Holes in Airport Security." *U.S. News & World Report,* April 25, 1988, 33–41.

Jain, Vinod K. "Thwarting Terrorism with Technology." *The World & I* 11, no. 11 (November 1996): 149–155.

Joyner, Christopher C. "Offshore Maritime Terrorism: International Implications and the Legal Response." *Naval War College Review* 36, no. 4 (July/August 1983), 17–32.

Laqueur, Walter. "Postmodern Terrorism." *Foreign Affairs* 75, no. 5 (September/October 1996): 24–36.

Stephens, Maynard M. "The Oil and Gas Industries: A Potential Target of Terrorists." In Robert Kupperman and Darrell Trent, eds. *Terrorism: Threat, Reality, and Response,* 45–63.

"Who Arms Iran? Almost Everyone." *U.S. News & World Report,* August 31, 1987, 8–14.

## Endnotes

1. See Michael J. Fenelo, "Technical Prevention of Air Piracy," *International Conciliation* 585 (1971): 28–41.

2. One CIA official (who requested anonymity) noted that in many less developed nations, the lack of any real security at airports constitutes "a terrorist attack waiting to happen."

3. "The Next Bomb," *Life,* March 1989, 130–138.

4. In an interview on April 8, 1982, Kupperman expanded on this theme (of the potential targets of terrorism), which he has previously described in his book *Terrorism: Threat, Reality and Response,* coedited by Darrell Trent (Stanford, CA: Hoover Institution Press, 1979).

5. Maynard M. Stephens, "The Oil and Gas Industries: A Potential Target of Terrorists," in *Terrorism: Threat, Reality and Response,* ed. Kupperman and Trent, 200.

6. Walter Laqueur. "Postmodern Terrorism," *Foreign Affairs* 75, no. 5 (September/October, 1996): 24–36.

7. "Protecting Public Transportation from Terrorists," *National Institute of Justice Journal* (March 1998): 17–24.

# Future Trends

*Terrorism is becoming commonplace—ordinary, banal and therefore somehow tolerable. . . . Extraordinary security measures no longer attract any comment. We expect diplomats to be assassinated and states to be involved.*

—Brian Jenkins

## Key Concepts

bureaucratic banality
institutionalized
"semipermanent subculture of
   terrorism"
trends in terrorism
volume
lethality
right-wing terrorism

Aryan Nations
"Identity"
generational difference
PFLP–General Command
Hamas
"unthinkable weapons"
victims
preferred tool

## BANALITY AND TERROR

The late Hannah Arendt, in her controversial book on the trial of Adolf Eichmann, coined the term "the banality of evil." She used this phrase to describe the way in which a "terrifyingly normal" person was able to help turn the murder of a people into an ordinary bureaucratic routine. Eichmann became the quintessential government bureaucrat—highly efficient and mindlessly, remorselessly obedient to orders.

Brian Jenkins, chief terrorism analyst for the Rand Corporation, suggests that terrorism has achieved a similar level of **bureaucratic banality:** its perpetrators carry out heinous crimes with increasing efficiency, while a worldwide audience becomes increasingly "unshockable" when viewing those acts. Terrorism has become so much the norm that it is "commonplace," not "unthinkable."

Moreover, terrorism has become increasingly **institutionalized.** As several reports have recently noted, some governments today not only provide logistical support for terrorists but actually create or designate government agencies to supervise relations with the terrorists. "Like any bureaucracy," notes Jenkins, such an agency "competes for influence and budget, promises results and resists dismantling."[1] In fact, in a seminar at Georgetown University's Center for Strategic and International Studies, Jenkins suggested that a **"semipermanent subculture of terrorism"** may be emerging, with shared personnel and some common sources of weapons and financing. Walter Lacquer, on a similar note in his 1987 study of the subject, compared terrorism to the "anonymous character of a multinational corporation."[2]

Recognizing what threatens to become a permanent part of the international landscape, many nations now spend billions of dollars every year trying to improve security, providing increasing protection for ordinary citizens and civilian facilities, and adopting special measures to ensure the safety of diplomats and government officials. Several nations have established commando units trained to combat terrorists. Large corporations now often provide their top executives with instruction in protecting themselves and their families.

The expense and the personnel involved both in terrorism itself and in the fight against it have, to a great degree in recent years, become institutionalized. Expenses for overseeing relations with terrorists, or for securing against terrorism, are today more often a part of the regular budget of both government and industry.

However, the 1990s have been a decade of significant change. Organizations such as the PLO and the IRA, which until the mid-1990s engaged in and supported terrorism, are becoming a legitimate part of the international community. The PLO began achieving diplomatic recognition from several states, and initiated diplomatic dialogue with the U.S. government in December 1988. It acted as a major participant in the peace process with Israel, resulting in the creation of semiautonomous Palestinian systems in Gaza and parts of the West Bank in 1994. PLO leader Yasir Arafat came to enjoy, by the mid-1990s, acceptance as chief executive of a legitimate organization, not a terrorist group. Required for this transformation was a renunciation of the threat to use terrorism as a means to secure political independence. The reality of the terrorist acts committed by the PLO were neither denied nor apologized for; instead, the leadership declared that terrorism would no longer be a tactic employed against its enemies.

We have, perhaps, come to accept the existence of terrorism. It has become in some parts of the world routine, commonplace, ordinary. The level of violence that society is willing to tolerate has risen in concert with the rise of terrorism in recent years. There is less talk of "eliminating" terrorism now and more emphasis on "limiting its effectiveness."

Success in peace efforts in the Middle East and Northern Ireland, although disrupted by bombings in London from time to time, generate optimism about the potential for ending terrorism by eliminating the political and social causes for which the terrorists fight. Yet in both cases, political solutions acceptable to a large faction of those who have felt alienated to the point of resorting in terrorism are not acceptable to all factions of the same people. While the PLO leadership appears willing to work with Israel toward settlement on the issue of Palestine, the Hamas faction continues to carry out violent attacks, particularly suicide bombings against Israeli targets. Similarly, the IRA in Northern Ireland has found it difficult to prevent smaller factions from continuing to carry out acts of terrorism against civilian targets, in London as well as in Northern Ireland.

Perhaps it is true, as Jenkins suggests, that there is no cure for terrorism. He refers to it as a condition, not a specific disease, that can be treated but not cured. If this view is true, then it seems likely that the prognosis for this "condition" will be a grim one. Terrorism could, in fact, grow worse, as the technology available becomes more sophisticated. N. C. Livingstone notes:

> As the nations of the globe learn to live with routine low-level violence, it can be expected that there will be a movement by terrorists toward more dramatic and increasingly destructive acts of terrorism designed to ensure that the public does not forget about them and their causes.[3]

The explosive growth of technology that has brought with it new vulnerabilities to superindustrialized societies will continue to provide incentives for increased destruction.

So our world is, and will for the foreseeable future continue to be, afflicted with the "condition" of terrorism, which will, in the view of most experts, probably get worse rather than better. As the general public worldwide becomes inured to low-level violence, that violence will escalate, perhaps in very undesirable ways using the incredible innovations of modern technology.

## TRENDS IN TERRORISM

The future of terrorism is a grim picture. But unfortunately it is a fairly accurate one, at least as accurate as any predictions of the future can be. Some specific **trends in terrorism** in recent years may help to bring this view of the future into better focus.

The **volume** of terrorist incidents, the number occurring annually, has begun to decrease. After the 1972 attack on Olympic athletes in Munich and continuing through the mid-1980s, the number of terrorist incidents rose at an annual rate of between 12 and 15 percent. This rate of increase was not constant throughout that time frame. In the 1980s, there was a marked acceleration, which brought the average rate up. From 1984 to 1987, for instance, a fairly dramatic annual increase occurred. Between 1989 and 1991, the escalation recurred, although certain types of incidents became less common (e.g., skyjacking).

However, in 1992, a total of 364 terrorist incidents were recorded worldwide, a decrease from the 666 recorded in 1987. The rise in the number of incidents in 1993 over those recorded in 1992 was caused by a campaign of 150 attacks carried out by the Kurdistan Workers Party against Turkish interests in Western Europe on two days, one in June and the other in November of that year. In 1994, the number of incidents fell again, this time to 321, according to U.S. State Department statistics. The number of incidents per year has continued to decline through the end of the 1990s.

Although terrorism has not increased in volume, it has increased in **lethality**— that is, in the number of people killed in attacks. There has been a tendency toward large-scale indiscriminate terrorist attacks in mundane, everyday locations such as airplanes or railway stations. A bomb on an Air India flight in June 1986 killed 329, and 115 people died from a bomb on a Korean Airlines flight in 1987. The bombing of Pan Am Flight 103 over Lockerbie, Scotland, in December 1988 resulted in the deaths of 270. Between 1969 and 1989, 1,128 people died as a result of bombs exploding aboard aircraft or in cargo containers on the ground. In 1993, 109 people were killed and 1,393 were wounded in terrorist incidents around the world, the highest casualty total in five years.

In the last four decades of the twentieth century, the number of incidents involving fatalities has increased by an estimated 20 percent over the number killed annually in the first six decades of this century. In 1983, for example, 720 people died in terrorist incidents, and another 963 were wounded. The number of attacks against ordinary citizens, often just businesspeople, has risen dramatically in recent years, by as much as 68 percent since the turn of the century.

Another trend has been in the surge in **right-wing terrorism,** carried out by militant, conservative, and fundamentalist individuals and groups. If the 1960s can be described in terms of left-wing terrorism, with the 1970s carrying that trend to its logical conclusion by witnessing the involvement of liberation struggles in terrorism, the 1980s and 1990s witnessed a resurgence of right-wing terrorism, particularly true in Europe and the United States. The activities of such organizations as the neo-Nazi youth groups against refugees from Eastern Europe in Germany have provided grim reminders of the existence of right-wing groups that are increasingly willing to resort to violence.

A brief examination of the growth of right-wing terror in just one nation may offer useful insights into this significant trend. While the United States' experience with domestic terrorism from the left in the 1960s was relatively modest compared to the more lethal violence produced by revolutionary and secessionist groups in Europe, its growing pattern of right-wing domestic terror indicates that the ideological pendulum swing may be putting the United States at the apex of this new trend in violence.

# CASE STUDY: RIGHT-WING TERRORISM IN THE UNITED STATES

The bombing attack in Oklahoma City in 1995 certainly raised concern over the possibility of violence generated by militia groups. But right-wing, racist, antiauthority, survivalist-type groups appear to abound in this country, and they are networked by common ideology and common enemies. Let us briefly examine one of these groups, the **Aryan Nations,** which experts have suggested may be the most deadly group operating in the United States at the end of the twentieth century.

This group traces its origins to the 1950s and early 1960s. Its current structure was organized in 1970 under the leadership of Richard Butler, with headquarters in Hayden Lake, Idaho. Its ideology is a mixture of theology and racism, being anti-Semitic and anti–African American. The literature of this group indicates that its beliefs are couched under the religious doctrine of **"Identity,"** which states that Jesus Christ was not a Jew but an Aryan, that the Lost Tribes of Israel were in fact Anglo-Saxon and not Semitic, and that Jews are the children of Satan.

The operational profile for this group derives from a book written by an American neo-Nazi, William Pierce. This book, *Turner's Diaries,* offers a blueprint for revolution in the United States based on a race war. It is a disturbing book, freely available on the market and used by many groups that have splintered from the Aryan Nations for tactical reasons, focusing on certain elements of the doctrine. These groups include, but are certainly not limited to, the Order, the Silent Brotherhood, the White American Bastion, Bruder Schweigen Strike Force II, Posse Comitatus, the Arizona Patriots, and the White Patriot Party.

These groups have been linked to armored car and bank robberies; counterfeiting; assassinations; and assaults on federal, state, and local law enforcement personnel and facilities. One leader in the Aryan Nations, who was also the head of Texas's Ku Klux Klan, proposed a point system to achieve "Aryan Warrior" status. One could achieve this status (which required achieving a whole point) by killing the following individuals:

Members of Congress = 1/5 point

Judges and FBI director = 1/6 point

FBI agents and U.S. marshals = 1/10 point

Journalists and local politicians = 1/12 point

President of the United States = 1 point (Warrior status)

With this kind of ideology and commitment to violence, it is not surprising that much of the more recent violence in the United States has come from this element. Moreover, right-wing groups have given evidence of several disturbing differences between the left-wing college radicals of the 1960s and 1970s. Unlike the isolated, crudely unsophisticated pipe bomb manufacturers who dominated most of the U.S.-based terrorist groups of the past, the right-wing extremists are well trained in the use of arms and explosives. They are skilled armorers and bomb makers, and they are adept at guerrilla warfare and outdoor survival skills. Coupled with their racial and religious intolerance and their apocalyptic vision of racial war, these groups bring more potential to engage in lethal and increasingly sophisticated terrorist operations, as the Oklahoma City bombing demonstrated.

This right-wing terrorism has wide-ranging geographic dimensions, a diversity of causes that its adherents espouse, and overlapping agendas among its member groups. There are right-wing groups from Idaho to California, Arizona to North Carolina, Georgia to Michigan, Texas to Montana. Almost every state has at least one such group, and most have several. These groups share motivations that span a broad spectrum: antifederalism, sedition, racial hatred, and religious hatred. Most have masked these unpleasant-sounding motives under a rather transparent veneer of religious precepts, as noted earlier. Their shared hostility to any form of government above the county level advocates overthrowing the United States government (or the Zionist Occupation Government, as some of them call it). Vilification of Jews and nonwhites as children of Satan is coupled with an obsession with achieving the religious and racial purification of the United States and a belief in a conspiracy theory of powerful Jewish interests controlling the government, banks, and media.

These facets of right-wing ideology give interesting insights, in light of the material discussed earlier concerning the images that terrorists have of their world, their victims, and themselves. To view the enemy as children of Satan is to dehumanize them, as terrorists must in order to kill. To view the struggle of the group as an effort to "purify" the nation is to view it as a battle between good and evil, as terrorists must. The view of a coming racial war fits the millennial view that terrorists maintain, as discussed in a previous chapter. A "Warrior" fighting in a cause to "purify" a state from the "children of Satan" will have little problem in justifying the use of lethal force.

Thus, right-wing terrorism in the United States is widespread, intricately linked by many overlapping memberships, and bound together in a political and religious doctrine that defines the world in terms that make the use of violence not just acceptable but necessary. Because many of the members of these groups are skilled in the use of weapons and use survival training in camps throughout the country, planning for an "inevitable" racial war, the impact of these groups may well be formidable in the twenty-first century.

## A GENERATIONAL DIFFERENCE

A **generational difference** between young militants and older leaders has been noted in terrorist groups operating today. Today's terrorists seem less likely to be involved in pickets and demonstrations before resorting to violence. Instead, they seem more willing to throw a bomb first and talk later (if at all) about their grievances.

This "do something now" mentality has caused some difficulties and even embarrassment to some of the older leaders of established movements. In the PLO, for instance, the 1990s has witnessed a number of splits, frequently between older, more "institutionalized" members of the organization, and younger members who want to take violent action now against the existing situation. Certainly Arafat, in his December 1988 speech promising that the PLO would not engage in terrorism, could not be sure that he spoke for the whole of that organization's membership.

George Habash's radical faction, the **PFLP–General Command,** strongly rejected any such renunciation of terrorist tactics, as have the fundamentalist **Hamas,** a radical element seeking the establishment of an Islamic state, which is supported by Iran and active in the West Bank and Gaza. The difficulties that Arafat experienced in governing Gaza during the 1990s illustrate the deepening splits between the older leadership, willing to compromise to achieve a portion of that for which they have fought, and the younger factions, willing to continue the struggle with violence and unwilling to settle for less than full success.

Terrorism has also contributed to changes in the mode of conflict both between nations and within nations. Conflicts today appear to be less coherent, at times exhibiting not two clear sides but several confusing and shifting alliances. Such conflicts are also less decisive, with no clear "winner" or "loser." As states use terrorism to engage in irregular warfare against other states, the stakes in the conflict become confused, the rules less clear, and the heroes hard to find.

## THE USE OF "UNTHINKABLE" WEAPONS

One further ominous trend in terrorism in the latter part of the 1990s has been the increased access to and willingness to use nontraditional, **"unthinkable weapons,"** the nuclear, chemical, or biological types. The 1995 attack on subways in Japan in which sarin gas was used, resulting in numerous casualties, indicated that those "unthinkable" weapons were not only in the hands of groups capable of violence but were already in use. Japan was fortunate, in that the group carrying out the attack had ample supply of the toxin but little experience in its effective use; consequently, the death count was low.

Similar "luck" befell the United States in 1993 in the bombing of the World Trade Center. While this sounds like an absurd statement, it is interesting to read more carefully the court accounts of the incident. In these records, it was revealed that those planning the attack had placed in the vehicle sodium cyanide as well as the explosive materials. The intent was to create sufficient heat to vaporize the sodium cyanide, creating a lethal cyanide gas, which would have been sucked into the north tower, killing thousands. Although the physical destruction and injuries caused by the bomb were dramatic, the death toll was very low compared to what was intended, had the materials been used correctly.

Evidence of similar efforts by individuals and groups within the United States to secure and even to use chemical or biological agents continues to grow. A list of only a few such attempts will make clear the reality of the threat:

1. In 1991, sheriff's deputies in Alexandria, Minnesota, learned of a shadowy group of tax protestors called the Patriots Council. One informant reported discussions of blowing up a federal building. Another turned over a baby food jar containing ricin, one of the most deadly poisons known. In 1995, three of the plotters, whose plans included the

assassination of IRS agents, were convicted under the Biological Weapons Anti-Terrorism Act.

2. In December 1995, an Arkansas man, Thomas Levy, who had survivalist connections, was arrested by the FBI for having possession of a biological agent for unlawful purposes. He had 130 grams of ricin, enough to kill thousands of people if used with skill.

3. In May 1995, an Ohio member of the Aryan Nations allegedly ordered bubonic plague bacteria from a Rockville, Maryland, research supplier. He received the bacteria, but the supplier became suspicious over the man's persistent phone calls for delivery of the material and alerted officials. Larry Harris was subsequently arrested.

Terrorists and groups appear to be more willing to experiment with the use of unconventional weapons such as these today. Recent alarming developments have occurred, too, concerning the probable access to and use of nuclear weapons by non-state actors. There is growing evidence of nuclear smuggling from the former Soviet Union, at first across Europe, but later in southerly directions where border controls were less stringent. While no individual or group has yet openly threatened to use, or used, such weapons to date, this tactic can no longer be dismissed as an "unthinkable" in the new century.

## GRAPHIC EVIDENCE

Ample evidence describes the trends in terrorism in recent years. The U.S. Department of State issues a summary report annually on patterns of global terrorism, in which it not only reveals interesting insights into terrorism during that year but also describes patterns of terrorism over the past several years. A brief look at some of these collective figures on terrorist incidents, victims, locations, and modes of operation may help us to understand both the scope of the problem of terrorism and its probable course in the next century.

Figure 13.1, culled from the 1997 edition of this report, illustrates the number of incidents of international terrorism from 1979 to 1997. Some observations can be made from this graph and the accompanying statistics in the report.

In 1987, 832 international terrorist incidents were reported by the U.S. Department of State. These incidents resulted in the deaths of 633 persons and the wounding of another 2,272. Much of this injury and loss of life resulted from terrorism in the Middle East and its spillover into Western Europe, which accounted for 295 deaths and 770 injuries. The Middle East had the highest incidence of terrorism in that year, unsurprisingly, of all of the world regions, incurring 371 attacks (about 45 percent of the worldwide total).

The annual report, released in April 1997, indicates a substantial decrease in terrorism worldwide since 1987. Only 305 incidents of international terrorism were recorded in 1997, with only about 1,000 casualties (dead and wounded). While these figures sound large, they are in fact considerably lower than those of 1987. It is worth

**FIGURE 13.1    Incidents of International Terrorism 1978–1997**
*Source:*  U.S. Department of State homepage (www.state.gov/www/global/terrorism/
              1997Report).

noting that the decline has not been consistent, since there was an increase in incidents in 1991, to more than 500. This rather diminishes the good news in the decrease of terrorism in the 1990s when compared to the 1980s, because the 1990s seem to have experienced both increases and decreases. However, as a whole, the 1990s indicate statistically a gradual decrease in the numbers of incidents.

The gradual (and somewhat erratic) decrease in number of incidents contrasts, however, with the casualties inflicted by these incidents. As Figure 13.2 indicates, casualties have actually increased, even as the number of incidents decreased. In 1995, for example, about 450 incidents produced a record 6,500 casualties, compared to the the 430 incidents that caused only about 1,500 casualties. This figure graphically illustrates the trend mentioned earlier—incidents, though becoming less frequent as a whole, are becoming increasingly lethal, inflicting more casualties.

Moreover, ordinary citizens, particularly businesspeople, were the **victims** of terrorist attacks in 1997. As Figure 13.3 illustrates, of the anti-U.S. attacks in that year, more than 90 percent were targeted were carried out against nonofficial, and often unprotected targets, such as businesses and tourists.

Nor is the United States the only nation experiencing this trend. As Figure 13.4 illustrates, terrorists worldwide tended, from 1992 to 1997, to choose businesses and other targets for attacks, rarely focusing on the diplomatic, government, and military facilities that had been for decades the primary targets. In the 1980s, less than 20 percent of the total number of terrorist attacks were against government, diplomatic, or military targets; in the 1990s, the choice of attacks on government, diplomatic, or military facilities continued to decline. It is obviously increasingly true, as Figure 13.4

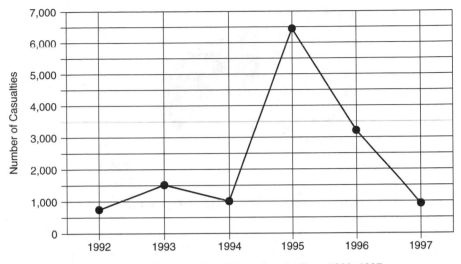

**FIGURE 13.2   Casualties of International Terrorism, by Year, 1992–1997**
*Source:* U.S. Department of State homepage, 1997.

indicates, that terrorist acts are carried out predominantly against innocent, noncombatant bystanders who are made the victims of violence in struggles of which they have no part.

Bombs remain the **preferred tool** of today's terrorists, with bombing attacks making up about 88 percent of the total number of terrorist incidents in the United States in 1997. While kidnappings still occurred, these events remain relatively

**FIGURE 13.3   Anti-U.S. Attacks, 1997, by Type of Targeted Victim**
*Source:* U.S. Department of State homepage, 1997.

**FIGURE 13.4    International Terrorist Incidents, by Type of Facility, 1992–1997**
*Source:* U.S. Department of State homepage, 1997.

infrequent in terms of the total number of terrorist incidents (only approximately 6.5 percent of the anti-U.S. incidents reported by the State Department in 1997). Figure 13.5 offers evidence of this trend.

On a positive note, there is evidence that, although some terrorists have begun to use Armageddon-type weapons (such as chemical or biological, but not thus far nuclear) in their attacks, such attacks have been the exception rather than the rule. However, there is increasing use of more sophisticated versions of more familiar tools. The Czech-made plastic explosive Semtex, which is colorless, virtually odorless, and almost completely undetectable by most modern security systems, has apparently come into recent use in aircraft bombing attempts, including the Pan Am Lockerbie explosion.

**FIGURE 13.5    Anti-U.S. Attacks, 1997, by Type of Event**
*Source:* U.S. Department of State homepage, 1997.

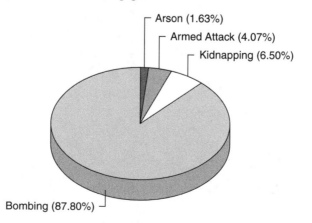

State Department records indicate that thus far, few terrorist attacks have involved the use of doomsday weapons. With the demise of the Soviet Union, the covert sale of nuclear weapons and weapons-grade materials has been of great concern to Europe and the United States. Four separate incidents, noted at the beginning of this text involving such sales, highlight the reality of nuclear options for terrorists in the twenty-first century. The lack of willingness on the part of governments, too, to limit nuclear proliferation, as more governments seek to enter the group of nuclear-capable states, will make it increasingly difficult for the international community to successfully prevent terrorist groups from acquiring or using nuclear weapons. The moral high ground of nuclear nonproliferation is rapidly eroding. The day when one small nation uses nuclear weapons against a larger opponent as a measure of "justified war" will certainly diminish any moral restraint on terrorist groups against the use of such weapons. Nuclear proliferation, as evidenced by India's and Pakistan's tests of nuclear devices, heightens the likelihood of such a war and its concomitant impact on terrorism.

As Figures 13.3 and 13.4 indicate, most of the victims of terrorism in 1997 were not diplomats, government officials, or soldiers. They were "others": men and women working for corporations with interests in more than one nation; elderly people taking the tour for which they had saved all of their lives; housewives who went to the wrong supermarket at the wrong time; children. Someone did, in fact, make war on these people. Terrorism, like other forms of warfare, is an act that maims or takes lives. In 1995, statistics indicate that terrorist acts were quite successful in this respect. More than 6,000 were wounded or killed in terrorist attacks around the world.

Figure 13.6 illustrates the casualties caused by international terrorist incidents, by region, from 1992 to 1997. The graph indicates the number of individuals killed or wounded in terrorist events, broken down according to the region in which the attack occurred. One interesting insight from this graph relates to the two areas in which the greatest number of deaths and injuries occurred: the Middle East and Asia.

In 1987, the war in Afghanistan resulted in government-directed attacks on Afghan refugees in camps along the Pakistani border. Since the defeat of the Communist regime in Kabul in April 1992, many of the non-Afghan Muslims who had fought in that war with the rebel forces have returned home and become active in insurgent movements. The cyclical nature of violence is again painfully illustrated.

Not all incidents in this area were caused by the war in Afghanistan. Sectarian violence increased throughout the region, particularly in the Philippines, with bombing of churches and mosques killing some and injuring far more.

Similarly, few of the incidents occurring in the Middle East in 1993 were a result of the conflict between Israel and its Arab neighbors. The civil strife in Egypt and Algeria contributed significantly to the large number of casualties, as did the attacks against UN and other humanitarian efforts in northern Iraq.

It is also significant to note that North America recorded one of the highest number of people wounded in terrorist incidents. This anomaly was created by the results of the bombing of the World Trade Center in New York City on February 26, 1993, which resulted in over 1,000 injuries.

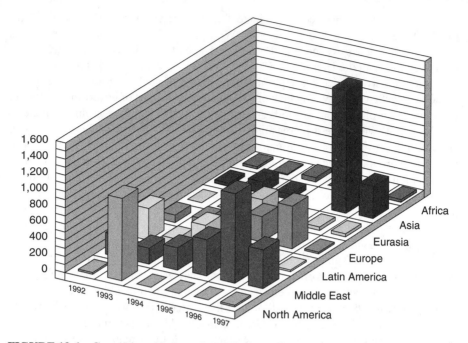

**FIGURE 13.6    Casualties of International Terrorism 1992–1997**
*Source:*  U.S. Department of State homepage, 1997.

Figures 13.6 and 13.7 illustrate the trends of such deaths and injuries by region over six years. It is interesting to note that, although Americans have frequently been targets for terrorism during those years, few individuals died or were injured as a result of terrorist incidents in this nation, with the exception of the bombings in New York City in 1993 and Oklahoma City in 1995.

Eurasia (which, according to the State Department, includes all of the former Soviet Union and Eastern Europe) has also had a marginal history of deaths or injuries taking place on its soil as a result of terrorist incidents. Casualties appear to have been marginal in Africa during most of this time; the other regions have experienced an erratic pattern of increase and decrease from 1992 through 1997, but Asia has clearly witnessed an increase in casualties from 1996 to 1997, as has Latin America. These data are insufficient to substantiate a trend, but it does look as though the 1990s may be indicative of increasing levels of casualties from terrorism in the twenty-first century throughout the world.

The graphs make it easier to effect an examination of international terrorist incidents over time, illuminating some interesting trends. About these trends certain generalizations can safely be made:

1. Statistics indicate that the number of terrorist incidents, although increasing at an alarming rate during the 1980s, was in 1992 approximately at the same level as that

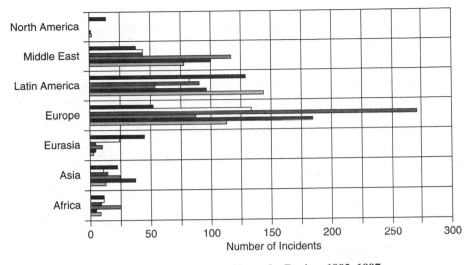

**FIGURE 13.7    International Terrorist Incidents, by Region, 1992–1997**
*Source:*  U.S. Department of State homepage, 1997.

recorded for 1975. From a low of fewer than 400 incidents reported in 1975, terrorism reached a peak of almost 700 such incidents in 1987, a staggering increase in just over a decade. These graphs indicate, however, that this pattern of rising numbers has reversed, and we are now witnessing a decrease in the number of terrorist incidents per year, throughout the world.

2. Certain regions of the world continue to experience a strong pattern of terrorist incidents. The greatest increases in terrorism have occurred in Latin America, the Middle East, and Europe. The latter two regions experienced some decline in incidents during the late 1980s, but significant increases in the 1990s. Political compromises in the 1990s between both the PLO and Israel, and the Hashamite Kingdom of Jordan and Israel, have removed at least some of the actors and sponsors of terrorism from the scene, leaving room for some optimism in that region.

3. In terms of both the type of facility targeted and the type of victim of terrorist attacks, there has been in recent years a continuous dominance of business as the target of choice for most terrorist attacks. During the 1990s, terrorists have apparently chosen businesses and businesspeople as targets, rather than the military, government, or diplomatic personnel who had in earlier years been the prime targets. The only other category that indicates a strong position as favorite for terrorist attacks is "other," which according the State Department includes grocery stores, restaurants, and other such "dangerous" places.

   In 1980, fewer than 100 of the attacks carried out by terrorists were aimed at this "other" category. Instead, most attacks were launched against diplomatic facilities. By 1997, 324 attacks were aimed at business facilities and 74 at "other"; only 41 of them were launched against diplomatic property, government facilities, or the military. The data indicate that terrorists have increasingly turned to attacking instead less protected areas: cafés, airplanes, supermarkets, trains, and other similar civilian facilities.

4. This trend is equally obvious in the statistics relating to the type of victims of terrorism during that time. Obviously, if terrorists attack business and other facilities with increasing frequency, then their victims are going to increasingly belong to those categories. It is, perhaps, a viable question as to whether terrorists make their choice based on the fact that the facility is less secure and thus more easily attacked, or they choose a particular group of "unthinkable" victims because their deaths, injuries, or capture will cause a greater stir worldwide. The fact remains that terrorists have rarely, during the latter twentieth century, chosen any of the traditional victims; instead, their victims are almost exclusively drawn from the category of innocent bystanders in someone else's war.

The final observation, to be drawn from Figure 13.5, is that, as noted in an earlier chapter, bombing has indeed become the preferred if not exclusive method of modern terrorists. Bombs have, of course, several advantages. They are impersonal. As attacks shift more and more toward what had been regarded in many societies as proscribed targets, it is psychologically less of a strain to launch or plant a bomb for a victim whom the attacker may never see than to kill deliberately at close range one of those proscribed targets.

Bombs are also easy to make, relatively inexpensive, and increasingly effective, thanks to modern technological advances. They can be detonated remotely, thus reducing the danger to the attacker. Their method of delivery can vary quite widely, to counter security measures. They can be sent by mail, wired under a car, dropped from a plane, driven into a compound on a truck, concealed in a briefcase, or carried aboard an airplane in luggage. Such diversity makes their use limited only by the attacker's imagination and the security countermeasures of the target area.

The love affair between terrorists and bombs has become increasingly evident in recent years, as bombs easily outstripped all other forms of attack in international terrorist incidents. In 1993, for example, bombing and firebombing accounted for more than 50 percent of the total events recorded for that year.

These graphs, then, reinforce the trends noted earlier: terrorism is becoming increasingly lethal (bombs are designed usually to kill masses, not individuals) and random, as the victimization of "others" becomes the rule rather than the exception in terrorist events. Terrorist incidents increased in number at an alarming rate during the 1980s and have begun to reflect a pattern of decrease in number of events, but with a related increase in lethality, in the 1990s.

One other group of statistics may be of interest in evaluating trends in terrorism. It has been stated repeatedly that terrorism has become "internationalized." One facet of such an internationalization has been discussed: the evolving of a network linking terrorist groups and their supporters worldwide. Another facet of this internationalization can be examined in the following statistics: the spillover of terrorist violence whose roots or causes lie in one region but whose attacks are carried out in a variety of different regions.

The "Patterns of Global Terrorism" publication by the State Department for 1987 details the spillover of Middle East terrorism into other nations in 1987. The State Department records indicate that 50 such spillover events occurred in that year.

Of these, 43 took place in Western Europe. Altogether, spillover events occurred in 16 different countries. Sixteen nations became victims, in many different ways, of one or more terrorist event whose real target was far away. Such nations are compelled to watch their cities and citizens become enmeshed in violent struggles over which they may have little direct control.

It is worth noting, then, that the increased movement toward peace in the Middle East may contribute to a corresponding decline in terrorism in Europe, because there will be less to "spill over." It is also possible that individuals and groups dissatisfied with the peace process, and not willing to make attacks that might cause the deaths of their own people, may seek to export terrorism to other regions. The World Trade Center bombing in New York could be an incident giving credence to this trend's potential, as could the hijacking of the French plane by individuals dissatisfied with the efforts to end the Algerian conflict. At this time, we have too few data to conclude that this will be true in the twenty-first century, but these are at least disturbing indications of this potential trend.

## CONCLUSION

> The world community is now required to deal with unprecedented problems arising from acts of international terrorism . . . which raise many issues of a humanitarian, moral, legal, and political character for which, at the present time, no commonly agreed rules or solutions exist.[4]

The world community must meet the challenge of terrorism. If it is indeed a condition for which there is no known cure, then let us at least seek to understand the phenomenon to better cope with its presence.

To recognize the existence of terrorism is not to recognize its right to exist or its inevitability. A doctor, faced with an epidemic, must first recognize the problem and then take steps to deal with it, at least in terms of containment and perhaps prevention. Similarly, students of world social, legal, political, and security issues today must study the phenomenon of terrorism to better cope with its presence in the world today.

Just as that hypothetical doctor facing that epidemic has restraints on how to handle the problem, so must nations searching for ways to cope with modern terrorism exercise restraint in their responses. They must weigh the cost, in terms of the loss of liberties and freedoms, against the gains in subduing terrorism, recognizing that to sacrifice too many liberties may well be giving terrorists the victory they seek: the destruction of the democratic systems. The cost of winning some battles against terrorism may be too great.

But to concede that there are some ways in which a nation or a people may not combat terrorism is not to concede that terrorism cannot be fought or is in any way acceptable. Regardless of the cause, terrorism is not an acceptable mode of behavior and cannot be permitted to prevail unchecked. The end does not, and can never, justify the means. To attempt to remedy perceived acts of injustice by committing even greater acts of injustice neither solves anything nor excuses anything. As Friedlander notes, "Human atrocity is not an excusing condition, but rather a moral wrong which affects all humankind."[5]

## *Evaluation*

Consider the following statements concerning the danger of terrorism in the modern world. Are they accurate assessments of the situation, or are there other overriding concerns that should be taken into consideration?

1. "The greatest threat posed by terrorists now lies in the atmosphere of alarm they create, which corrodes democracy and breeds repression. . . . If the government appears incompetent, public alarm will increase and so will the clamor for draconian measures." (Brian Jenkins, "Upgrading the Fight against Terrorism")
2. So in the Libyan fable it is told
   That once an eagle, stricken with a dart,
   Said when he saw the fashion of the shaft,
   "With our own feathers, not by other's hands
   Are we now smitten." (Aeschylus, *Wisdom of the Ages*)

## *Suggested Readings*

Friedlander, Robert A. "Terrorism and National Liberation Movements: Can Rights Derive from Wrongs?" *Case Western Reserve Journal of International Law* 13, no. 2 (Spring 1981), 47–69.

Livingstone, N. C. "Taming Terrorism: In Search of a New U.S. Policy." *International Security Review* 7, no. 1 (Spring 1992), 12–19.

Nanes, Allan S. *The Changing Nature of International Terrorism.* Washington, D.C.: Congressional Research Service, March 1, 1985.

"Patterns of Global Terrorism: 1987." 1997 U.S. Department of State Publication No. 9661. Washington, D.C.: Government Printing Office, August 1988.

Schultz, G. P. "Terrorism and the Modern World." *Terrorism* 12 (January 1985): 431–447.

Wright, Robin, and Norman Kempster. "Experts Fear New Bombings: Terrorist Attacks May Be Increasing." *Miami Herald,* January 1, 1989, A1–A3.

## *Endnotes*

1. See Brian Jenkins's paper on "The Future Course of Terrorism" (Santa Monica, CA: Rand, 1989), 3.

2. Walter Lacquer, *The Age of Terrorism* (Boston: Little, Brown, 1987), 291.

3. N. C. Livingstone, "Taming Terrorism: In Search of a New U.S. Policy," *International Security Review* 8, no. 1 (Spring 1992): 17.

4. Statement by Kurt Waldheim, made July 9, 1976, before the UN Security Council at the beginning of the debate over the Israeli Entebbe raid. See the *New York Times,* July 10, 1976, reprinted in the *Wall Street Journal*, July 29, 1976, p. 10, col. 4.

5. Robert A. Friedlander, "Terrorism and National Liberation Movements: Can Rights Derive from Wrongs?" *Case Western Reserve Journal of International Law* 13, no. 2 (Spring 1981): 310.

# Index